AF681433

# RENT CONTROL

# RENT CONTROL

## CONCEPTS, REALITIES, AND MECHANISMS

MONICA R. LETT

CENTER FOR URBAN POLICY RESEARCH

THE CENTER FOR URBAN POLICY RESEARCH
RUTGERS—THE STATE UNIVERSITY OF NEW JERSEY
BUILDING 4051—KILMER CAMPUS
NEW BRUNSWICK, NEW JERSEY 08903

Cover design by Francis G. Mullen

Copyright, 1976, Rutgers–The State University of New Jersey

All rights reserved. Published in the United States of America by the Center for Urban Policy Research, New Brunswick, New Jersey 08903.

ISBN: 0-88285-034-2

Library of Congress Cataloging in Publication Data

Lett, Monica R. 1942-
Rent control: concepts, realities, and mechanisms.

Bibliography: p.
1. Rent control–United States. I. Title.
HD7293.L48 352'.75 76-18791

352.75
L569r

*To F.F.R.*

FUNDERBURG LIBRARY
C.1
MANCHESTER COLLEGE

# Contents

# Exhibits

# Preface

Spiraling inflation and the shrinking power of the dollar have generated the rebirth of rent control legislation in many areas of the United States.

This handbook explores the theory and practice of rent control in an attempt to provide insight and practical guidelines for policymakers, tenants, landlords, and all those sectors of the general public that will either affect or be affected by rent control legislation.

Too frequently the rent control issue is viewed simply as a conflict between landlords and tenants. In reality, however, housing policy significantly affects the wealth and viability of an entire community or city and must, therefore, be examined within a comprehensive framework.

Consequently, in my investigation of this issue I have attempted to provide an overview of rent control concepts, legislation, judicial interpretation, and past and current implementation. The scope of authority and cost of regulating rent-controlled housing will be discussed along with a critical description of various administrative and rent adjustment mechanisms. Also included are case studies of the Boston, New York City and Fort Lee, New Jersey areas which provide an empirical basis for analysis of the realities of rent control administration and the impact of rent control on the fiscal operation of rental housing.

# Acknowledgments

The empirical data used in this study draw heavily upon two major research efforts undertaken by the Rutgers University Center for Urban Policy Research during 1974-1975: "The Realities of Rent Control in the Greater Boston Area," and "Rent Control in Fort Lee, New Jersey." Given the scope of these efforts, the many individuals and agencies to whom acknowledgment and gratitude is due are too numerous to cite. However, these studies would not have been possible without the cooperation and assistance provided by the U.S. Department of Housing and Urban Development, the Boston Housing Authority, the Massachusetts State Finance Agency, and the personnel of the rent control boards of Boston, Brookline, Cambridge, and Fort Lee. Special credit must also be given to Jack Burritt, Ilona Bernath, Brian Sullivan, and Edward Burroughs for their diligence in carrying out the numerous research tasks involved in these studies.

Also included in this volume is data derived from the report, "A Review of Rent Guidelines and the Economics of the Stabilized Sector of New York City's Housing Market," which was undertaken by Franklin James and myself for the Rent Stabilization Association of New York City. The full report was subsequently submitted to the Rent Guidelines Board for consideration in determining rent guidelines. Acknowledgment is here made of the cooperation and assistance provided by the Rent Stabilization Association and the Conciliation and Appeals Board.

A special note of thanks is owed to my colleagues here at the Center for their sustained support and assistance over the past year. Dr. George Sternlieb, in particular, made a substantial contribution to this effort in terms of his encouragement and insight into the problems under investigation. Thomas P. Norman, Esq., also offered helpful comments on the manuscript.

Under the supervision of Mary Picarella and Joan Frantz, Joan Dalton, Anne Hummel, and Lydia Lombardi typed the manuscript in steadfast fashion. Kathleen Agena, Cynthia Koch, and Barry Jones edited and shaped the manuscript. Any errors that remain are mine.

Monica R. Lett

# Part I: The Prevailing Controversy: Rent Control Past and Present

# Chapter 1
# The Historical Perspective in the United States: Federal, State, and Municipal Regulations

## *THE WORLD WAR I ERA*

Rent controls were initially imposed in the United States as a result of emergency housing shortages during World War I. These shortages were engendered by decreases in housing construction as resources (material and labor) were shifted to defense production, and they were exacerbated by large and rapid shifts of population to areas of wartime defense production.

The initial thrust of state and federal rent controls enacted during World War I were "limited to servicemen and their families and to workers engaged in the production of war material."[1] Such legislation was designed to protect these servicemen and their families from eviction; it generally prohibited eviction during the term of military service.[2] Toward the end of World War I rent regulation was extended to the general public housing market as "rent profiteering" became pervasive. Although specific rent control laws were enacted in many states and cities, the most common response to wartime rent profiteering came from the citizens' committees organized to direct public attention against the exploitation of housing shortages.[3] Eighty-two locally organized committees were established; their creation was promoted by the federal government through the Bureau of Industrial Housing and Transportation.[4] Representing a cross-section of public interests, these committees were instrumental in reducing speculative rent gouging. However, because these committees had no real legal authority and relied primarily on public pressure, their activity and effectiveness declined abruptly with the cessation of hostilities.

Most of the committees disbanded after the war. Some communities, however, particularly in northern urban centers which were experiencing an extremely tight housing market, extended wartime measures and gradually replaced them with formal methods of rent control. In New York City, for example, more than 100,000 dispossession proceedings were pending by 1920.[5] This critical housing situation prompted the New York State legislature to enact its first rent control law.[6] Other states followed,[7] and constitutional challenges accompanied the enactment of these postwar statutes. The challenges centered on the controversy regarding the validity of extending emergency measures after the war.

The first two cases to reach the United States Supreme Court, in a series of rent law cases heard by the Court between 1921 and 1924, were decided on the same day by a 5 to 4 majority. These decisions upheld the constitutional validity of a District of Columbia rent law enacted in 1919 by Congress and a New York State statute enacted in 1920.[8] *The existence of an emergency housing situation was of crucial importance in these decisions,* which upheld the exercise of police power.

The creation of rent commissions with authority to handle rent adjustments and evictions in a number of jurisdictions mitigated the problems of the post-World War I period and eased the transition from a wartime to a peacetime economy.[9] Other factors, such as major revisions in state laws governing landlord-tenant relationships, also were important during that transitional period. The introduction of tax-exemption legislation to encourage new housing construction was a significant factor in facilitating the normalization of conditions and eliminating rent controls in New York State.[10]

## *WORLD WAR II RENT CONTROLS*

### *Federal Controls*

The United States' entry into World War II marked the first use of rent control on a national scale as a result of the enactment of the Emergency Price Controls Act of 1942 (EPCA). Authority for the administration and development of rules and procedures of the measure was delegated to the Office of Price Administration (OPA). The rent division of OPA initially attempted to encourage the formation of voluntary fair rent committees in cities confronting increased housing demand; however, when it became apparent that success for such an approach was unlikely due primarily to insufficient statutory authority to handle evictions, federal rent regulations were drafted. By March 1941 a large number of "defense-rental areas" were designated for possible federal rent regulation providing adequate local action was not taken within a statutory sixty-day period.[11] Formal federal controls began in June 1942 in Altantic and Pacific port cities and inland cities with major war-related industries and military installations. Although the EPCA was not intended to cover all areas of the United States, the entire country was designated for potential rent control in

October 1943. Some sections, however, were never brought under regulation. Federal controls applied to all premises defined as "housing accomodations" located in the designated defense-rental areas. The definition included any buildings, structures, or any real property rented or offered for rent for dwelling purposes and all privileges, services, furnishings, furniture, and facilities connected with the occupancy of the property.[12]

During the 1940s many areas of the country were subject to emergency controls from one or more governmental levels. Federal controls were substantially continued through 1952, although interim legislation allowed for some decontrol and the easing of eviction regulations.[13] The Housing and Rent Act of 1947 initiated the eventual termination of federal controls; it also provided for state and local determination in the extension and decontrol of areas within their jurisdiction, in compliance with guidelines established by the Office of the Housing Expeditor. The "Declaration of Policy" of the Housing and Rent Act of 1947 reaffirmed the existence of an emergency and stated that in order to halt inflation and maintain rent stability, "it is necessary for a limited time to impose certain restrictions on rents charged for rental housing accomodations in defense-rental areas."[14] Contrary to the practice in earlier periods of rent regulation, in the 1947 legislation continued restrictions were intended to be administered with consideration for prompt adjustments to property owners receiving inadequate rents. The adjustment process depended on the discretion of local boards and involved only minimal participation by the central agency.[15]

The Housing and Rent Act of 1948 authorized extension of the Office of Housing Expeditor until March 31, 1949, but in amending the 1947 act maintained the 1947 "Declaration of Policy" intact.[16] The 1948 act further authorized the Housing Expeditor to facilitate the housing of veterans in newly constructed rental housing units or in acquiring homes. The Housing Expeditor administered rent controls by issuing regulations consistent with the 1947 act in regard to maximum rents, living space and services, and uncontrolled premises. He was, however, no longer empowered to rule on evictions; the new regulations placed such cases totally under the jurisdiction of local courts. Furthermore, the 1948 act prohibited any recontrol of areas decontrolled by the 1947 act and the control of any new areas. 1948 rent control was restricted to those places designated as "defense-rental areas" prior to March 1, 1947. Premises decontrolled by the 1947 and 1948 acts were hotels, motor courts, tourist homes, new construction, and nonhousekeeping units. The Housing Expeditor exempted additional classes of housing and removed maximum rents on others which met certain conditions.[17]

The Housing and Rent Act of 1949 placed more responsibility for the decontrol of federal rental areas upon states and municipalities than the 1947 and 1948 legislation. Under the 1949 act, entire states or portions of states were decontrolled or state control substituted for federal control. The Housing Expeditor's authority to disapprove recommended decontrol of areas under his jurisdiction was continued as was his authority to decontrol those areas. Federal controls extended by this act ended June 30, 1950. Due to the Korean conflict, however, controls were extended through June 1952. Controls were relaxed at each extension, however; and some decontrolled areas became recontrolled in 1951.

### *State and Local Controls*

By 1948, ten states, including Connecticut, Illinois, Maryland, Minnesota, Missouri, New Jersey, New York, Rhode Island, Virginia, and Wisconsin had enacted rent control laws. With the exception of Rhode Island and Wisconsin whose laws went into effect concurrently with federal controls, the other state laws were "standby" statutes which became effective at the termination of federal controls.[18] The gradual termination of federal controls which was initiated with the 1947 act specifically involved the decontrol of hotel and other accommodations and the cessation of federal eviction controls. This federal action led to the enactment of local rent control ordinances which recontrolled these accommodations and instituted eviction restrictions. The local ordinances superseded state, and continued federal controls. New York City was one of the first municipalities to recontrol decontrolled accommodations and reimpose eviction restrictions under a locally enacted ordinance. This local enactment was later confirmed by the New York State legislature. Subsequently, Baltimore, Buffalo, Chicago, Los Angeles, Minneapolis, Philadelphia, St. Louis, and San Francisco enacted local ordinances similar to New York City's.

Although the constitutionality of rent control was established during World War I, legal challenges at a number of judicial levels accompanied the enactment of many statutes during the World War II period. The initial imposition of rent controls under the Emergency Price Controls Act of 1942 led to a challenge of the act on grounds that it constituted an unlawful delegation of powers to the OPA and that the OPA regulations failed to guarantee landlords a profit.[19] Congressional power to regulate rents during the wartime emergency was not an issue. The Supreme Court upheld the constitutionality of the 1942 act. The Court also established the constitutionality of other regulations, notably postwar regulations which were challenged on the argument that the constitutional basis for rent control—the wartime emergency—was no longer applicable.[20] The 1948 decision upholding post-World War II regulations was the last rent control case to be heard by the Supreme Court.

Subsequent to termination of federal controls in 1950, a number of state and local statutes were challenged on the basis of municipal authority, state preemption, and due process issues (see chapters 2 through 4 for more discussion of these issues). Although many of these were upheld, a number of these statutes were declared unconstitutional. Municipal ordinances were declared unconstitutional primarily due to a lack of municipal authority in the absence of state legislation or on grounds of state preemption where such legislation existed. Several decisions resulted in the termination of both state and local controls, particularly in cases involving attempts to extend municipal controls upon the expiration of state statutes.[21]

By the mid-1950s, all areas, with the exception of some New York State localities, had been completely decontrolled. New York State is thus an anomaly in rent control history and New York City has had the most active and turbulent role in the history of rent control. A summary of the New York City experience is included at the end of this chapter.

## *FROM WORLD WAR II TO THE PRESENT*

Broad-based rent control did not resurface on a national scale until 1971 when the Nixon Administration initially invoked a 90-day absolute freeze on all wages, prices, and rents.[22] The freeze was replaced by Phase II stabilization measures constituting a "flexible system of wage and price controls" with a goal of reducing the annual rate of national inflation to 2 to 3 percent by the end of 1972.[23] It was under Phase II, which lasted thirteen months (November 13, 1971 through January 11, 1973), that actual rent regulation took place. This regulation allowed restricted annual rent increases of 2.5 percent plus specified allowable cost increases.[24] Although the overall stabilization program proceeded through Phase IV (decontrol), the introduction of voluntary restraint under Phase III in January 1973 marked the end of formal rent control and the abolition of the Rent Advisory Board.[25]

Numerous state and local rent control ordinances both preceded and followed these federal regulations. These statutes have been labeled "Second Generation Rent Controls,"[26] and are the subject of Chapter 3.

## *DEVELOPMENT OF RENT CONTROL MECHANISMS*

The regulatory mechanisms effective during World War I consisted primarily of conciliatory activities of voluntary citizens' committees which were legally limited in authority and dependent solely upon public pressure for influence. Although the post-World War I extension of controls in many areas necessitated the definition of methods and principles for adjusting rents,[27] "the lack of scientific basis for determining fair rents and the discrepancies in judicial interpretation brought about confusion and resentment both by landlords and tenants."[28]

In 1937 a historical account of World War I rent controls was undertaken to provide insight to the problems encountered in past rent control measures and to make recommendations for handling similar future measures.[29] Subsequent to this seminal research—which provided an international overview of prior experience and detailed recommendations for legislative action in New York State—the National Defense Advisory Commission recommended that rent controls be handled at the state and local levels and published a draft of a model state rent control law.[30] It became apparent, however, that some form of federal legislation was inevitable, and congressional hearings on such legislation were begun in late 1941.[31]

The specific focus of these hearings, which included testimony from real estate and housing experts, was the problem of how to control rents and the basis for rental evaluation on a national scale.[32] Although acceptance of federal controls was gradual, and intense controversy surrounded the issue, "the question was not why rent control was necessary but how it was to be accomplished."[33] Eventually, the following criteria for rent control regulation were developed:

> 1. A fair method which would reflect the average return on property under normal times and conditions.
> 2. A method which would have exactness and be so objective that there could be uniformity of application throughout the country.
> 3. A method which would eliminate long drawn out disputes and avoid simulation of court procedure under condemnation action.
> 4. A method which could be put into operation immediately.
> 5. A method which ould be easily administered with the minimum number of personnel.[34]

Although it was recognized that rent prices were normally derived as a function of real property appraisal the primary objective for congressional leaders was the determination of a fair weekly or monthly rental value as opposed to a units capital value. Following are the various methods of rent evaluation which were considered during this period in the history of rent control:

> 1. There was, what might be termed, the appraisal method. Appraise the total value of the subject property, and then say that the gross rent to be received monthly should be one-twelfth of a given percentage of total appraisal value. This has also been dubbed the 'fair return upon fair value' approach.
> 2. There was the comparability or grading method, which would classify various types of housing into grades and determine the most common rental found for a given grade, then assign that figure to the particular grade.

3. There was the so-called 'fair rent' method. Inexperienced persons believed that by some legerdemain process or by the waving of an appraisal wand, a fair, equitable, just (or any other synonym) price could be arrived at, ipso facto. It was a method that might have had its roots in Thomas Aquinas' theory of the 'just' price of canonistic days. There could be no basis for evaluation unless supported by one of the other methods. Hence, this was a nebulous concept, existing only in the minds of the most optimistic Pollyannas.
4. There was the fixed date, maximum rent date, or 'freeze' date method—one that was to be applied subsequently to other commodities under OPA regulations. This method would set a date and allow rents that were being charged on that date.[35]

In consideration of the diversity of the units and types of properties to be regulated (e.g., apartments, hotels, single-family homes) and the intention to temporarily stabilize rental rates, the fourth method was selected for implementation.[36] The presumption that current rent prices had been determined between landlord and tenant under free market conditions before housing shortages were severe supported the attractiveness of the "freeze" date method. According to Daniel Gage,

> the chief attributes of the freeze date principle [were] . . . its objectivity, . . . the rapidity with which control could be effected, and . . . the ease of administration. Most important, the freeze date by-passed the need for total evaluation of the property which was not the desideratum but only the means to the end.[37]

As rent control became effective under the 1942 Emergency Price Controls Act, there was continued clamor for regulation providing a guaranteed "fair return." The seminal federal case upholding the constitutionality of rent control regulatory mechanisms was heard by the U.S. Supreme Court in 1944.[38] Regarding the "fair return" issue, the Supreme Court reversed a district court ruling and found Congress under no constitutional necessity to provide a system ensuring a "fair return" to property owners and although the legislation may have resulted in reducing the value of the regulated property there was no "taking of it."[39]

The form of the federally controlled regulatory mechanism changed substantially during its implementation. The initial impetus leading to the introduction of rent adjustment provisions was a recognition that the freeze-date method—like any method applied across-the-board—produced some inequities in individual cases.[40] By the end of World War II, fourteen grounds for adjustment had evolved. They can be classified according to the following categories:

1. Situations where the landlord had made a substantial capital improvement in the housing accommodation since the freeze date, or had added a substantial increase in services rendered the tenant.
2. Situations where there had been a substantial increase in the number of persons then occupying the premises. This was not one of the original grounds, but, with crowding in and doubling up, it was necessary to make this amendment to cover a situation not previously encountered in rental practices to any extent.
3. Situations where, due to blood, special relationships or peculiar circumstances the rent charged on the freeze was substantially below the rent common for subject type of housing accommodations, and where free bargaining was absent on the freeze date.
4. Situations where the net income received under rent control was substantially below that which had been received in the year before rent control was invoked. This was one of the later amendments and resulted from aggressive action taken by real estate trade bodies.[41]

The second catalyst leading to a redefinition of the regulatory mechanism evolved out of the postwar extension of controls. Initiated with the enactment of the Housing and Rent Act of 1947, this change in the mechanics of rent control involved gradually terminating federal controls and transfering rent control regulation to states and localities. The goal of rent control methods at this stage was to allow gradual increases in maximum rental levels while effecting minimal impact on the nation's overall economy pending complete decontrol.[42] An important factor in the postwar relaxation of rent control, the relaxation and decontrol of other commodities, strove to achieve parity between rent and other commodities and relieve property owners' hardship while granting prompt adjustments. The maximum rents carried forward under the 1947 act were subject to three methods of modification:

1. Adjustment by the Housing Expeditor under his independent powers to change maximum rents;
2. Adjustment by the Housing Expeditor on recommendation of a local advisory board; and
3. Voluntary execution of a lease by a landlord and tenant providing for a rent increase not in excess of the 15 percent limit specified in the 1947 Act, as amended.[43]

Although generally applicable to individual units, adjustments were also made for entire buildings when the grounds were hardship or operating loss and the adjusted increase was applied to all units on a proportional basis.[44]

Not until 1949 did the concept of "fair net operating income" (FNOI) enter the administration of federal and subsequent state and local rent control mechanisms. A gross rent formula (see chapter 4) was used to derive the FNOI rather than the return on some valuation because any other formula was considered unworkable by Congress.[45]

The adjustment standard was derived from a 1939-1946 study of operating costs which examined "representative" rental housing accommodations both before and during rent control.[46] Using the standard adjustment, small structures of one to four units qualified for rent increases if their net operating income was less than 25 percent of the gross income; increases were allowed to yield net operating incomes of up to 30 percent. Large structures of four or more units qualified if the net operating income was less than 20 percent and increases in rent would not yield more than 25 percent of gross income.[47]

The provision of a "fair return" based on the federal model was included in some subsequent state and local rent control legislation; however, in general formulas based on the property's value tended to prevail. For example, the New York Temporary State Housing Rent Commission defined fair return in 1951 as 4 percent on assessed property valuation plus a 2 percent allowance for depreciation. The standard was raised in 1953 to 6 percent plus 2 percent for depreciation and equalized valuation rates were used.

## *SUMMARY: THE CYCLE OF RENT REGULATION*

Although specific methods of rent control have varied over the years, the primary purpose of rent control has always been and continues to be the "stabilization" of rents. Salient differences in the nature of controls at any period in time were determined by the severity of the crisis and decisions regarding the scope of the control mechanism to be applied. Present-day controls do not involve absolute freezes on rent levels as was the case during the initial World War II and 1971 Phase I controls; rather they provide mechanisms for regulated increases. Three important features characterized the earlier "freeze" periods: (1) they were applied on a broad scale; (2) they were relatively short-term in duration; and (3) they were accompanied by freezes on most other commodities. Both of the freeze periods were inevitably followed by regulatory periods which permitted gradual adjustments upward, necessitating the creation of complex systems of regulation. Typically, these transition periods in rent control history paralleled gradual price adjustments on other commodities as large-scale price controls were removed or relaxed.

The methods of rent control regulation currently used generally derive from those initiated during World War II. However, some very recent rent control statutes have been enacted during normal rather than "emergency" conditions; thus, they have bypassed the first phase in traditional rent control legislation–the freeze. More important, with the exception of controls enacted during Phase II (November 13, 1971 through January 11, 1973),[48] these recent measures were enacted in the absence of price controls on other commodities. The specific regulatory methods initially employed as temporary mechaisms are now established in what appear to be permanent rent control systems in many communities. However, since these regulatory mechanisms are still regarded as temporary from a legal standpoint, they are often administered in a haphazard, makeshift fashion.

## *THE NEW YORK THIRTY-THREE YEAR EMERGENCY*

An explanation of New York City's retention of rent control as a permanent housing policy, necessitates analysis of the many integral factors of the New York City housing market, the city's demography, and, perhpas most importantly, its politics. A study of that nature is beyond the scope of this investigation; however, research related to these issues has been undertaken over the years by leading experts in the fields of housing and economics: Frank Kristof, Ira Lowry, Leo Grebler, Chester Rapkin, George Sternlieb, and the New York City Rand Institute.[49] These investigations have to varying degrees resulted in changes in rent control administration and policy in New York City.

Surprisingly, a large number of other localities in New York State have retained rent control under state administration. A list of one hundred communities including those in which state-administered rent control continues to exist and those with expanded rent control in the form of rent stabilization can be found in the summary of currently enacted legislation in chapter 3.

Unitl 1974, New York State-administered rent control was applicable outside New York City only to units constructed prior to 1947. The enactment of the 1974 New York State Emergency Tenant Protection Act (ETPA) gave communities in Westchester, Nassau, and Rockland counties (all within the New York City metropolitan area) the option to extend rent regulation to post-1947 buildings via a more flexible stabilization program instituted in New York City in 1969.

The primary basis for continuing rent control in New York City and other state localities was a 1951 statutory privision dictating mandatory decontrol of properties having vacancies in excess of a 5 percent vacancy-rate standard. Mandatory decontrol applied to all or to a particular class of housing accommodations.[50] With the exception of decontrol at various times for certain high-rent apartment categories, no housing classifications have been made persuant to this 1951 provision.[51] Since 1951, a number of communities have been totally decontrolled as a result of the mandatory 5 percent vacancy-rate standard. Albany's units, for example, were decontrolled in 1960 when the total rental vacancy rate exceeded 5 percent; however, controls were reimposed in 1962 on units which rented for $80 or less in 1960. A number of communities, primarily smaller ones with few units subject to control, have opted to decontrol all units despite vacancy rates lower than 5 percent. This was possible because the 5 percent level was a standard for decontrol not for required controls—a significant distinction that has frequently been a point of debate.

Over the years in New York, a number of amendments and changes in regulation and exemption categories have occurred, including the transfer of legislative authority and administration of New York City's rent control from the state to the city in 1962.[52] The ultimate effect of the administrative transition is described in the following evaluation:

> The deterioration of the rent control situation became complete under its administration by the City of New York. Trapped by its own campaign rhetoric, the city's administration of rent control became harsh relative to the state's. Evictions granted for rehabilitation dropped sharply. The state's liberalized return on equity technique was scrapped. Only two formulas, the 15 percent rent increase permitted when apartments became vacant, and reasonable allowances for the replacement of equipment such as refrigerators, gas stoves, kitchen closets, and other items, remained as a ready source of increased revenues to owners.
>
> In short, the motivation for owners to maintain the condition of their rent-controlled properties weakened as the benefits from full occupancy and reduced services wore off and vanished with the termination of state controls and the inauguration of regressive city controls. It was during this period that the serious deterioration of rent-controlled housing began.[53]

The most significant action taken in New York City resulting in expanded rent regulation was the 1969 enactment of the Rent Stabilization Law (RSL).[54] Constituting a far less stringent form of regulation than the extant "rent control" law, rent stabilization applies controls to buildings constructed subsequent to 1947 and never previously controlled.[55] RSL provides a more liberal rent adjustment mechanism than previous regulations,[56] and its administration is delegated to the real estate industry via a tripartite sturcture: the Rent Stabilization Association (RSA), the Conciliation and Appeals Board (CAB), and the Rent Guidelines Board (RGB).[57] Building owners' compliance and cooperation with the regulations of the RSL is more or less guaranteed through the threat of mandatory imposition of regular rent control.

The rent stabilization approach to rent regulation is apparently more acceptable to both building owners and policymakers. It is an easier system to administer than the earlier rent control laws and major day-to-day responsibilities are handled by the real estate industry via RSA. Theoretically, if the real estate industry did not make a concerted effort to maintain stabilization standards, it jeopardized both its delegated authority and the program itself.

One of the long-term impacts of New York State's 1974 ETPA is the gradual phasing out of the original rent control mechanism transferring these units to rent stabilization through a vacancy decontrol process. The 1974 act eliminated the "vacancy decontrol," provision passed in 1971 applicable to the City and nearby metropolitan counties. Under 1971 vacancy decontrol vacated units were freed of all controls and could be rented at prices determined through negotiation between landlord and tenant. Under 1974's ETPA "rent-controlled" units' rents can increase to current market prices when vacated. Like under vacancy decontrol, the specific prise is negotiated between landlord and tenant. However, it is subject to rent stabilization guidelines for future rental increases,[58] and the initial negotiated rent can be appealed to the CAB for adjustment. Adjustment is possible when the CAB finds "that the presence of unique or peculiar circumstances materially affecting the initial legal regulated rent has resulted in a rent which is substantially different from the rents generally prevailing in the same area for substantially similar housing accommodations."[59] This adjustment appeal provision also applied to units decontrolled or destabilized under "vacancy decontrol" between July 1, 1971 and June 30, 1974 and which became subject to stabilization July 1, 1974.

A historical summary of rent control in New York City is presented in the following exhibit.

## *EXHIBIT 1–1*
## *SUMMARY OF NEW YORK CITY RENT CONTROL*

| *Enabling Legislation* | *Major Policy/Administrative Changes* | *Consequence/Impact* |
|---|---|---|
| *New York State "Standby" Law* (Chapter 274, Laws of 1946). | 1946-1950–Extended yearly. To be effective upon termination of federal controls. | Effective 7/1/46–7/25/46 during expiration of federal act until reinstated. |
| *Emergency Housing Rent Control Law* (Chapter 250, Laws of 1950). | State administered rent control by Temporary State Housing Rent Commission effective May 1, 1950 and superceded New York City rent control statute (Local Law #54 [1947]. | Established maximum rents as the lower of federal controls or maximum rents set by local law with adjustments granted after March 1, 1949. |
| | *Rent Increase Provisions* (1) Increased services or facilities, substantial rehabilitation, major capital or other improvements; (2) Voluntary lease agreements (two year term, 15% increase); (3) Increased occupancy or subletting; (4) Unique or peculiar circumstances (below prevailing rent for similar accommodations); (5) Net Annual Return (See Fair Return below); (6) Unavoidable increase in operating costs in small structures; (7) Unavoidable increases in specified structures; (8) Other necessary adjustments not inconsistent with act. All increases for any one ground limited to 15% above maximum rent and new lease increase once in two year period. | |

*EXHIBIT 1–1*
*(continued)*
*SUMMARY OF NEW YORK CITY RENT CONTROL*

| *Enabling Legislation* | *Major Policy/Administrative Changes* | *Consequence/Impact* |
|---|---|---|
| Amendments: (Chs. 36 & 443, Laws of 1951). | 1951: Fair Return–4% on equalized assessed valuation plus 2% operating expense allowance for depreciation. Fair return increases no more than 15% in any one year. | |
| | 1951: Five percent statutory vacancy decontrol established for any class or all housing accommodations within community. | |
| Amendments: (Chs. 320 & 321, Laws of 1953). | 1953: Across-the-board equalization adjustment up to 15% above 1943 maximum rents (where increases, excluding service increases, had not been granted). | |
| | 1953: Fair return raised to six percent on equalized assessed valuation or sales price plus two percent depreciation allowance. | |
| Amendments: (Ch. 755, Laws of 1957) Decontrol Order No. 51. | 1957: Luxury decontrol of units of four rooms or less with monthly rents on 1/1/57 in excess of $416 unfurnished and $500 furnished effective 3/16/58. | |
| Amendments: (Ch. 337, Laws of 1961). | 1961: Changes in criteria for defining value under Fair Return adjustment provision. Use of most recent state equalization rates, rather than 1954 rates. Restricted use of sales price. | |
| | Eliminated retroactive rent adjustment orders. Orders effective as of date of issuance. | |

*EXHIBIT 1-1*
*(continued)*
*SUMMARY OF NEW YORK CITY RENT CONTROL*

| *Enabling Legislation* | *Major Policy/Administrative Changes* | *Consequence/Impact* |
|---|---|---|
| *Local Emergency Housing Rent Control* (Ch. 21, Laws of 1962). | Transferred total administration of rent control in cities with population in excess of one million (New York City). (1) City authorized to enact local legislation; (2) State to bear reasonable and necessary costs; (3) Freeze imposed on maximum rents previously established pending transfer of jurisdiction. | |
| *New York City Rent and Rehabilitation Law* (Local Law No. 20 of 1962) (Title Y, Sec. Y51-1.0 to Y51-18.0 of the Administrative Code of the City of New York) "City Rent and Eviction Regulations" of the Rent and Rehabilitation Administration. | 1962: Administered by Rent and Rehabilitation Administration. With some exceptions city law similar to state law. Exempt: (1) units in post-2/1/47 buildings; (2) units in one- and two-family homes; (3) nonpermanent resident hotels and rooming houses. Vacancy decontrol: (1) converted units with major capital improvements with floor plan changes before 5/1/62; (2) units in owner-occupied buildings of six units or less. | |
| | Rent Increase Provisions (based on certification of code compliance and maintenance of all essential services): same as above state provisions with following additions/changes: (1) increased value as a result of substantial rehabilitation since 3/1/59; (2) sales price for fair return/hardship could not be used for a two-year period following transaction; (3) added | *Approved Rent Increases 1967:*[a] (units in thousands)<br>156.8–New Lease<br>12.6–Hardship<br>41.1–Equalization and Labor Costs |

*EXHIBIT 1–1*
*(continued)*
*SUMMARY OF NEW YORK CITY RENT CONTROL*

| *Enabling Legislation* | *Major Policy/Administrative Changes* | *Consequence/Impact* |
|---|---|---|
| | 1967: equalization and labor costs pass-along (a) where units have not had average of two increases since 1943 and (b) for increased labor costs of union and nonunion contract employees. | 136.7–Increased services<br>55.7–Major Capital Improvements<br>2.4–Other Provisions<br>405.3–Total (out of 1,300,000 units) |
| | Rent Decreases: (1) reduced services, facilities, etc.; (2) hazardous conditions; (3) uncorrected code violations. | 1967: Average unit reduction of $10 per month for 43,000 units granted. Applications filed for 311,000 units.[b] |
| City Rent and Eviction Regulations Sec. 2 f (14)(15). | Luxury Decontrol: 1964–units vacant on or after 3/26/64 having monthly rents on 4/1/60 in excess of $250 unfurnished and $300 furnished. (Exception allowed for households with school-aged children and four or more related persons.) Later extension decontrolled units vacant on or after 1/29/68 with rents effective 4/1/65. | |
| *New York City Rent Stabilization Law* (Local Law No. 16 of 1969) (Title YY Sec. YY51-1.0 to YY51-7.0 of the Administrative Code of the City of New York). | Regulated rents, services and evictions in all privately-owned buildings of six or more units constructed between 2/1/47 and 3/10/69, and most units formerly under rent control and previously decontrolled. Also covered post-1969 buildings receiving partial tax exemption under Sec. 421 of New York State Real Property Tax Law for 10-year period of abatement.<br><br>Program supervised by New York City Housing and Development Administration and administered by industry via Rent Stabilization Association. | 1970 registered units: 350,855.<br><br>1975 registered units: 652,534[c] (see 1974 ETPA). |

*EXHIBIT 1–1*
*(continued)*
*SUMMARY OF NEW YORK CITY RENT CONTROL*

| *Enabling Legislation* | *Major Policy/Administrative Changes* | *Consequence/Impact* |
|---|---|---|
| | Rent Increase Provisions:<br>Rent Guidelines Board established annual guidelines for rent increases based on length of lease entered or renewed during the particular period. Rents initially rolled back to rent effective 5/31/68 plus allowed increase per guidelines. Order No. 1 for 6/68-6/70. | Annual Percent Increase granted[d] (on 1- 2- 3-year leases):<br>6/68 6/70: 10.0/10.0/15.0<br>7/70–6/71: 6.0/8.0/11.0<br>7/71–6/72: 8.0/10.0/13.0<br>7/72–6/73: 6.5/8.5/10.5<br>7/73–6/74: 6.5/8.5/10.5<br>7/74–6/75: 8.5/10.5/12.0<br>7/75–6/76: 7.5/9.5/12.5 |
| *Maximum Base Rent Program* (MBR) Local Law No. 30 of 1970). | Introduced a cost-plus-profit formula for granting increases and closing the gap between existent and economic rents. MBR established for every eligible unit allowing no more than 7.5 percent increases annually. Required correction of all rent-imparing violations and 80% of other housing code violations prior to rent increase orders. | Estimated that 65,000 buildings[e] (1 million units) applied in 1970 to program.<br><br>1975: Approximately 800,000[f] units in program, but does not reflect number granted increase orders. |
| | Interim increases of up to 15% for period 8/1/70 to 12/31/71 granted to MBR applicants. | Increase determined by previous increases. |

*EXHIBIT 1-1*
*(Continued)*
*SUMMARY OF NEW YORK CITY RENT CONTROL*

| *Enabling Legislation* | *Major Policy/Administrative Changes* | *Consequence/Impact* |
|---|---|---|
| *New York State Vacancy Decontrol* (Ch. 371, Laws of 1971). | Allowed for total decontrol of rent-controlled and rent-stabilized units. | Estimates range from 240,000 to 325,000 rent-controlled units decontrolled between 7/71 and 12/73.[g] Estimated 88,000 rent-stabilized units destabilized 7/71 to 12/73.[h] |
| *New York State Emergency Tenant Protection Act of 1974* (ETPA)(Ch. 576, Laws of 1974). | Placed units completed between 3/11/69 and 12/31/73 under rent stabilization. Eliminated vacancy decontrol. Placed units decontrolled and destabilized under vacancy decontrol (1971-1974) under rent stabilization. Allowed rent-controlled units vacated after 5/1/74 to be transferred to rent stabilization. | Placed approximately 400,000[i] additional units under stabilization. |

*EXHIBIT 1–1*
*Sources*

a. F. Thomas Kingsley, "A Review of the Operations of Rent Control in New York City," *Rand Limited Document* (March 11, 1969), p. 4.

b. Ibid., p. 12.

c. Rent Stabilization Association Files cited in F. James and M. Lett, "A Review of Rent Guidelines and the Ecomomics of the Stabilized Sector of New York City's Housing Market" (June 23, 1975, unpublished).

d. Rent Guidelines Board, order nos. 1–6 found in the Rent Stabilization Association's supplement to reference booklet of August, 1973 (May 1975); and order no. 7 (July 1, 1975) (Mimeo).

e. State Study Commission For New York City, "The Management of the Maximum Base Rent (MBR) Program By the Housing and Development Administration of New York City from June 1970 to October 1972," p. 31.

f. Per telephone conversation: Mr. Bernstein of Rent and Housing Maintenance Division, 11/75. 1974 *New York Times* estimate of 900,000–1,000,000 cited in Real Estate Research Corporation, "A Policy Review of Rental Housing in New York City" (New York: Coalition to Save New York, 1975), p. II-8.

g. Frank Kristof, "Vacancy Decontrol In New York City: July 1971–December 1973" (January 28, 1974) – Estimate 250,000 to 300,000. New York City HDA estimates an average of 10 percent per year between 240,000 and 325,000 – See Real Estate Research Corporation (cited above), p. II-33.

h. Stein Commission, "Report on Housing and Rents of the Temporary State Commission on Living Costs and the Economy of the State of New York to the Governor and the Legislature" (January, 1974) (Mimeo).

i. Real Estate Research Corporation, p. II-40. Assuming the Stein Commission estimate of 88,000 destabilized units 7/71 to 12/73 correct, a more precise number is 383,000.

## *NOTES*

1. Edith Berger Drellich and Andrée Emery, *Rent Control in War and Peace* (New York: National Municipal League, 1939), p. 11.

2. In early 1917, Delaware, Maine, Massachusetts, Connecticut, and Nevada enacted legislation (on a limited basis) with Virginia following suit in 1918. The governor of New Jersey issued a proclamation which requested public cooperation in reporting rent profiteering and theatened criminal action against violators. In March, 1918, Congress passed the Soldiers and Sailors Civil Relief Act, protecting servicemen against excessive rent increases and evictions. In May 1918, Congress further passed a resolution which governed evictions in the District of Columbia. See Ibid., p. 11.

3. "Residential Rent Control in New York City," *Columbia Journal of Law and Social Problems*: 3 (1967): 31.

4. The Bureau of Industrial Housing and Transportation within the Department of Labor was an outgrowth of the activities of the Council of National Defense which was charged with "the coordination of industries and resources for the national welfare" during the war. Subsequently, Congress authorized the creation of the United States Housing Corporation, which assumed the housing responsibilities of the bureau. The Home Registration Service and Information Division created under the Housing Corporation maintained registries of inspected vacant rooms, flats and houses available in eighty-eight industrial centers.

5. "Residential Rent Control in New York City," p. 31.

6. April Housing Laws, N.Y. Session Laws, 1920, Ch. 131-38; September Housing Laws, N.Y. Sess. Laws, 1920, Ch. 942-52. See Drellich and Emery, pp. 109-13. One Statutory provision (Ch. 136) provided, "that if an action [was] brought for the payment of rent, defense [could] be based on the unreasonableness and oppressiveness of the agreement. This was the sole statute permitting the courts to fix maximum rents; the remaining provisions were largely amendments to the Code of Civil Procedure designed to curb landlords' powers to evict tenants."

7. Massachusetts General Acts 1920, Ch. 555, 578; New Jersey Ch. 340 (1920); Illinois Law of Landlord & Tenant, amended 1921, 52nd General Assembly; Arizona Laws, 1921, Ch. 126; Delaware Laws, 1921, Ch 215; Oregon Laws, 1919, Ch. 63; Maine Laws, 1919 (Special Session), Ch. 256. Municipal ordinances were also enacted in Jersey City, Los Angeles, Baltimore, and Denver.

8. Block v. Hirsh, 256 U.S. 135 (1921) and Marcus Brown Holding Co v. Feldman, 256 U.S. 170 (1921).

9. Successful rent commisions were established in Washington D.C., Denver, Colorado, and the state of Wisconsin. The most comprehensive series of laws was enacted by New York State. The following summarizes the substantive elements

of these measures which constitute a change in the landlord-tenant relationship, giving the tenant:

a) longer terms in notices to vacate, and permitting oral leases;

b) extension of terms for stays in summary proceedings, and also prohibition of summary proceedings for nonpayment of "unjust rents";

c) more substantial defense, based upon unjust rents and oppressive agreements, in legal proceedings for holdover or nonpayment of rent;

d) safegards against annoyances from landlords wanting to rent at higher prices;

e) the court's judgement instead of the landlord's as to the tenant's "undesirability";

f) protection in case the tenant paid or was willing to pay the rent after issuance of a dispossess warrant.

The Washington, D.C. law was abruptly ended in 1924 by court decision (Peck v. Fink, 2 Fed [2d] 912, [1924]) on the basis that there was no longer an emergency, thus no longer a constitutional basis for the legislation, although the act had been extended by Congress until May 22, 1925. The Washington Real Estate Board voluntarily handled complaints to minimize the problems of sudden termination.

10. Laws of 1920, Ch. 942 applied throughout the state. It authorized counties, cities, towns, villages and school districts to exempt from taxation for local purposes until 1/1/32 all new residential dwellings completed after 4/1/20 or begun before 4/1/22.

11. Prior to the enactment of the 1942 act, statutes were enacted in the District of Columbia and Virginia, although the Virginia law was never implemented. See Willis, "A Short History of Rent Control," *Cornell Law Quarterly 36 (1950):* 79-89. A "defense-rental area" generally consisted of a county or group of counties surrounding a metropolitan area. It was not initially the plan to cover the total United States, as rural areas and communities not affected by factors of the war would have no need for controls of rents. See Daniel D. Gage, "Wartime Experiment In Federal Rent Control," *The Journal of Land and Public Utility Economics,* 23 (1947): 52.

12. For detailed information pertinent to controls over this entire period at all governmental levels, see Bernard Friedlander and Anthony Curreri, *Rent Control: Federal, State, and Municipal* (New York: Central Book Co., 1948, 2nd ed., 1950).

13. Federal controls which lapsed for a twenty-five day period in 1946 were extended by the Price Controls Extension Act of 1946, Ch. 67; 60 Stat 664. The Housing and Rent Act of 1947, Ch. 163 decontrolled rooming houses, hotels, and apartment hotels and eased eviction controls for all rental accommodations. The 1947 act also provided for local rent advisory board recommendations for decontrol. Further the 1947 act designated the administra-

tion of federal rent control to the Office of Housing Expeditor, which was initially established by executive order in 1946 and given statutory status by the Veterans Emergency Housing Act of 1946 to carry out programs chiefly for veterans.
15. Ibid.
16. U.S. Public Law 464, 1948.
17. Friedlander and Curreri, pp. 28-38.
18. Ibid., pp. 247-48.
19. Bowles v. Willingham, 321 U.S. 503 (1944).
20. Woods, Housing Expeditor v. Clowyd W. Miller, 333 U.S. 138 (1948).
21. Prior to the expiration in 1956 of New Jersey's state rent control legislation, Newark passed an ordinance which was subsequently struck down by the New Jersey Supreme Court in Wagner v. City of Newark (24 N.J. 467, 132 A.2d 794 (1957]). The court held that the ordinance was outside the municipality's authority in the absence of state enabling legislation. This opinion was overturned in 1973 by the New Jersey Supreme Court in *Inganamort* v. *Borough of Fort Lee* (120 N.J. Super. 286, 293 A. 2d 720 [L. Div. 1973]).
22. U.S., Office of the President, Executive Order 11615, August 15, 1971.
23. U.S., Office of the President, Executive Order 11627, Section 11A, October 15, 1971.
24. *United States Code of Federal Regulations,* Title 6, Part 301, "Economic Stabilization," revised October 1972, exempted newly constructed and rehabilitated units (occupied after 8/15/71), single-family units and multifamily units of which an owner owned no more than four such units, and units renting for $500 per month (later lowered to $400). Base rents on applicable units were established as those effective at the time of the freeze, August 15, 1971.
25. U.S., Office of the President, Executive Order 11695, Section 10 (d), January 11, 1973. Also see U.S., Department of the Treasury, IRS Stabilization Program Guidelines, "Introducing Phase III" (January 12, 1973).
26. See Richard E. Blumberg, Brian Quinn Robbins, and Kenneth K. Baar, "The Emergence of Second Generation Rent Controls," *Clearinghouse Review,* 8 (August 1974): 240-249.
27. The need for a set of guiding principles during the period of controls prompted the United States Home Registration Service to compile a list of the various devices used by committees. These were grouped into three types in the U.S. Housing Corporation Report, as found in Drellich and Emery, pp. 18-20.

1) A basic date was fixed from which increases were calculated in proportion to increases in maintenance and living costs.

2) Fair rents were determined on a gross basis, i.e., an amount up to 10 percent gross return on investment was fixed as the standard. Alternatively, it was determined that the yearly rental should equal 10 percent of the assessed valuation, increased by one-third. Chicago defined three classes of apartments based on services provided and set the annual rental at 10, 15,

and 18 percent of the appraised value to provide the owner with a 6 percent return on the appraisal value.

3) Fair rentals were computed on the basis of net return on the investment. Figures of 6 to 8 percent were used as return to the owner.

28. Drellich and Emery, p. 22.

29. Drellich and Emery, p. 5. This research task was sponsored by the still active Citizen's Housing Council of New York.

30. Proposals to reinstitute rent control began as early as 1932 in Washington, D.C. as it was purported that rents had declined less there than anywhere in the country at a time when government employees' pay was being cut. Rents in the District averaged 20 percent higher than the rest of the country. In New York City, a housing shortage became apparent as early as 1936, but subsequent state legislation in 1940 failed to pass. See Willis, pp. 77-80.

31. Willis, p. 78.

32. Gage, p. 50.

33. Ibid.

34. Ibid.

35. Ibid., p. 51.

36. Ibid.

37. Ibid.

38. Bowles v. Willingham.

39. Ibid., at 517-19.

40. Gage, p. 53. Gage also notes that some of the freeze dates may have been set too far back. These freeze dates, set for defense-rental areas as it became necessary on the basis of demand and shortage, ranged from a three-month to a year rollback in rents. According to Gage, as the national office gained experience, freeze dates were selected with increased care and accuracy.

41. Gage, pp. 53-54. Friedlander and Curreri, pp. 198-218. Those grounds identified were: (1) major capital improvements after the effective date yielding a difference in rental value as the standard for rent increases; (2) change (increase) in value or services prior to maximum rent date; (3) substantial increase in space, services, furniture, furnishings or equipment; (4) varying rents as provided in lease effective maximum rent date allowing for future automatic rent increases; (5) seasonal rent variations; (6) substantial increases in occupancy; (7) priority-constructed accomodations for which no federally-approved rent increase was previously obtained; (8) inequitable rents below level for comparable premises; (9) substantial hardship from increase in operating expenses; (10) rental to employee of landlord; (11) change from year-round to seasonal renting; (12) priority-constructed housing accomodations for which a rent increase has been approved by a federal agency; and (13) operating loss.

42. Friedlander and Curreri, p. 24.

43. Ibid., p. 49. For grounds, see note 41.
44. The 1947 act as amended also provided for decreases in maximum rents, initiated by a tenant objection or on area rent director's initiative. Grounds for such decreases were: (1) rents higher than generally prevailing rents; (2) substantial deterioration in accomodations; (3) decreases in living space, services, furnishings, or equipment; (4) special relationship between landlord and tenant or peculiar circumstances; (5) varying rents through landlord-tenant agreements; (6) seasonal rental variations; (7) substantial decrease in occupancy; (8) rent concessions previously agreed upon (only in New York City); (9) reduction where hardship increase granted and the necessity for such increase is eliminated.
45. Friedlander and Curreri, p. 245 (1950).
46. Ibid.
47. Ibid., pp. 238-45. Regulations defined net operating income as that remaining after the payment of all operating expenses and depreciation allowances. Operating expenses did not include payments for interest or amortization of mortgages. Applications for increases in net operating income were based on annual income and expenses during a "test" year, consisting of the previous calendar or fiscal year or the most recent twelve-month period. Many costs were, however, projectable.
48. It should be noted that the controls on most commodities allowed for increases on the basis of increased costs for production and raw materials.
49. Extensive analysis of the dynamics of the New York City housing market are to be found in the following: Ernest Fisher, "Twenty Years of Rent Control in New York City," in *Essays in Urban Land Economics* (Los Angeles: University of California, Real Estate Research Program, 1966), pp. 31-67; Frank Kristof, *People, Housing and Rent Control in New York City* (New York: Rent and Rehabilitation Administration, 1964); Paul Niebanck, *Rent Control and the Rental Housing Market* (New York: Housing and Development Administration, 1970); Chester Rapkin, *The Private Rental Housing Market in New York City, 1965: A Study of Some Effects of Two Decades of Rent Control* (New York: Rent and Rehabilitation Administration, 1966); George Sternlieb, *The Urban Housing Dilemma: The Dynamics of New York City's Rent Controlled Housing* (New York: Housing and Development Administration, 1972); George Sternlieb and James Hughes, *Housing and People in New York City* (New York: Housing and Development Administration, 1973); Ira Lowry et al., *Rental Housing in New York City* (New York: Rand Institute, 1970-71), vol. 1, *Confronting the Crisis* (1970) and vol. 2, *The Demand For Shelter* (1971).
50. "Residential Rent Control in New York City," p. 61.
51. Ibid. The 1964 New York City law decontrolled unfurnished units renting for more than $250 per month and furnished units $300 per month or more, unless the tenant had children in elementary or secondary school or more than four relatives residing with him.

52. In 1962 the state passed the Local Emergency Housing Rent Control Act which provided and mandated local determination and establishment of local legislation for continuation after May 31, 1962 in cities with populations over one million.
53. Frank S. Kristof, "Housing: The Economic Facets of New York City's Problems," in *Agenda for a City,* Lyle C. Fitch and Ann Marie H. Walsh, eds. (New York: Institute of Public Administration, 1970), p. 313.
54. New York City Administrative Code, Sections YY 51-1.0 to YY 51-7.0. Can be found in *McKinneys Unconsolidated Laws,* book 65, pp. 587-623.
55. Exempted from RSL control were cooperatives and condominiums, buildings for which a certificate of occupancy was obtained after March 10, 1969, and structures of less than six dwelling units in the Class-A category. Unlike standard rent control, the RSL applies to publicly assisted housing, and, under separate regulations to nontransient hotel accomodations renting for less than $350 per month or $75 per week on May 31, 1969.
56. The RSL provides for an annual determination of fair rent increases by an impartial rent guidelines board on the basis of objective data which reflects current economic conditions including operating costs, financing costs, and housing supply and demand factors. An annual "Price Index of Operating Costs for Rent Stablilized Apartments in New York City" is prepared by the U.S. Bureau of Labor Statistics, under contract to the city, for the express purpose of guideline determination by the RGB.
57. The Rent Stabilization Association is organized by the industry and consists of the owners of not less than 40 percent of the units covered by the law. The RSA was required to formulate and adopt a code, consistent with the guidelines of the law, subject to the approval of the New York City Housing and Development Administration. As the primary administrative agency, the RSA operates on the basis of mandatory dues paid by all affected members and funds the operation of the CAB. The CAB, composed of an impartial chairman and eight members, four representing the public and four the real estate industry, handles all tenant grievances and complaints, determines hardship increases, and functions in a quasi-judicial manner. The RGB, appointed by the mayor, makes the annual determination of rent guidelines representing fair rental increases as described in above note. See: "The New York City Rent Stabilization Law of 1969," *Columbia Law Review* 70 (1970): 156 and "Rent Stabilization Law of 1969" *Brooklyn Law Review* 37 (1970): 307. Also see: 8200 Realty Corp. v. Lindsay, 1970, 27 N.Y. 2d 124, 313 N.Y.S. 2d 733, 261 N.E. 2d 647, appeal dismissed 91 S. Ct. 367, 400 U.S. 962, 27 L.Ed.2d 381, and Edward Lukashok, "There Is a Way to Stabilize Residential Rents" *Real Estate Review* 70, no.1 (Spring 1970): 96-99.
58. For housing accomodations which were regulated pursuant to the city rent and rehabilitation law (standard rent control) on the local effective date of the

Emergency Tenant Protection Act of 1974 and thereafter became vacant, the rent agreed to by the landlord and tenant and reserved in a lease or provided for in a rental agreement provided that such initial rent may be adjusted on application of the tenant pursuant to subdivision b of section YY51-6.0.2 of New York City's Administrative code.

59. New York City Administrative Code, Section YY 51-6.02 (b)1.

# Chapter 2
# The Conceptual Frame: Defining the Rent Control Issues

## *RENT CONTROL AND THE QUESTION OF HOUSING EMERGENCIES*

Of the many prevailing issues and controversies surrounding rent control, the issue concerning "emergency conditions" is critical and is inextricably tied to the constitutionality of rent controls. Rent control has been justified in many communities on the grounds that an emergency housing situation exists which needs to be addressed by the public control of rents. This was certainly the case during and immediately after World War II when a national housing emergency existed. New York City and other communities retained and expanded rent control statutes after the World War II period on grounds that emergency housing conditions continued to exist.

Today, municipalities in Massachusetts and New Jersey, as well as Miami Beach and other localities, have enacted rent control legislation in response to an avowed local housing emergency. The incorporation of a declaration of emergency in the preamble of all rent control legislation has become routine procedure. These declarations may identify a single cause for the emergency as in the Fort Lee, New Jersey ordinance, which cites "increases in rent . . . determined by [this] government body to be exorbitant, speculative, and unwarranted,"[1] or they may be as broad as the Massachusetts State Enabling Act declaration, encompassing nearly all of the economic forces impacting upon housing supply and demand.

> The general court finds and declares that a serious public emergency exists . . . which . . . has been created by housing demolition,

> deterioration of a substantial portion of the existing housing stock, insufficient new housing construction, increased costs of construction and finance, inflation and the effects of the Vietnam War, and which has resulted in a substantial and increasing shortage of rental housing accommodations for families of low and moderate income and abnormally high rents.[2]

Underlying such declarations is the question of exactly what constitutes emergency housing conditions.

*Why The Emergency Linkage?*

The emergency requirement as legal justification for upholding the constitutionality of rent control dates from the first rent control laws enacted subsequent to World War I. At that time the United States Supreme Court ruled that rent control was justified in response to a wartime emergency on the basis of the state's inherent emergency police power.[3] The first Supreme Court opinions–later described by one of the justices as on the "verge of the law"[4]–were narrowly decided 5 to 4 and written on "narrow" grounds:

> The [rent control] regulation is put and justified as a *temporary* measure. A limit in time, to tide over a passing trouble, well may justify a law *that could not be upheld as a permanent change.* [emphasis added].[5]

Students of rent control agree that the application of the emergency requirement as a prerequisite to the use of police power resulted from the early twnetieth century concept of "economic due process."[6] However, in a Supreme Court decision during the New Deal era the Court retreated from the economic due process concept as a basis for regulating rates in private industry.[7] Such interpretations suggest that the emergency requirement is no longer constitutionally viable. However, it has also been suggested that the emergency declaration remains necessary because of the two-pronged nature of most rent control measures, i.e., the regulation of rents and the limitation of the owners' power to evict. This argument states:

> In order to justify eviction controls, rent legislation has always been upheld under broad emergency police powers of the state, even though there would be no need to rely on this broad power to justify the regulation of rent rates alone. Since *Nebbia v. New York* it has been clear that rent rates, like other prices generally, could be regulated in the absence of an emergency.[8]

Although recent legal challenges have not focused on the emergency requirement as a central issue, the courts have continued to consistently hold that emergency is a necessary prerequisite to rent regulation.[9]

Constitutional challenges accompanying the imposition of rent controls can be classified as issues concerning (1) the emergency doctrine; (2) preemption of municipal police-power authority; and (3) procedural and substantive due process of law.[10] The latter two issues are discussed in subsequent chapters; the emergency doctrine is treated below.

In a recent 1975 decision the California Court of Appeals upheld a lower court decision invalidating a Berkeley City Charter amendment which enacted rent control through a voter initiated referendum.[11] Although the court in this decision acknowledged the municipality's authority under the California State constitution to enact rent control, the charter amendment was invalidated on the basis that "there was not such a widespread rental housing shortage and exorbitant rents as to constitute a 'serious public emergency.' "[12] Although the primary issue in the invalidation of a 1969 Miami Beach ordinance was municipal authority, the Florida Court also held that the prevailing housing conditions did not sufficiently constitute the type of emergency required to justify the use of rent controls.[13] However, the emergency requirement has not been the central issue in some recent cases which have challenged the constitutionality of rent control.[14]

Concerning rent control, there appears to be general judicial consensus regarding the constitutional necessity for emergency housing conditions;[15] however, considerable judicial controversy persists concerning two aspects of the emergency question: the extent of judicial review vis-a-vis the existence of a housing emergency and the criteria for defining an emergency housing situation.

### *Judicial Notice versus Judicial Review*

Well-established principles of judicial review have evolved from the separation of powers doctrine; this fact is exemplified in the following excerpt from a recent rent control decision. "Judicial inquiry is limited to consideration of the constitutional issue whether legislation has gone so far as to reach the point where police power ceases and leaves only that of eminent domain."[16]

The courts are also concerned with the question of "reasonableness" particularly as related to the stated goals of legislation. It is the function of the legislature to formulate policy and determine the need for given regulations. On finding a reasonable basis for legislation the courts generally refrain from weighing the wisdom of legislation or interfering with legislative policy.[17] Therefore, in reviewing challenges to rent control most courts "have given great deference to the legislative finding of emergency, no matter how pro forma it appears."[18] In *Inganamort v. Borough of Fort Lee* the trial court took judicial notice of the existence of emergency housing conditions: "The population growth and the rent increase fluctuations are matters of common knowledge not requiring the taking of testimony."[19] And upon appeal, the New Jersey Supreme Court also took notice: "We must assume there is a critical shortage of the housing covered by the several ordinances here involved and that tenants, trapped by the fact, are being exploited."[20]

However, in deciding on rent control legislation, the judiciary may not always defer to legislative wisdom concerning the determination of a housing emergency.[21] For example, in *Chastleton v. Sinclair* (1924) the Supreme Court "made it clear that legislative declarations of emergency would not be accepted at face value if unsupported in fact and that the courts would scrutinize legislative findings of emergency whenever necessary."[22] In the *Inganamort* decision, the factual premise of a housing emergency was not challenged, either as a central issue or on pretrail motion.[23] In that situation the ordinances were upheld on the basis of municipal authority to enact rent control pursuant to the police power vested in them by the state.[24] In the previously cited Berkeley California case concerning the rent control charter amendment, rent control was acknowledged as a legitimate constitutional exercise of police power; however, its exercise was invalidated on the basis that an emergency did not exist.

In the Berkeley case the California Court of Appeals also acknowledged the principles of judicial review. While it presumed "that the legislative body [had] investigated and ascertained the existence of those facts [establishing the existence of an emergency] before enacting the laws," it

> upheld the rights of an interested party [landlord] to challenge the validity of rent control legislation by presenting evidence that a serious housing emergency, which is the basis of rent control legislation, either did not exist at the time the legislation was enacted, or no longer exists. . . . The fundamental issue in this case is therefore whether the respondents–Landlords sustained their burden of showing that no critical shortage of rental housing resulting in exorbitant rents, constituting a serious public emergency, in fact existed at the time the charter amendment in question was enacted.[25]

This decision is not unlike those in a number of rent control cases where the constitutionality or validity of legislation is dependent upon the existence of certain facts. Relying on *Chastleton v. Sinclair,*[26] the California Court of Appeals, in reviewing the essential facts found by the trial court, concluded that the trial courts' finding of fact supported its conclusion–that "there was not such a *widespread* rental housing shortage and exorbitant rents as to constitute a *'serious public emergency.'* " [emphasis added].[27]

The extent of the court of appeal's scrutiny of the essential facts may be related to the process enacting the law in question. In that situation there was no legislative determination of emergency; in fact, the Berkeley City Council had refused to place the referendum on the ballot.[28] What is of most significance in this case, however, is the lack of specific criteria upon which the conclusion was based. How wide is "widespread?" And at what point are rents "exorbitant?" Acknowledging that the judgment of the court was conscientiously made and may have well been accurate, the lack of consensus as to what constitutes an emergency poses a crucial question in the imposition of rent controls.[29] Contributing to this lack of consensus is an unclear understanding of the nature of the urban housing market. Therefore, it seems appropriate to briefly address the vagaries of this complex market before proceeding to define an emergency housing situation.

## *TOWARD AN UNDERSTANDING OF THE HOUSING MARKET*

> The twin controversies of whether rent control is justified and whether it has adverse effects on housing markets and on the supply of rental housing are largely rooted in judgments of how closely the rental housing market comes to the competitive norm and how rapidly the housing supply adjusts to both short run profits and loses.[30]

The principles of supply and demand are generally accepted as the crucial variables in any competitive market. There are, however, several conditions which must be met, in order for a truly competitive market to exist: (1) numerous buyers and sellers; (2) a small number of sales or purchases of individual units in relation to the aggregate volume of transactions; (3) no buyers' or sellers' collusion; (4) free market entry and exit for both producers and consumers; (5) producers and consumers must possess perfect information concerning prevailing prices and current bids and take advantage of every opportunity to increase profits and utility, respectively; (6) artificial restraints must not be placed on demands for resources used to produce that service; (7) housing service must be a homogeneous commodity.[31]

Urban housing markets do not always provide a representative picture of what, theoretically, constitutes a competitively sound market. The distinctive characteristics of housing markets makes the application of conventional market theory difficult and further contributes to cloudy understanding of its functioning. These unique characteristics have been defined according to: (1) structural features and (2) operational consequences. These definitions proposed by Jerome Rothenberg are summarized as follows:

*Characteristics of Housing Market*

A. *Structural Features*

1. *Localization* –For an overwhelming proportion of households, housing consumption occurs within a single geographic location during each conventional economic period (say one year). It is this localization that creates the concept of residential neighborhood and household accessibility and hence deeply links the economic dimension of housing with the sociological and political dimensions.

2. *Durability* – Housing capital is by far the most durable capital incorporated in consumer goods. Durability means more than simply the continued physical existence of a structure. It means that a structure does not necessarily lose its marketability just because it is older. An older unit remains a good substitute in the market for units just built, even at advanced age.

3. *Heterogeneity* – Housing units in an urban area are heterogeneous, not homogeneous. They differ markedly in a number of ways. Differences in the physical units themselves are well known–embracing size, number of rooms, architectural layout and style, structural amenities, and condition, among others. But a housing unit comprises more than simply the structure, because of the localization function referred to above. It is a package, consisting of the structure, the land lot, the neighborhood and the configuration of accessibility to desirable destinations within and without the urban area.

4. *Convertibility of Existing Units* – Housing units are highly durable. But continued viability in the market requires continued maintenance and repair. Indeed, more than the economic survival of the unit is at stake. A unit constructed to render one type of service at a certain time can be converted during its lifetime to render other types of services. The quality of the unit may also be converted.

5. *Capital Market* – In urban America, a housing unit is a very expensive commodity. Most people occupy units which have a market value at least three times as great as the annual income of their occupants and greater than the total portfolio of assets of their occupants. The durability of housing makes it possible to accommodate the budgets of occupants by two means: 1. high mortgages on ownership claims; 2. the rental market. Both of these market patterns lead the housing sector to make very heavy demands on loanable funds, especially long-term funds. Housing is one of the largest clients of the national capital market.

6. *Moving Costs* – To a much greater extent than with other types of consumer goods, a change in consumption of housing is costly–in

terms of time and money in search, acquisition and physical moving. These costs are even greater for owner occupants and in the case of tenure changes from renter to owner occupancy.

7. *Public Constraints* – Because of the close connection between physical housing conditions and health and safety, housing has been the target of a variety of public interventions–including zoning regulations, health and building codes, and rent control, among others. These can exercise substantial constraints on the actions of suppliers and demanders in the market, and on the operation of the market itself. The housing market is not a perfectly free market.

*Some Operational Consequences*

1. *Preexisting Stock and New Units* – Because of the durability of housing, units of many ages will be on the market at any given time. Indeed, in any year all but a minute percentage of all units will have been built before the beginning of the year. The preexisting stock is the paramount component in the supply of housing in any period. Newly produced units are a small part of the story, although they may have influence disproportionate to their numbers in some respects. The preexisting stock is not a static component of the supply of housing. Owners of existing units can modify them in directions suggested by changing market opportunities. Thus, there are two forms of actual supply response to market forces: 1. the building of new units, and 2. the conversion of older units.

2. *Information* – The great variety of housing units and the importance of tastes regarding differences in those units lends importance to the dissemination of information about the housing units. Both the providers of housing and housing consumers must be adequately informed about alternatives.

3. *Market Segmentation* – The great diversity of housing units indicates segmentation of the housing market. Housing units are not substitutive one for another. The housing market actually consists of several markets, each providing a different quality and type of housing and appealing to different sectors of the consumer public.

4. *Transactional Friction* – The high costs of active participation in the market–search, transactions, and moving costs–imply that the benefits of making a change in housing may have to be quite substantial to warrant making the change. For most households, participation in the housing market occurs sporadically, with long periods of nonparticipation in between. This in turn implies that in each period the particular lineup of units available and households seeking units is very important in determining the outcomes of transactions.

5. *Neighborhood Externalities* – The localization function of the housing market lends significance to the neighborhood of the housing unit. Changes in neighborhood can affect the desirability of a housing unit, independently of the actions of its owner or changes in taste of the housing consumer. Thus, the relatively external factor of the neighborhood can have a profound affect upon the housing market.
6. *Vulnerability to Capital Market* – The heavy dependence of the housing market on the national capital market makes the housing market especially vulnerable to aggregate forces that can impinge on the capital market for reasons that have little to do with the worthwhileness of housing versus other production or consumption sectors. Macroeconomic conditions may have effects on housing far greater than on other production and consumption sectors.
7. *Dynamics* – Most of the foregoing suggests that timing is very important in the housing market. Indeed, they even raise the question of whether equilibrium ever exists in any but very special and limited circumstances in the housing market.[32]

Of this broad group of characteristics the two most important features are the localization of consumption of housing services and the durability of housing capital. They underlie all other features of the housing market and directly affect the scope of the market's operation. At the same time, however, it should be noted that the importance of market segmentation in defining local housing conditions is often underrated. According to Rothenberg,

> one consequence of this segmentation is that the different submarkets can experience an independent margin of variation relative to one another: one can have excess demand, another excess supply, another be well-balanced. So housing prices may move diparately among them. Another consequence is that variation initiated within one subsector will have very uneven repercussions on the other subsectors: in general, the closer the relatedness the more nearly parallel the repercussion in direction and intensity.[33]

In sum, this broad spectrum of factors places constraints on the ability of the housing market to react to changes in demand and thus makes the definition of an emergency housing situation extremely complex.

## *WHAT IS AN EMERGENCY HOUSING SITUATION?*

A shortage of housing units is most often equated with a housing emergency. Such shortages are traditionally defined in terms of projected duration.

> *A short-run housing shortage* is said to exist if, and only if, the quantity of housing service demanded at the existing market price is greater than the quantity of housing service supplied. Short-run shortages will be eliminated by a rise in the prise of housing service for bundles of the size which are in excess demand initially.*A long-run housing shortage* is said to exist if, and only if, the quantity of housing service demanded at the long-run equilibrium price is greater than the quantity of housing service supplied. Long-run shortages are eliminated by maintenance, repairs, alterations, and additions as well as by new construction. Clearly, a housing shortage can exist by these definitions even if everyone who wants to occupy a separate dwelling unit at the relevant price is doing so because everyone may want to occupy better housing (i.e., to consume a greater quantity of housing service) at this price than they presently occupy and none may be available.[34]

The declarations of emergency, included in all rent control legislation, differ widely in identifying the nature of housing emergency—from a single cause to a multiplicity of causal factors—encompassing nearly all of the economic forces which may directly or indirectly impact housing supply and demand. An analysis of currently enacted legislation (discussed in detail in the following chapter) reveals seventeen factors which have been used as indicators of the existence of an emergency housing situation.

An examination of Exhibit 2-1 reveals the variation and ambiguous nature of many of these emergency indicators, as well as the lack of precision used in, and thus the unquantifiability of, measures reflecting the relative existence of these indicators. The most frequently cited grounds for the imposition of rent controls are: (1) the existence of a housing shortage; and (2) excessive rent increases which adversely affect or threaten the health, safety, and general welfare of the residents of the state or municipality. The latter is generally included to justify the use of the police power. Only two of the four statutes in Exhibit 2-1 supplying references to vacancy rates provide quantifiable criteria,[35] and none of the twelve rent control statutes cite actual rental increase percentages or increase patterns. Two interrelated factors warrant special attention in light of the significance they play in any rent control controversy.

1. The *rent* factor—are absolute local rental levels placing decent housing beyond the means of a large portion of the population?

*EXHIBIT 2-1*
*EMERGENCY CRITERIA FROM SELECTED RENT CONTROL STATUTES*

| | Alaska | Berkeley, California | District of Columbia | Miami Beach Florida #1 | Miami Beach. Florida #2 | Maine | Maryland[4] | Massachusetts | Fort Lee, New Jersey | New York Emergency Housing Rent Control | New York Rent Stabilization | New York: ETPA |
|---|---|---|---|---|---|---|---|---|---|---|---|---|
| 1. Housing Shortage | ✓ | ✓ | ✓ | ✓ | ✓ | ✓ | ✓ | ✓ | | ✓ | ✓ | ✓ |
| 2. Rent Increases | | ✓ | ✓ | | ✓ | ✓ | | ✓ | ✓ | ✓ | ✓ | ✓ |
| 3. Overcrowding serious threat to Public Health | | | ✓ | | | | | | | | | |
| 4. Safety and General Welfare | ✓ | ✓ | ✓ | | ✓ | ✓ | | ✓ | ✓ | ✓ | ✓ | ✓ |
| 5. Evictions | | | ✓ | | | | | | | | ✓ | |
| 6. Population Growth | ✓ | | | | | | | | | | | ✓ |
| 7. Economic Conditions | ✓ | | | ✓ | | | ✓ | ✓ | | | ✓ | ✓ |
| 8. Vacancy Rate[1] | ✓ | ✓ | | | | | | | | | ✓ | ✓ |
| 9. Disruption of free housing market | ✓ | | | | | | | | | ✓ | ✓ | ✓ |
| 10. Tenant Hardship | | ✓ | | | ✓ | | | | ✓ | ✓ | ✓ | ✓ |
| 11. Environmental Crisis | | | | | | | ✓ | | | | | |
| 12. Housing Demolition | | | | | | | | ✓ | | | | |
| 13. Housing Deterioration | | ✓ | | | | | | ✓ | | | | ✓ |
| 14. New Construction[2] | | | | | | | | ✓ | | | ✓ | |
| 15. Cost of New Construction | | | | | | | | ✓ | | | | ✓ |
| 16. War[3] | | | | | | | | ✓ | | ✓ | ✓ | ✓ |
| 17. Reduced Federal Subsidies | | | | | | | | | | | | ✓ |

*Notes:* 1. Only Alaska and New York ETPA specify a vacancy rate; the other two references are only to "low vacancy."

2. Generally refers to the absence or insufficient quantity of new construction.

3. The Massachusetts declaration cites the Vietnam War while New York references the conditions created by World War II and the Korean conflict.

4. Maryland further cites the termination of federal controls as a justification.

*Source:* Kenneth Baar and W. Dennis Keating, "The Last Stand of Economic Substantive Due Process–The Housing Emergency Requirements For Rent Control," *Urban Lawyer* 7, no. 3 (Summer 1975): 490 (modified slightly).

2. The *vacancy* factor—does the area have an extremely low vacancy rate thereby leading to abuses in the housing market, i.e., rent gouging?

*The Rent Factor*

Vacancy rates are traditionally viewed as crucial in explaining housing shortages, since rents and vacancy rates vary inversely within a critical zone of occupancy.[36] It is, however, necessary to identify the range of factors which contribute to vacancy rate changes, and to rental increases which appear to occur in the absence of vacancy rate changes. These include both supply and demand factors. Demand factors include:

1. Increased numbers of households resulting from population growth and new household formation which leads to a scarcity of housing at current rents and contributes to rising rents. In the short-run, rising rents somewhat reduce demand and tend to encourage new and continued investment (barring the presence of any other factors).
2. Increased incomes of the population in general may increase the demand for housing thus leading to higher rents. Much of this increased demand will be directed toward higher quality units. The number of households seeking units may also increase as rising income will allow some present members of overcrowded households to seek residences of their own.

On the supply side:

1. The costs of operating housing may increase, leading to higher rents necessary to cover relatively fixed operating expenses.
2. The costs of construction may increase at such a pace that new construction is inadequate to keep pace with demolitions and other losses, thus resulting in a reduced housing stock. Even in the absence of an increase in absolute demand (as reflected above) the demand upon existing units will intensify and will lead to rising rent levels for the reduced numbers of available units.

Increased investment and construction generally follows rising rents as a result of demand-pull inflation in the housing market. However, the rapidly rising rent levels of the 1970s are but one manifestation of the cost-push variety of inflation rampant in the economy as a whole. This brand of inflation led to the recent pattern of rising rent levels in new and existing multifamily units.

These higher rent levels, in turn, have been defined as exorbitant and unwarranted in the declarations of emergency in some rent control statutes.

Relying upon legal precedent,[37] it has been held that "*an increase in the cost of living (an inflationary spiral) alone is not a justification for rent control legislation.*" [emphasis added].[38] Furthermore the propriety of utilizing rent control as a measure to combat inflation in only one sector of the economy when that inflation is pervasive throughout the economy raises a serious question. Given excess demand within the housing market, rent control may be an appropriate device to reduce exorbitant and speculative increases while market forces seek equilibrium. But, are rent increases as a result of cost-push inflation exorbitant if they are commensurate with increases in operating costs? Unlike rental increases generated by demand-pull inflation these rent levels will not decline significantly in an excess supply market.[39]

A standard by which to gauge speculative and exorbitant rent increases has not evolved out of recent emergency debates; rather, in the instances in which rental increases were a central issue, subjective judgments have been made by public officials and the courts on the basis of arbitrary and often conflicting testimony and data.[40]

Rent controls have been adopted to protect low-and-moderate-income households and particularly the elderly poor who bear the heaviest burden during periods of rapidly escalating rents. The Washington Area Federation of Tenants Associations, for example, argued for the adoption of rent regulations in Washington, D.C. "because sharp rent increases most adversely affect the large concentration of low-income, fixed-income and aged citizens who live in the District, and probably more than it affects the more affluent suburban areas."[41] Harvard University economist, John Kain, commenting on Cambridge, Massachusetts rent control summarized generally utilized arguments in support of rent control:

> First, market forces (growth in demand for property in Cambridge) has and will likely continue to cause a rapid rise in the rents of Cambridge properties. Second, this rapid rise in rents is causing serious hardship for many long-term, elderly, and low-income residents of Cambridge. Increasingly, these Cambridge residents are confronted with the unenviable choice of paying a growing fraction of their small, and frequently fixed, incomes for rent or with moving from Cambridge to surrounding communities where rent increases have been smaller.[42]

Yet, while rent control has often been defended as a protection for the elderly on fixed incomes, it is clear that the majority of tenants who benefit from such regulations are not in this category. Rental housing may have once been "a poor man's good," but life style and consumer preferences have altered this conception as middle-income and luxury structures have become popular. However, an increasingly larger proportion of the population, including the middle-income strata, is finding that decent housing–if not beyond its means altogether–is taking a larger bite from its disposable income. Housing costs have increased as a much faster rate than real spendable income in recent years, particularly since 1970. Thus, rent control has evolved as a form of subsidy to tenants.

The widening "gap" between tenants' ability to pay and the increased rentals required to operate and maintain a unit represents the essence of the rent control dilemma. A substantial proportion of rent controlled units are occupied by tenants who pay 25 percent or more of their income for rent.[43] However, the property owners argue that the provision of rent subsidies is a governmental function not a property owner's, and is, therefore, clearly beyond the scope and intent of the rent control mechanism.

### *The Vacancy Factor*

More than any other variable, the vacancy rate provides a measure of the degree to which existing housing stock is being utilized, and is, consequently, a fairly good indicator of the current state of excess demand in the market. A "low" vacancy rate has frequently been used as evidence of an emergency housing condition and as justification for enacting rent control. The few judicial attempts to analyze the validity of legislatively declared housing emergencies have focused primarily on vacancy rates. There is widespread agreement that a critical vacancy situation can lead to such undesirable consequences as rent gouging, but there is little consensus in the definition of what constitutes a low vacancy factor.

A definition of low vacancy rate as 5 percent or less dates from as early as 1923.[44] The 5 percent vacancy standard is derived from theories of the optimal level necessary to maintain equilibrium in the housing market.[45] According to one housing expert, vacancy ratios exceeding 3 to 5 percent are indicative of either overpricing or an oversupply of rental space.[46] According to another housing specialist, before World War II "a 4 or 5 percent gross vacancy was considered normal and not dangerous. Since the war, it has been shown, the vacancy rates have generally been lower than this. . . . No single vacancy rate can be considered 'normal.' "[47] The latter is true because the optimal rate necessary to guarantee a competitive market varies between housing markets and is determined by such factors as the size of communities, proportion of rental units to the total stock, and distribution of units on the basis of price and unit types.[48] Thus, for any community two vacancy rate standards are needed because the same vacancy rate cannot be both "optimal" and an indicator of a "critical" housing shortage. That is, if a 5 percent vacancy rate provides equilibrium in the housing market then disequilibrium does not occur at 4.9 percent—but certainly may at 3 percent.

Rent control statutes may set vacancy standards as gauges for determining the existence of an emergency housing condition. The 1974 New York State Emergency Tenant Protection Act cites a vacancy factor of 5 percent or less as the basis for emergency declaration by a local legislative body. The New Jersey communities of Atlantic City and Haddon Township also include a 5 percent vacancy standard in their rent control ordinances. Further, the 5 percent vacancy rate has been established since 1951 in New York State rent control legislation as the standard for statutory decontrol. That legislation states that

> Whenever the city rent agency shall find, after making such studies and investigation as it deems necessary . . . that the *percentage of vacancies in all or any particular class of housing* accommodations in the city, as such class is determined by the city rent agency, *is five per centum or more, [then] the controls imposed* on rents and evictions by and pursuant to this title, with respect to the housing accommodations as to which such finding has been made, *shall be forthwith scheduled for orderly decontrol.* [emphasis added].[49]

The five percent standard is not, however, sacrosanct. Lower vacancy factors have and are currently used as indicators of a public emergency. Alaska's rent control enabling legislation, for example, employs the following operational definition:

> A housing emergency exists when the rate of vacancies in residential rental housing is so low that there is a substantial impairment of free choice in residential rental housing or when the average vacancies in residential housing rental *falls below three per cent in the area, or areas, affected and remains below three per cent for a period of at least 90 days.* [emphasis added].[50]

In the Berkeley, California case in which the courts determined no emergency existed, a 3.1 percent rate existed within the City of Berkeley. More significantly, however, the court decision involved an acceptance of evidence of vacancy rates in communities adjoining Berkeley:

> In determining that a rental housing emergency does in fact exist, it is necessary that the rental housing availability in the adjacent incorporated and unincorporated areas, as well as the subject municipality be considered.[51]

This utilization of a regional framework in analyzing a metropolitan area is not a novel approach. However, due to the realities of legislative boundaries, it is a factor which has largely been ignored in rent control emergency debates.

### *Defining the Housing Market*

In addition to the absence of a consistently updated data base, the difficulties in measuring housing availability are compounded by the necessity to determine those adjoining communities which should be included in a given housing market.

The Federal Housing Administration defined a housing market as the geographic entity within which nonfarm dwelling units are in mutual competition.[52] Similarly, Ernest and Robert Fisher noted that a housing market is defined by the area over which units in the standing stock are assumed to be substituted for one another.[53] Charles Abrams refers to a housing market area as "the geographic area within which dwelling units are closely substitutable for one another—that is, which contain all the units that are likely to be considered potential housing accommodations by the resident population."[54]

It is difficult to draw the boundary lines of a housing market with any degree of precision—largely because of the difficulty in determining which housing units are in competition with one another.[55] However, many housing market surveys have been conducted making no attempt to delineate the area where housing units are in mutual competition or are clearly substitutable.[56]

There is widespread consensus that the length of journey to work has a major influence on the purchase or rental of a dwelling unit. David Blank and Louis Winnick, for example, noted that the most important factor in determining where an individual will locate is the travel or distance from his or her job or business. Similarly, the FHA noted that the location of employment centers and the availability of transportation facilities are among the major considerations in the choice of housing locale among the working population.[57] Ernest and Robert Fisher, as well as Charles Abrams, also concur that the most important factor in analyzing a local housing market is distance to employment centers.[58] This theory is supported by a 1964 survey conducted by the University of Michigan's Survey Research Center in which more than half of the sample population said that living close to the head of household's place of work was *important,* and almost one-third felt this to be a *very important* factor.[59] A 1967 survey conducted by the *Oakland Tribune* indicated that proximity to work was the single most important consideration in selecting housing.[60]

Utilization of the previously discussed components of the housing market facilitates a reasonable delineation of a housing market region. Although absolute precision in identifying the boundaries of a housing market is not possible, at least one thing is certain: a housing market cannot be realistically defined according to artificial political boundaries.

## *THE DYNAMICS OF THE RENT CONTROL CONTROVERSY*

Rent controls adopted during a public emergency such as war are generally accepted by the public with a minimum of controversy. Such a consensus has not been characteristic of peacetime controls. In fact, as more and more jurisdictions adopt rent control regulations, the debate over the benefits and costs of these public measures has intensified. According to one student of the controversy, "Rent control has been subjected to as much criticism, vilification and abuse, as almost any type of social legislation."[61]

Although the existence of an emergency housing condition is the primary legal justification for rent control there are other reasons, largely economic ones, which account for the treatment of rent controls as "emergency measures." In the recent Berkeley California case the judge stated that:

> while these [other] reasons are not always articulated clearly, they are implicit in the effect that rent controls have on the community. . . . In contrast to the myriad of regulations of businesses and use of property under the police power, rent control regulations adversely affect not only the owners of the regulated property, but also the community at large.[62]

The economic consequences of rent control, both direct and indirect, coupled with the embedded principles of inalienable property rights, serve to perpetuate the emergency rationale in the private housing market, regardless of judicial economic due process interpretations in other areas of private enterprise. Therefore, a brief discussion of these economic consequences–both advantageous and disadvantageous–is in order. The purpose of this discussion is not to assess the merits and demerits of the various arguments but merely to present them in summary form.

### *The Benefits of Rent Control*

The desired benefits of rent control are directly related to the objective to be derived from rent control legislation. A typically stated prupose for enactment is "to protect tenants from unreasonable or exorbitant rents during a shortage of rental housing, and at the same time provide landlords with reasonable rents."[63] Supports of rent control often base their arguments on the following points:

1. The special nature of the housing market demands rent control.
2. The special nature of housing as a commodity demands rent control.

3. Rent controls are needed to house the poor and other vulnerable social groups.

The Nature of the Market

In most competitive markets, rising demands generate increased production and eventually supply meets demand. However, as suggested earlier in this chapter, housing markets have distinctive characteristics which are not representative of most competitive markets. Given these characteristics and the combination of factors which may prevail in a period of housing shortage—curtailed financing, housing cost, household income disparity, and the presence of other controls such as growth moratoriums—an adjustment lag in inevitable. During this adjustment period, while housing supply catches up to demand, undesirable practices such as rent gouging may take place. Rent control is viewed by its proponents as one strategy for alleviating such practices.

Housing As a Consumer Commodity

The unique characteristics of housing consumption are cited as another reason demanding special protection for the housing consumer through rent controls. As summarized by one author:

> Most elements of the ordinary family's budget have some element of flexibility. If food costs go up, the family can usually exist on less food, or on cheaper food stuffs. If clothing costs rise, old clothes can be made to do. If the family budget no longer balances—either because costs have gone up or because the family income has gone down—economies can be made in various ways. But rent is an inflexible charge. If it goes up, the tenant has little choice but to pay more or to move to a less expensive lodging, and in times of housing shortages the latter alternative is an illusory one. The result is a monopoly situation in which the state has to intervene—just as it will intervene in other cases where monopolistic control of some element of the economy in which there is an intense public interest makes oppression probable.[64]

Rent Control As A Social Function

Rent control is also viewed by its advocates as a strategy for providing housing protection for the poor, and especially for the elderly on fixed incomes.

A number of studies have confirmed that tenants in rent-controlled housing pay less rent than they would in an uncontrolled market.[65] One of these researchers stated that rent control reduced "the proportion of housing expenditures to total consumption expenditures, *for those who were protected by rent control. . . .* [Thus] rent control was a factor not only in the maintenance of consumption standards, but in the rise of relative consumer expenditures for food, clothing, recreation, radios, television, and so forth."[66]

Another study indicated that about 80 percent of New York City's poor live in rent-controlled housing; however, it also indicated that about 45 percent of those who live in controlled housing were not poor. Both the poor and prosperous reaped substantial benefits, paying an average of about $650 a year less than the market value of the housing they occupied in 1968; in addition, the greater benefits accrued to the more prosperous tenants.[67]

Other studies have attempted to estimate the benefits of rent control not only in terms of reduced rent but also in terms of the consumption of nonhousing goods.[68] Their assumption is that the existence of rent control facilitates this consumption.

It has been suggested that the value of rent control to the tenant declines as time passes.[69] Nonetheless, one author has concluded "given certain conditions, rent control can be the most expedient short-term response the legal system has to offer in providing decent housing the poor can afford."[70]

### *The Disadvantages Of Rent Control*

Critics of rent controls cite the following arguments:

1. Rent controls discourage housing production.
2. Rent controls adversely affect housing quality.
3. Rent control often leads to inequities in the housing market.
4. Rent control contributes to the erosion of the local community tax base.[71]

#### Housing Production

If rent control is imposed due to a housing shortage of emergency proportions, then new construction is essential to ending the shortage. Those who are critical of rent control argue that it discourages new construction or at best has a dampening impact on new housing production. The charge is based quite simply on the assumption that investors will be unwilling to invest in a market in which the likelihood of receiving a profit is uncertain. Specifically, as one rent control critic argues, "investment will move away from those areas in which price is less than average total cost and toward those areas in which price is greater than total average cost."[72]

Although new construction is generally exempt from controls, the housing industry is often wary of possible future extensions of controls. Consequently, opponents of rent control maintain that investors may turn to communities without such controls or abandon the rental market entirely and focus on the construction of fee-simple, owner-occupied housing, particularly since there has been increased demand for condominiums.

Additionally, critics maintain that even if the investors are willing to build rental units in rent control jurisdictions, lenders may be hesitant. They may abandon such areas for more lucrative markets, charge higher interest rates, or grant smaller mortgages for buildings in rent control areas. In a recent survey of leading institutions, a significant portion of the respondents indicated that, although specific evaluations of building income, condition and expenses were necessary in making a mortgage loan determination, the existence of rent control would have a definite impact on the proportion of the total amount which they would extend.[73] Such practices in rent control jurisdictions combined with hesitation to invest in the constructiion of rental housing can significantly reduce new housing construction, thereby tightening the housing market.

In 1952, Leo Grebler appraised the implications of rent control utilizing preliminary data from the 1950 Census of Housing.[74] Regarding new construction, Grebler concluded that "odds are that the volume of housing construction in the United States would not have been substantially larger without rent control, . . . But rent control was in all probability an important factor in reducing the volume of new rental housing."[75] A number of years later, Ernest Fisher proposed to test some of Grebler's principal hypotheses by using a more complete set of data for New York City.[76] Fisher confirmed Grebler's hypothesis and further emphasized some of the implications relative to the distribution of the volume of new construction. He found that "the volume of housing construction may not be affected seriously, but the "mix" of kinds of facilities built, the prices or rents at which they are brought onto the market, and the sources of both finance and initiative will probably be different from what they would be in an uncontrolled market."[77]

Thus, both theoretical and empirical conclusions suggest that in the past new construction shifted to owner-occupied dwellings and to higher cost rental units where the demand from high income families is most effective.[78]

### Housing Quality

Of the four arguments cited against rent control that concerning impact upon the quality of housing is most reflective of the long-term adverse impact of rent controls. It should be noted here again that some economists distinguish between the consumer good of *housing services* provided by a rental unit and the investment good of the *housing stock,* thus identifying different types of housing "quality"—the latter more readily observable than the first.[79]

Of the major categories of operating expenditures—real estate taxes, fuel and utilities, maintenance and repair, payroll costs, management-administrative fees, insurance costs, and debt service requirements including principal and interest—all are relatively fixed costs. That is, they must be borne regardless of the level of occupancy; some must be carried whether a building is occupied or not. The one expenditure providing a degree of flexibility is that of maintenance and repair; it becomes the major adjustment mechanism for the property owner under rent control. As operating costs increase owners may: 1. increase rents proportionately; 2. decrease or defer expenses; or 3. absorb short-term losses. With the first possibility excluded under rent control and the third minimized or eventually negated due to rising inflation, it has been argued that rent controls force property owners to reduce their level of maintenance and repairs and, thus, eventually lead to a gradual deterioration of the housing stock. Economists also suggest that rent control may result in a short-term reduction of housing services. That is, the reduction in quality and thus the quantity of housing services provided results in a higher cost for providing housing services in a rent-controlled apartment than in an uncontrolled market.[80] Jerome Rothenberg concludes that "at this first impact stage rent control will induce general disinvestment in rental housing capital by systematic downward conversions throughout the quality spectrum while holding nominal prices constant."[81]

Economists suggest that the "optimal economic life of a rent controlled building" is shortened by rent control.[82] They also suggest that "rent control results in a faster than optimal rate of deterioration."[83] A recent analysis of maintenance patterns in New York City—using size, age, and quality of housing as constants—confirmed the relationship between owner's income from rent and maintenance of rented units. This study concluded that

> during a period of inflation, rent control lowers the optimal level of maintenance. In the absence of rent control and given the nature of housing costs (long-term, high fixed costs), adjustments in dynamic equilibrium are optimally made by price change. To the degree that rent control imposes a cost on price adjustments the burden of adjustment falls on maintenance.[84]

### Inequities In The Housing Market

Rent control is also charged with producing severe inequities in the housing market by creating two categories of housing—controlled and uncontrolled—and two classes of claimants for the available housing supply.[85] The criteria for determining which housing will be exempt from controls necessarily varies according to the particular characteristics of the housing stock in a given community and the exigencies of the defined emergency. The classification of claimants is more varied. Generally, the first group of claimants consists of the tenants in rent-controlled units who reap the benefits of lower rents simply by virtue of being there first. The second category consists of those persons who either compete for whatever, if any, controlled units become available or pay the higher uncontrolled market price. Thus the benefit of rent control are randomly distributed. It has been suggested that this division of the population into two groups without regard for the income earning potential of either group, "is perhaps the most serious effect of rent control, and one that is indefensible on either economic or social criteria."[86]

Those in favor of rent control often argue that it serves as a redistributive mechanism, but as one author has suggested, it is highly inequitable in this regard:

> In one sense, rent control may be regarded as a means of redistributing the costs and benefits of housing that exist in the uncontrolled market. The redistribution operates not only between landlords and tenants of rent controlled housing but also between owners of controlled and exempt buildings and between protected tenants and other housing consumers. To the extent that the costs and benefits of rent control are arbitrarily distributed among various groups, it may be considered an inequitable and inefficient remedy for the problem of housing costs.[87]

Critics of rent control also claim that rent control regulations encourage an inefficient consumption of housing "since controlled rents tend to lower turnover, [and] as a group, tenants occupy more housing space than if rents followed the market standard."[88] This situation is particularly true of older adults whose space needs decrease as their children leave home but who are less inclined and often less able financially to move since they would have to pay more rent for smaller quarters in the uncontrolled market.

A recent study in Sweden presented evidence indicating that rent control also contributes to a change in the demand pattern for housing, specifically a growth of demand among single adults desiring to live alone and finding it economically possible to do so. The proportion of married couples without dwellings of their own remained constant despite increases in the supply of housing.[89]

### The Broad Economic Consequences

Analyses of the disadvantages and benefits of rent control have generally focused on its impact on tenants and owners. However, the long-term impacts of rent control have significant reverberations from the broader community. This phenomenon is explained in a recent study of rent control in Greater Boston.

> *A substantial part of the wealth and viability of a community lies in its housing stock.* The care, maintenance and improvements of this stock therefore is of very considerable relevance to the community as a whole. Its relevance lies not merely in where people will live today as opposed to tomorrow, not only on how attractive the community will be to newcomers as well as those who seek alternate housing facilities within the community; but also, *given our heavy dependence on local real estate taxes, on the long term value of the fixed capital investment in the community, and its physical structures,* the economic viability of the residential structures is an absolute requirement if they are to be maintained, and this certainly is, or should be, front and center in the consideration of the citizenry of the community as a whole and its officials [emphasis added].[90]

Increasing deficits in many municipal budgets and the threat of impending default in New York City have generated yet another issue in the debate over the economic consequences of rent control. The essence of this current issue is the contention that rent control contributes to the erosion of the local tax base as reflected in 1. reductions in the tax base due to decreased assessed valuation; and 2. increased tax delinquency. Reduction in the tax base occurs as a result of increased applications for tax abatements and lowered tax assessments. The value of a property is substantially related to the income it produces; limitations on income due to rent controls result in the decreased value of the affected property, and, consequently, reduced assessed valuation. Increased tax delinquencies occur when operating expenses significantly exceed allowable rent increases and an owner is confronted with the decision of defaulting either on taxes or the mortgage.

Recent data reflect both reduced tax bases and increased tax delinquency in rent-controlled communities.[91] Court ordered reductions in tax assessments in surburban New York communities in 1974-1975, where rent regulation was expanded in 1974, ranged from 15 to 30 percent.[92] Beyond the initial abatements and reduced valuation, the ultimate effect is on the resale value of controlled structures. Apartment buildings in desirable locations on Manhattan's upper east side sold, as recently as 1973, for five to six-and-one-half times the rent roll, but by 1975 owners found it difficult to secure buyers for two to three times the rent roll.[93]

## *NOTES*

1. Borough of Fort Lee, New Jersey Ordinance 72-1, February 2, 1972.
2. Massachusetts General Laws, Ch. 842 Sec. 1 (1970).
3. Block v. Hirsh, 256 U.S. 135 (1921); Marcus Brown Holding Co. v. Feldman, 256 U.S. 170 (1921). Both cases were decided the same day by a 5-4 decision, and were the first of a series of "rent law" cases handed down by the U.S. Supreme Court between April 1921 and April 1924. See also Levy Leasing Co. v. Siegel, 258 U.S. 242 (1922) and Chasteleton v. Sinclair, 264 U.S. 543 (1924).
4. This description of the rent law cases written by Justice Holmes, (who wrote the lead opinion in *Block v. Hirsh*) in invalidating a nonrelated regulation case, *Pennsylvania Coal Co. v. Mahon* (260 U.S. 393, 416 [1922], was directed toward affirming the unique "public interest" arising out of the war-created emergency which justified use of the police power during this era of judicial interpretation.
5. Block v. Hirsh, 256 U.S. 135 at 157.
6. Richard E. Blumberg, Brian Q. Robbins and Kenneth K. Baar, "The Emergence of Second Generation Rent Controls" *Clearinghouse Review* 8, no. 240 (1974): 242. This concept was based on the protection of private property rights guaranteed by the due process clauses of the Fifth and Fourteenth Amendments and applied both substantively and proceedurally. During this era, price controls and regulatory ratemaking legislation was upheld when the area to be regulated was "affected with a public interest." Two independent elements of this test were monopoly control and a temporary public emergency. The regulations to be imposed were then further examined to determine if they met a "rational relations test." For a comprehensive discussion of the historical evolution of judicial interpretation see Kenneth K. Baar and W. Dennis Keating, "The Last Stand of Economic Due Process–The Housing Emergency Requirement for Rent Control," *The Urban Lawyer* 7, no. 3 (1975):447-509.
7. Nebbia v. New York, 291 U.S. 502 (1934).
8. "Residential Rent Control in New York City,"*Columbia Journal of Law and Social Problems* 3 (1967): 31.
9. Blumberg, Robbins, and Baar, p. 242.
10. See for example, Block v. Hirsh; Marcus Brown Co. v. Feldman; Chastleton v. Sinclair; Levy Leasing Co. v. Siegel; Bowles v. Willingham, 321 U.S. 503 (1944); Housing Expeditor v. Cloyd W. Miller Co., 333 U.S. 138 (1948); Teeval Co. v. Stern, 301 N.Y. 346, 93 N.E. 2d 884, cert. den. 340 U.S. 876 (1950); Heubeck v. City of Baltimore, 205 Md. 203, 107 A.2d 99 (1954); Russell v. Treasurer & Receiver General, 331 Mass. 501, 120 N.E. 2d 338 (1954); Jamouneau v. Harner, 16 N.J. 500, 109 A. 2d 640 (1954); Brookchester, Inc. Section 1 v. Ligham, 17 N.J. 460, 111 A. 2d 737 (1955); Warren v. City of Philadelphia, 382 Pa. 380, 115 A. 2d 218 (1955); Kress, Dunlap & Lane, Ltd. v.

Downing, Virgin Islands 193 F. Supp. 874 (1961); Bucho Holding Co. v. Temporary State Housing Rent Com'n. of N.Y., 11 N.Y. 2d 469, 184 N.E. 2d 569 (1962); Israel v. City Rent and Rehabilitation Administration, 285 F. Supp. 908 (1968); Amsterdam–Manhattan, Inc. v. City Rent & Rehabilitation Administration, 15 N.Y. 2d 1014, 207 N.E. 2d 616 (1965); Marshal House, Inc. v. Rent Control Board of Brookline, 358 Mass. 686, 266 N.E. 2d 876 (1971); Inganamort v. Borough of Fort Lee, 62 N.J. 521, 303 A. 2d 298 (1973); Albigese v. Jersey City, 127 N.J. Super. 101, 316 A. 2d 483 (1974), modified at 129 N.J. Super. 567, 324 A. 2d 577. Constitutionality upheld over arguments: (1) violated landlords' rights to due process of law–Block v. Hirsch, Bowles v. Willingham; (2) equal protection of the law–*Woods* v. *Cloyd W. Miller Co.;* (3) protection from impairment of the obligations of contract–*Marcus Brown Co.* v. *Feldman* and Huard v. Forest Street Housing, Inc. 316 N.E. 2d 505 (1974); (4) taking of property without compensation–*Teeval Co.* v. *Stern*.

11. Birkenfeld v. City of Berkeley 428971 Cal. Super. Ct. (1972); Court of Appeals, 1 Civil 34378 (1975).

12. Ibid., p. 19 (Court of Appeals). Also unconstitutional because it failed to provide a method of termination when emergency no longer existed and measure does not establish a gauge by which to adjudge the continuance of emergency conditions.

13. City of Miami Beach v. Fleetwood Hotel Inc., 261 So. 2d 801 (1972). See also "Rent Control as a Municipal Function in Florida," *Urban Law Annual* 7 (1974): 356-361 and "Rent Control by Municipal Ordinance–Not Within Home Rule Power," *University of Miami Law Review* 27 (1973): 518-524.

14. The last U.S. Supreme Court decision in a rent control case was 1948 in which the court relied upon constitutional war powers to justify the postwar extension of emergency rent controls. Subsequent state court decisions avoided addressing the issue of an emergency requirement and upheld or invalidated rent control on other grounds. The emergency doctrine was only an issue insofar as assessing whether the legislative determination was sufficient. Appellants and intervenors in Birkenfeld v. Berkeley, cited above, sought to introduce into the appeal a challenge to the emergency requirement. The court, however, based its consideration (beside the view of the court that it was necessary) on the specific language of the amendment itself and determined that the amendment "must be judged in light of its stated purpose." (The amendment contained in its statement of purpose three references to the existence of an emergency.)

15. The consensus has not, however, been absolute. A month before the initial U.S. Supreme Court decisions, the New York Court of Appeals in People, ex rel Durham Realty Corp. v. La Fetra ([1921] 230 N.Y. 429, 130 N.E. 601) upheld a New York law under broadly defined use of the police power and rejected the necessity of an emergency as a prerequisite to rent control: "even in the absence of an emergency the state may pass wholesome and proper laws to regulate the use of private property" (at 606).

16. Helmsley & Schwartz et. al. v. Borough of Fort Lee et. al., Sup. Ct. Bergen County Docket no. L-11348-74 (1975), p. 8. (unreported).
17. Birkenfeld v. Berkeley, p. 9.
18. Blumberg, Robbins, and Baar, p. 242.
19. Inganamort v. Borough of Fort Lee, 293 A. 2d 720 (1972) at 737.
20. Inganamort v. Borough of Fort Lee, 303 A. 2d 298 (1973) at 301.
21. The following should also be noted: "The general rule is that an ordinance need not recite the reasons or necessity for its enactment. Even where the charter or statute provides that in certain ordinances the necessity for the passage of an ordinance be declared, the view has been taken that failure in this respect does not render the ordinance void, since its passage is equivalent to declaring its necessity. The law, when enacted, furnishes its own reason." E. McQuillin, "The Law of Municipal Corporations," 16.15 at 151-52 (3d ed. 1969) found in "Municipal Governments–Police Power–New Jersey Municipalities Have The Power to Enact Rent Control Ordinances," *Seton Hall Law Review* 4 (Fall/Winter 1974) 360.
22. Chastleton v. Sinclair, 264 U.S. 543 (1924). See also Baar and Keating, p. 465.
23. Inganamort v. Borough of Fort Lee, 303 A 2d 298, at 301.
24. Although it is not implied that the Inganamort decision would have been different had the existence of an emergency been a central issue; it is clear that the absence of this issue precluded its invalidity on these grounds.
25. Birkenfeld v. Berkeley, pp. 14, 15-16. Given the nature of the enactment, it is highly probable that the initiative process of enactment in this case (as opposed to legislative enactment) in the court's view mandated thorough scrutiny, as there had not been such a legislative finding and in fact the Berkeley City Council had refused to place the referendum on the ballot.
26. Chastleton v. Sinclair, 264 U.S. 543 (1924).
27. Birkenfeld v. Berkeley, p. 19.
28. In technical terms, under the California constitution as amended in 1974 (Article XI, Sec. 3[a]), charter amendments by the initiative process "have the force and effect of legislative enactments". (Birkenfeld v. Berkeley, p. 5).
29. As noted earlier, the absence of an emergency was but one of the issues for which the rent control charter amendment was invalidated and was affirmed only in the lead opinion of Judge Scott. Judge Devine concurred with the lead opinion in the affirmation of the judgment but based his concurrence on the lack of method of termination, citing his inability to concur with the absence of an emergency primarily on the difficulty involved in making such a "subjective" judicial judgment–"upon vague or arbitrary norms." He further stated, "For what standards does a judge use as his measure? The charter amendment states none. Here the judge found a 3.1 percent vacancy rate. Is this rate high enough to preclude emergency? How are judges to know?"
30. John Kain, Testimony on Rent Control (Delivered before the Massachusetts

MANCHESTER COLLEGE

State Legislature, March 21, 1975), mimeographed, p. 4.

31. Edgar O. Olson, "A Competitive Theory of the Housing Market," *American Economic Review* 59 (September 1969): 612-22. The author, in noting the objections which may be raised to all of these assumptions relative to housing markets, cites specifically the lack of plausibility of the seventh homogeneity. In setting forth his theoretical construct he introduces an unobservable entity called "housing services" and delineates two housing markets: (1) *Housing services* constitutes the demand for and supply of a consumer good. It is the one and only thing in a dwelling unit to which consumers attach value. The quantity of housing services contained in a dwelling unit can be thought of as an index of all of its attributes, including both space and quality. (2) *Housing stock* constitutes the demand for and supply of an investment good. See also Edgar O. Olson, "An Econometric Analysis of Rent Control," *Journal of Political Economy* 80 (1972): 1081-2000, in which this theoretical construct is applied.

32. Jerome Rothenberg, *Urban Housing Markets and Housing Policy: Selected Readings in Urban Policy Analysis,* Massachusetts Institute of Technology, Department of Economics, Working Paper no. 150 (Cambridge, 1975), pp. 1-13.

33. Ibid., p. 10.

34. Olson, "A Competitive Theory"; reprinted in: Jon Pynoos et al., eds., *Housing Urban America* (Chicago: Aldine Publishing Co., 1973), pp. 228-38.

35. New York State Emergency Tenant Protection Act (1974) and Alaska Emergency Residential Rent Regulation and Control (1974). The Atlantic City and Haddon Township, New Jersey ordinances also include a five percent vacancy rate among criteria.

36. Lawrence B. Smith, "A Note on the Rent Adjustment Mechanism for Rental Housing," *American Economic Review* 64, no. 3 (June 1974): 478-81.

37. Chastleton v. Sinclair.

38. City of Miami Beach v. Fleetwood Hotel, Inc., 261 So. 2d 801 at 804.

39. It is recognized that over the long-term, cost-push inflation also impacts upon the forces of supply and demand as the economic feasibility of new investment declines thereby constraining the "normal" growth of the inventory and increasing the demand on the extant stock.

40. In the Berkeley case, the court found that the evidence of exorbitant rents was "minimal" based on a finding that in the various areas of the city between 85 and 98 percent of all rental housing was available for $200 per month or less. Survey results of what rental increases had been in the first quarter of 1973 were presented in public hearings on the need for rent control in Washington, D.C. This survey found: 39 percent of the units–no increase; 26 percent of the units–less than 5 percent increase; 29 percent–between 5 and 10 percent increases; and 6 percent–more than 10 percent increases. Although these results were challenged, the legislation pending before Congress to authorize rent control was enacted. See U.S., Senate, Committee on the District of Columbia, Public Hearing on H.R. 4771, July 24, 1973.

41. U.S. Senate public hearing on H.R. 4771 (cited above) entitled "To Authorize the District of Columbia Council to Regulate and Stabilize Rents."
42. John Kain, "An Alternative to Rent Control," (Lecture delivered before the Cambridge Massachusetts League of Women Voters April 1, 1969), p. 2.
43. Available 1970 statistics for New York City indicate that approximately 40 percent of all rent-controlled units are occupied by tenants who pay 25 percent or more of their incomes for rent. The bulk of these people pay more than 35 percent.
44. Edith Berger Drellich and Andrée Emery, *Rent Control In War and Peace* (New York: National Municipal League, 1939), p. 55.
45. These ratios are generally further differentiated by rental vs. sales housing with a higher ratio viewed as necessary for rental housing. The U.S. Department of Housing and Urban Development in its former Workable Program requirements utilized a 3 percent ratio for low- and moderate-income housing.
46. Alfred A. Ring, *Real Estate Principles and Practices* (Englewood Cliffs, N.J.: Prentice-Hall, 1972), p. 43.
47. Glen H. Beyer, *Housing: A Factual Analysis* (New York: Macmillan Co., 1965), p. 284.
48. Glen H. Beyer, *Housing and Society* (New York: Macmillan Co., 1965), p. 134.

1) In general, large communities tend to have higher vacancy ratios than small communities.
2) Communities with a high proportion of rental units tend to have higher vacancy ratios than communities with a high proportion of owner-occupied units.
3) Communities with a large proportion of multifamily structures show tendencies toward higher vacancy rates than localities that contain predominantly single-family houses.
4) Vacancy rates tend to be highest in the lowest- and the highest-priced classes, indicating that most stable occupancy is found in the middle-type bracket where shifts in demand upward and downward in price have the least net effect.
5) Vacancy ratios in all price classes are consistently highest in the smaller units, decreasing as the size of the units increases.
6) No consistent relationship has been found between vacancies and the proportion of units overcrowded.

49. *McKinney's Unconsolidated Laws,* vol. 65, New York City Administrative Code, Sec. Y51-12.0.
50. Alaska Statutes Supplement, Sec. 34:06, 020 (1974).
51. Birkenfeld v. City of Berkeley, p. 17: "Although not necessary for determination of this case, we also believe it to be the better view that if the rental housing within a municipality is adequate to negate the existence of a

rental housing emergency, rent control legislation within that municipality would be constitutionally prohibited as being in excess of the police power of the municipality, regardless of the condition of rental housing outside the municipality."

52. U.S., Department of Housing and Urban Development, FHA Economic and Market Analysis Division, *FHA Techniques of Housing Market Analysis* (Washington, D.C.: Government Printing Office, 1970), pp. 9-11. This definition originally proposed in Chester Rapkin, Louis Winnick, and David Blank, *Housing Market Analysis: A Study of Theory and Methods* (Washington, D.C.: Housing and Home Finance Agency, 1953), p. 9.

53. Ernest and Robert Fisher, *Urban Real Estate* (New York: Henry Holt and Co., 1954), p.223.

54. Charles Abrams, *The Language of Cities,* p.142.

55. Rapkin, Winnick, and Blank, p.9.

56. Ibid, p.7.

57. David Blank and Louis Winnick, "The Structure of the Housing Market," *Quarterly Journal of Economics* 67 (May 1953): 187; and FHA *Techniques of Housing Market Analysis,* p.12.

58. Fisher and Fisher, p.225; and Abrams, *The Language of Cities,* p.143.

59. John B. Lansing and Eva Mueller, *Residential Location and Urban Mobility,* Survey Research Center, Institute for Social Research, University of Michigan (Ann Arbor, 1964), p.41.

60. *Oakland Tribune,* May 28, 1967, cited in: Association of Bay Area Governments, *Regional Housing Study,* Supplemental Report RA-4, October, 1969, p.26.

61. John W. Willis, "A Short History of Rent Control Laws," *Cornell Law Quarterly,* 36 (1950): 84.

62. Birkenfeld v. Berkeley, p.13.

63. Ibid. With minor variations in language similar definition of the purpose of rent control have been cited in the following recent cases: Marshall House Inc. v. Rent Control Board of Brookline et al., 266 N.E. 2d 876 (1971); City of Miami Beach v. Forte Towers, Inc., 305 So. 2d 764, 768 (1974); Foti v. Heller, 137 A.2d 10 N.J. App.(1957).

64. Willis, p.57.

65. Ira Lowry et al., *Rental Housing In New York City* (New York: Rand Institute, 1971), vol. 2, *The Demand For Shelter;* Edgar O. Olson, "An Econometric Analysis of Rent Control," *Journal of Political Economy* 80 (Nov.-Dec. 1972) 1081-1100; Leo Grebler, "Implications of Rent Control Experience In the United States," *International Labor Review* 65 (1952): 462-485; Ernest M. Fisher, "Twenty Years of Rent Control in New York City," in *Essays on Urban Land Economics* (Los Angeles: University of California, Real Estate Research Program, 1966), pp.31-67.

66. Grebler, p.474.
67. Lowry et al.
68. Olson, "An Econometric Analysis," pp.1081-1100.
69. Edgar O. Olson, *The Effects of a Simple Rent Control Scheme in a Competitive Market,* Rand Corporation, (Santa Monica, Working Paper P-4257, 1969), p.1.
70. Emily P. Achtenberg, "The Social Utility of Rent Control," in John Pynoos et al., eds., *Housing Urban America* (Chicago: Aldine Publishing Co. 1973), p.434.
71. Although longer lists have been proposed, most criticisms fall into these broad categories. See William M. Shenkel, "Rent Control: A Critical Review," *Journal of Property Management* 39 (May-June 1974): 101-110, and Willis, pp.54-94.
72. William D. Grampp, "Some Effects of Rent Control," *Southern Economic Journal* 16 (April 1950): 438.
73. George Sternlieb et al., *The Realities of Rent Control in The Greater Boston Area* (New Brunswick, N.J.: Rutgers University, Center for Urban Policy Research, 1975).
74. Grebler, p.470.
75. Ibid, p.470.
76. Fisher, p.34.
77. Ibid., p.34.
78. Grampp, pp.425-447; and Lloyd Rodwin, "Rent Control and Housing," *Social Research* 27 (September 1950): 302-19.
79. See note 32.
80. Olson, "An Econometric Analysis," p.1098.
81. Rothenberg, p.53.
82. John C. Moorhouse, "Optimal Housing Maintenance Under Rent Control," *Southern Economic Journal* 39 (July 1972): 100.
83. Olson, "An Econometric Analysis," p.1098.
84. Moorhouse, p.105.
85. Kain, "An Alternative."
86. Grebler, p.483.
87. Achtenberg, p.439.
88. Shenkel, p.102.
89. Sven Rydenfelt, "Rent Controls Thirty Years On," in *Verdict on Rent Control: Essays on the Economic Consequences of Political Action to Restrict Rents in Five Countries,* F.A. Hayek et al., eds. (London: Institute of Economic Affairs, 1972), pp.63-78.
90. Sternlieb et al, p.1.
91. Ibid., chapter 5.
92. Betsy Brown, "Rent Curbs Stir Westchester," *New York Times,* Real Estate Section, September 7, 1975, p.1. See also Glenn Fawbe, "City's Realty-Tax

Need Added to Rent-Control Debate," *New York Times,* August 26, 1975.
93. Charles Kaiser, "Prices of Buildings in Manhattan Falling Sharply," *New York Times,* Real Estate Section, October 26, 1975, p.1. See also: Frank S. Kristof, "Rent Control Within The Rental Housing Parameters of 1975," (Paper presented at the annual midyear meeting of the American Real Estate and Urban Economics Association, Washington, D.C., May 30, 1975), p.11.

# Part II: Second Generation Rent Controls

# Chapter 3
# Scope of Currently Enacted Legislation

The delineation of current rent controls as "second generation" is essentially related to the economic conditions prompting their imposition; specifically, they are peacetime economic controls as opposed to war-related emergency controls. The shift in national economic policy under the economic stabilization programs initiated in 1971 is frequently cited as a major factor precipitating the current wave of locally enacted rent controls. The current movement toward increased use of peacetime rent regulation, however, antedates the imposition of federal controls and initially occurred in the form of conciliatory rent review boards which handled grievances and complaints. Such voluntary rent review boards were established in Boston and Brookline, Massachusetts in 1968 and 1969, respectively.[1]

In 1969 Boston moved to enact a stronger, though still tenant-initiated, grievance system.[2] Boston's authority to enact rent control was confirmed by the state legislature in late 1969;[3] and in 1970 the legislature passed a state enabling act authorizing cities and towns with populations over 50,000 to enact local rent control ordinances.[4] Subsequently Cambridge, Somerville, Boston, and Lynn enacted ordinances under the provisions of this act (the Lynn regulations were later repealed). Under a separate law which was enacted concurrently with the statewide local option law Brookline developed a rent control mechanism. The scope of the Massachusetts rent control movement has placed it at the forefront of this current era in the history of rent control.

Also in 1969 Connecticut passed state rent control legislation which provided for the creation of fair rent commissions of limited jurisdiction.[5] Seven Connecticut communities have adopted local ordinances under the provisions of the state act.[6] Although the Connecticut commissions have the power to order rent reductions in specific instances, they cannot establish across-the-board controls and neither the state legislature nor any of the localities have moved toward initiating a stronger regulatory system.

State enabling legislation has recently been adopted in Maine (1973) and Alaska (1974) and Maryland adopted a statewide rent control statute in 1973. Approximately 100 of New Jersey's 567 municipalities have adopted local ordinances and their authority to do so in the absence of state enabling legislation was upheld by the New Jersey State Supreme Court in 1973.[7] Miami Beach, over a series of legal challenges and additional pending litigation; has implemented controls. And Washington, D.C. has rent control authorized by Congress. Rent control was significantly expanded in the state of New York with the enactment of the Emergency Tenant Protection Act of 1974. The ETPA embodies a less rigid form of control than existed under the New York State Rent Control Act and extends rent stabilization measures introduced in New York City in 1969. (see chapter 1). With the exception of Alaska's, all rent control legislation currently enacted is on the east coast.

The number of states which have actually enacted legislation does not reveal the extent of the rent control movement. Proposed legislation and study commissions have surfaced across the country. In Oregon, for example, rent control legislation was proposed only to die in committee. Recommendations by a citizens' study commission in Ann Arbor, Michigan suggested that a proposed general rent control policy was unwarranted.[8] Rhode Island's Department of Community Affairs undertook a similar study which found that the availability of housing, specifically the extant vacancy rate, made rent control unnecessary, and a rent arbitration board initially proposed in 1971 in Boulder, Colorado lost support through a dispute over mandatory arbitration of all rental increases. The eventual compromise in Boulder was the creation of separate landlord and tenant "helplines" to handle complaints and disputes. Rent control proposals in Madison, Wisconsin and Philadelphia, Pennsylvania were defeated, although the issue continues to surface in Philadelphia. Minneapolis, Minnesota and Hawaii are at this writing considering proposals. A charter amendment enacted through a voter initiated referendum in Berkeley, California was declared unconstitutional and the decision was appealed only to be invalidated on the basis that no emergency housing situation existed.[9] A similar initiative in Palo Alto, California was defeated.

A summary of enacted rent control statutes is included in Exhibit 3-1; however, the recitation of proposed and enacted legislation does not constitute a full treatment of the subject. To that end, these aspects must be addressed:

1. variation in legislative approaches;
2. variations in the regulatory mechanisms; and
3. an identification of the factors which account for enactment of rent control.

*EXHIBIT 3–1*

*NATIONAL SUMMARY OF RENT CONTROL LEGISLATION*

| *Area Legislation Status* | *Emergency Declaration/ Definition* | *Applicable Units/ Exemptions* | *Base Rent/ Rent Adjustment Provisions* | *Other Provisions Administrative/ Implementation Mechanism* |
|---|---|---|---|---|
| *Alaska* | | | | |
| State enabling legislation, "Emergency Residential Rent Control," enacted 1974.<br><br>Alaska Statute 34.06.010. On 5/6/75 emergency declared in Fairbanks and Valdez. | "[When the] rate of vacancies . . . is so low that there is substantial impairment of free choice . . or when the average vacancies . . . falls below three percent for a period of at least 90 days" (34.06.020). | All residential housing accommodations/ Rent upon initial occupancy in new construction, transient units; units owned, operated by public authority. | Tenant initiated complaint of unwarranted rent increase submitted to local Emergency Rent Review Board which shall recommend to the commissioner whether or not a proposed rent increase shall be approved or denied. | Commissioner of Commerce charged with administration of chapter, promulgation of regulations, establishment of maximum rents, and classification of residential housing accommodations. |
| *Connecticut* | | | | |
| State enabling legislation, "An Act Enabling Municipalities to Create a Fair Rent | No emergency declared. Authorized creation of commissions to control and eliminate excessive rental charges. | All housing accommodations/ Seasonal units rented less than 120 days per year. | Tenant initiated complaint of excessive rental charges submitted to commission which is empowered to order a rent reduction. May suspend rent | Common Pleas Court has jurisdiction to handle appeals and enforce orders. |

*EXHIBIT 3–1*
*(continued)*
*NATIONAL SUMMARY OF RENT CONTROL LEGISLATION*

| *Area Legislation Status* | *Emergency Declaration/ Definition* | *Applicable Units/ Exemptions* | *Base Rent/ Rent Adjustment Provisions* | *Other Provisions Administrative/ Implementation Mechanism* |
|---|---|---|---|---|
| Commission," enacted 1969 with subsequent amendments. Conn. Gen. Stat. Ann. Sec. 7-148. | | | payment if housing is in violation of code statutes until conditions corrected. | |
| *Maine* | | | | |
| State enabling legislation, "Municipal Rent Control," enacted 1973. Me. Rev. Stat. Ann tit 30, ch. 2114 §5373 (No community has adopted ordinance under the provision of this act). | Emergency declared, no specific criteria for definition. | All residential units/ Rental units owned, operated, financed or subsidized by government agency-authority of imposition would result in cancellation or withdrawal of financing on subsidy. Co-op units and institutional units. | Fair Net Operating Income through individual or general adjustments to assure rents are established at levels to yield a fair net operating income. May make determination to increase or decrease based on changes in property taxes; operating and maintenance expenses; capital improvements, living space, services, etc.; substantial deterioration; failure to perform ordinary repair, replacement and maintenance. | Municipality may determine whether to appoint an administrator or rent control board who shall have authority to promulgate regulations and implement provisions of this act and any other provisions contained in the municipal ordinance. |

*EXHIBIT 3–1*
*(continued)*
*NATIONAL SUMMARY OF RENT CONTROL LEGISLATION*

| *Area Legislation Status* | *Emergency Declaration/ Definition* | *Applicable Units/ Exemptions* | *Base Rent/ Rent Adjustment Provisions* | *Other Provisions Administrative/ Implementation Mechanism* |
|---|---|---|---|---|
| Maryland | | | | |
| Statewide statute, "Limitation on Rental Fee Increases," enacted 1973 (Ch. 794) with subsequent amendments.<br><br>Md. Ann. Code Art. 53 §45; (1973) expired 7/1/74. Revised Md. Ann. Code Real Property §209 (1974). Subsequent to expiration of state statute (6/75), additional counties enacted ordinances (see Exhibit 3-2). | Emergency declared, no specific criteria for definition. | Apartments, townhouse, house, mobile home or mobile home lot of which a landlord rents four or more units/ Federally financed projects where the rent is determined as a percentage of tenant's income and rental fees of nonprofit educational institution units. | Rent in effect 1/11/73 upon termination of federal controls. Five percent of base rent plus pass-through on increases in real estate taxes, water, and sewer charges, utility rates, heating fuel charges and actual costs of capital improvements incurred from 1/11/73 in proportionate charges. Calculation based on rules established under federal rent stabilization under Title 6 Federal Regulations 301.101 (a) (3) and (b) as applicable. | Rental for vacant unit may be increased to highest permitted rent for comparable unit in the same facility. May be superseded by laws enacted by governing body of any county or city of Baltimore or the reinstitution of federal rent stabilization.<br><br>Attorney General may take appropriate injunctive action to prohibit rental increases above permissible limits. |

*EXHIBIT 3–1*
*(continued)*
*NATIONAL SUMMARY OF RENT CONTROL LEGISLATION*

| *Area Legislation Status* | *Emergency Declaration/ Definition* | *Applicable Units/ Exemptions* | *Base Rent/ Rent Adjustment Provisions* | *Other Provisions Administrative/ Implementation Mechanism* |
|---|---|---|---|---|
| *Massachusetts* | | | | |
| State enabling legislation, "An Act Enabling Certain Cities and Towns to Control Rents and Evictions."<br><br>Mass. Gen. Laws Ch. 842 (1970). Boston, Brookline, Cambridge, Lynn and Somerville enacted local ordinance under the provisions of Ch. 842. Lynn subsequently rescinded. Brookline has specific enabling legislation under Ch. 843. | Emergency declared, no specific criteria for definition. | All rental units with the exception of those specifically exempted/ Transient units; units completed or converted after 1/1/69; units owned, operated, financed, subsidized or rents regulated by a governmental agency; cooperative units, units in 2-or 3-family,owner-occupied house; non-profit institutional housing. Municipality may also exempt units for which rent charges exceed a specified limit, not to exceed 25 percent of total units. | Rent in effect six months prior to local enactment/ Individual or general adjustments (upward or downward) as necessary to assure a Fair Net Operating Income. Determination includes increases/decreases in property taxes/operating and maintenance expenses; services, space, etc., capital improvements, substantial deterioration. | Municipality shall determine whether act administered by Rent Control Board or Rent Control Administrator who shall have authority to promulgate regulation and implement provisions of this act and other provisions contained in local ordinance. |

*EXHIBIT 3-1*
*(continued)*
*NATIONAL SUMMARY OF RENT CONTROL LEGISLATION*

| *Area Legislation Status* | *Emergency Declaration/ Definition* | *Applicable Units/ Exemptions* | *Base Rent/ Rent Adjustment Provisions* | *Other Provisions Administrative/ Implementation Mechanism* |
|---|---|---|---|---|
| *New Jersey* | | | | |
| General Summary of Municipal Ordinances.<br><br>No state enabling legislation exists in New Jersey. The New Jersey State Supreme Court in 1973 found rent regulations to be in the purview of the municipal police power. *Inganamort* v. *Fort Lee,* 62 N.J. 521 (1973). The Fort Lee ordinance initially adopted 2/2/72 has been the model for most of the New Jersey ordinances (see Exhibit 3-2). | Emergency declared, generally no specific criteria for definition Seven communities use 5% vacancy rate. | Rental structures of 2/3/4 or more units/ Transient units and initial rental in newly constructed buildings. Some cases 2-to-3 unit owner-occupied structures. Units owned and/or operated by public authority. | Rent in effect at a specified date preceding enactment of ordinance (within preceding year).<br>Increase may not be greater than the percentage difference between the Consumer Price Index a previously established number of days prior to the expiration of the lease and the Consumer Price Index at the date the lease was entered into. Some communities have amended their ordinances, specifying a maximum percent increase. | Provisions are generally included for pass-throughs for real estate tax increases and increases based on capital improvements. Some ordinances also allow for surcharges for unavoidable increases in utilities and operating costs. Such charges are generally not included in the base rent for calculation of annual rent adjustments.<br><br>Rent Board or Administrator as determined by the local governing body. |

*EXHIBIT 3–1*
*(Continued)*
*NATIONAL SUMMARY OF RENT CONTROL LEGISLATION*

| *Area Legislation Status* | *Emergency Declaration/ Definition* | *Applicable Units/ Exemptions* | *Base Rent/ Rent Adjustment Provisions* | *Other Provisions Administrative/ Implementation Mechanism* |
|---|---|---|---|---|
| *Miami Beach* | | | | |
| "Rent Stabilization Law" enacted 1974. | Emergency declared, no specific criteria for definition. | Apartments 3 units or more and units in residential hotels rented one year prior to 10/16/74./ Buildings which posted bonds pending litigation. | Rent effective 10/16/74. | Capital Improvements and Real Estate Tax pass-through. |
| Ordinance 74-2018 effective 1/1/75 although litigation pending. Previous 1969 ordinance (69–1791) declared unconstitutional as outside scope of municipal authority. State legislation in 1973 enacted Ch. 73-129 granting authority to municipalities. 1973 ordinance (73–1978) found invalid–guidelines deemed confiscatory. | | | Increase allowed commensurate with operating cost increments to maintain 1973 ratio of Net Operating Income. | Rent Control Board. |

*EXHIBIT 3–1*

*(continued)*

*NATIONAL SUMMARY OF RENT CONTROL LEGISLATION*

| *Area Legislation Status* | *Emergency Declaration/ Definition* | *Applicable Units/ Exemptions* | *Base Rent/ Rent Adjustment Provisions* | *Other Provisions Administrative/ Implementation Mechanism* |
|---|---|---|---|---|
| *Washington, D.C.* | | | | |
| "District of Columbia Rent Control Act" of 1973.<br><br>Public Law 93-157. D.C. Council adopted local ordinance August 1, 1974, Regulation No. 20, amended 1975. | Authorized council to determine whether emergency exists and upon such findings to adopt such rules as necessary. | All residential units and rooms/Publicly owned units, initial rental in new construction, transient and institutional living quarters. | Rent Effective 2/1/73.<br><br>Four percent 1973; 8 percent 1974; proposed 1975: 4 percent or 6 percent if two utilities provided and 8 percent if all utilities provided. | Increases based on hardship provision related to fair return. Increases for capital improvements.<br><br>Pursuant to Council adoption, a temporary District of Columbia Housing Rent Commission was established. |
| *New York State* | | | | |
| State enabling legislation, "Emergency Housing Rent Control Act," | Emergency exists for any class of housing if the vacancy rate and any class or all housing is not in excess of five | Residential units completed before 2/1/47./ Transient units, units constructed after 1947 and substantially | Rent charged in 1943 with an allowance for a 15 percent increase granted in 1953. | Statutory provisions vary for different locations (cities/counties) within the state. As of July 1, |

*EXHIBIT 3–1*
*(continued)*
*NATIONAL SUMMARY OF RENT CONTROL LEGISLATION*

| *Area Legislation Status* | *Emergency Declaration/ Definition* | *Applicable Units/ Exemptions* | *Base Rent/ Rent Adjustment Provisions* | *Other Provisions Administrative/ Implementation Mechanism* |
|---|---|---|---|---|
| enacted 1946 with subsequent amendments.<br><br>*McKinney's Unconsolidated Laws,* book 65 §8581-8597, §8601-8617 | percent. Sec. 8592 of 1962 "Local Emergency Housing Rent Control Act" mandated local determination and administration in cities over one million population (NYC only). | rehabilitated or converted units built before 1947. Monthly rentals of $250 or more. Units owned or operated by public authority, institutional units (specific owner-occupied per city and or county regulations). | Beyond the 15 percent allowed general adjustment in 1953, increases granted on basis of increases in expenses for operating and labor costs increases in services provided, change in occupancy, and if the income yielded an annual return of less than 6 percent of the assessed valuation. All increases subject to the approval of the administrator. Also allows for adjustment based on unique circumstances. | 1964 the Division of Housing and Community Renewal assumed the administration previously vested in the temporary State Housing Rent Commission. |
| "Emergency Tenant Protection Act" enacted 1974.<br><br>Laws of New York. Ch. 576. | Local determination of emergency if vacancy rate for any class or all housing accomodations is "not in excess of five percent." | Buildings of 6 or more units constructed before 12/31/73 in City of New York and Counties of Nassau, Westchester and | Initial Legal Regulated Rent determined upon local adoption or for controlled unit upon vacancy as negotiated subject to adjustment. Subsequent rental increases as authorized annually by Rent Guidelines Boards. | ETPA amends existing laws. Extended regulation to newer units and stabilization to counties outside NYC. Eliminated |

*EXHIBIT 3–1*
*(continued)*
*NATIONAL SUMMARY OF RENT CONTROL LEGISLATION*

| *Area Legislation Status* | *Emergency Declaration/ Definition* | *Applicable Units/ Exemptions* | *Base Rent/ Rent Adjustment Provisions* | *Other Provisions Administrative/ Implementation Mechanism* |
|---|---|---|---|---|
| | | Rockland/ Exempt Publicly owned and or operated, transient, institutional. | | vacancy decontrol in these areas but transferred units to stabilization. |
| *New York City* | | | | |
| Rent and Rehabilitation Law" enacted 1962 with subsequent amendments.<br><br>N.Y.C., Administrative Code Y51-1.0 to Y51-18.0 | Vacancy determined to be 1.79%. Emergency exists for any class of housing if the vacancy rate for all housing is not in excess of five percent. (Implied Sec. Y51-12.0: Decontrol on Basis of Vacancy Rate.) | Units controlled under State Rent Control Act built before 2/1/47 and rented prior to 5/1/50./ Publicly owned, leased, financed or subsidized units; transient units. Vacancy decontrol conversions and other provisions allowed for further exemptions. | Rent control authority and regulations transferred from state regulation.<br><br>Effective 1/1/72: Maximum Base Rent Formula, revised biannually based on a cost-plus-profit formula which determines a MBR for every rent-controlled unit. After 1/1/72 increases not in excess of 7.5 percent granted until the maximum rent for the unit reached, unless the unit is vacant at which point the MBR could be changed. Factors | Administered by the Rent and Housing Maintenance Division of the Housing and Development Administration. |

*EXHIBIT 3–1*
*(continued)*
*NATIONAL SUMMARY OF RENT CONTROL LEGISLATION*

| *Area Legislation Status* | *Emergency Declaration/ Definition* | *Applicable Units/ Exemptions* | *Base Rent/ Rent Adjustment Provisions* | *Other Provisions Administrative/ Implementation Mechanism* |
|---|---|---|---|---|
| | | | included in calculating the formula are: real estate taxes. water and sewer charge, reasonable allowances for operating and maintenance expenses, vacancy and collection losses, and 8.5 percent return on the equalized assessed valuation. | |
| "Rent Stabilization Law" enacted 1969 with subsequent amendments.<br><br>N.Y.C., Administrative Code, YY51-1.0 to YY51-7.0. | | Class A structures of 6 units or more, completed after 2/1/47 and units built before 1947 previously decontrolled. Some residential hotel units/ Buildings completed after 12/31/73. Co-op and condominium units. Publicly owned, | Rent charged 5/31/68 or Initial Legal Regulated Rent upon vacancy as negotiated by new tenant but subject to adjustment by CAB.<br><br>Annual increases established by Rent Guidelines Board by length of lease. | Applicable only to eligible buildings, the owners of which are members of the Rent Stabilization Association and must register with HDA. Nonregistered although eligible buildings are subject to rent control imposition. Regulations |

*EXHIBIT 3–1*
*(continued)*
*NATIONAL SUMMARY OF RENT CONTROL LEGISLATION*

| *Area Legislation Status* | *Emergency Declaration/ Definition* | *Applicable Units/ Exemptions* | *Base Rent/ Rent Adjustment Provisions* | *Other Provisions Administrative/ Implementation Mechanism* |
|---|---|---|---|---|
| | | leased, financed or subsidized units, transient units. | | are promulgated and administered by the association. A Conciliation and Appeals Board established to handle grievances and complaints |

## *EXHIBIT 3-2*
## *LOCALITIES WITH ENACTED RENT REGULATION*

*Alaska*
- Anchorage
- Fairbanks
- Valdez

*Connecticut*
- Danbury
- East Norwick
- Enfield
- Hartford
- New Britain
- New Haven
- Stamford

*District of Columbia*

*Florida*
- Miami Beach

*Maryland*
- Anne Arundel County
- Baltimore City
- Baltimore County
- Harford County
- Howard County
- Montgomery County
- Prince Georges County
- Wicomico County

*Massachusetts*
- Boston
- Brookline
- Cambridge
- Somerville

*New Jersey*

Atlantic County
- Atlantic City
- Pleasantville City[1]

Bergen County
- Bergenfield Boro
- Cliffside Park Boro
- Dumont Boro
- East Rutherford Boro
- Edgewater Boro
- Elmwood Park Boro
- Englewood City
- Fair Lawn Boro
- Fairview Boro
- Fort Lee Boro
- Hackensack City
- Hasbrouck Heights Boro
- Leonia Boro
- Little Ferry Boro
- Lodi Boro
- Lyndhurst Twp
- Maywood Boro
- New Milford Boro
- North Arlington Boro
- Palisades Park Boro
- Ridgefield Boro
- Ridgefield Park Vlge.
- River Edge Boro
- Rutherford Boro
- Teaneck Twp
- Wallington Boro

Burlington County
- Southhampton Twp

Camden
- Bellmawr Boro
- Clementon Boro
- Gloucester City
- Haddon Twp
- Lindenwold Boro
- Oaklyn Boro
- Pine Hills Boro

*EXHIBIT 3-2*
*(continued)*
*LOCALITIES WITH ENACTED RENT REGULATION*

Camden cont'd

Somerdale Boro
Stratford Boro
Winslow Twp

Essex County

Belleville Town
Bloomfield Town
Caldwell Boro
Cedar Grove Twp.
East Orange City
Irvington Town
Maplewood Twp
Millburn Twp[2]
Newark City
Nutley Town
Orange City
South Orange Vlge.
Verona Boro
West Orange Town

Hudson County

Bayonne City
Hoboken City
Jersey City
North Bergen Twp
Union City
Weehawken Twp
West New York Town

Hunterdon

Flemington Boro

Mercer County

Princeton Boro

Middlesex County

East Brunswick Twp
Edison Twp
Highland Park Boro
Madison Twp
Metuchen Boro
Middlesex Boro
New Brunswick City
No. Brunswick Twp
Perth Amboy City
Piscataway Twp
Sayreville Boro
South Brunswick Twp
Woodbridge Twp

Monmouth County

Freehold Twp
Red Bank Boro

Morris County

Morristown Town
Parsippany-Troy Hills
Randolph Twp

Ocean County

Jackson Twp
Lakewood Twp

Passaic County

Clifton City
Little Falls Twp
Passaic City
Paterson City
Wayne Twp
West Paterson Boro

*EXHIBIT 3–2*
*(continued)*
*LOCALITIES WITH ENACTED RENT REGULATION*

Somerset County
- Franklin Twp
- No. Plainfield Boro

Union County
- Clark Twp
- Elizabeth City
- Linden City
- Roselle Boro
- Roselle Park Boro[3]
- Springfield Twp
- Union Twp

*New York State*

Albany County
- Cities
  - Albany
  - Watervliet
- Towns
  - Bethlehem
  - Green Island
  - New Scotland
- Villages
  - Green Island
  - Voorheesville

Erie County
- Cities
  - Buffalo
- Towns
  - Cheektowaga
- Villages
  - Depew
  - Sloan

Nassau County
- Cities
  - Glen Cove
  - *Long Beach
- Towns
  - Hempstead
  - *North Hempstead
  - Oyster Bay
- Villages
  - Baxter Estates
  - Bayville
  - Bellerose
  - Brookville
  - *Cedarhurst
  - Centre Island
  - Cove Neck
  - East Hills
  - East Williston
  - Farmingdale
  - *Floral Park
  - *Flower Hill
  - Freeport
  - *Great Neck
  - Great Neck Estates
  - **Great Neck Plaza
  - Hempstead
  - Hewlett Bay Park
  - Hewlett Harbor
  - Hewlett Neck
  - Kensington
  - Kings Point
  - Lake Success
  - Lattingtown
  - Laurel Hollow
  - Lawrence
  - Manorhaven
  - Massapequa Park

*EXHIBIT 3–2*
*(continued)*
*LOCALITIES WITH ENACTED RENT REGULATION*

Nassau County cont'd

Matinecock
Mill Neck
*Mineola
Munsey Park
Muttontown
New Hyde Park
North Hills
Old Brookville
Old Westbury
Oyster Bay Cove
Plandome
Plandome Hghts.
Plandome Manor
Port Washington No.
Roslyn
Roslyn Estates
Roslyn Harbor
*Russell Gardens
Saddle Rock
Sands Point
Sea Cliff
South Floral Park
Stewart Manor
Upper Brookville
Valley Stream
Westbury
Williston Park
**Lynbrook
**Rockville Centre
**Thomaston

Rensselaer County

Cities

Rensselaer

Towns

Hoosick
North Greenbush

Villages

Hoosick Falls

Rockland County

**Spring Valley

Schenectady County

Towns

Niskayuna
Princetown

Westchester County

Cities

*Mount Vernon
*New Rochelle
*White Plains
*Yonkers

Towns

Cortlandt
*Eastchester
*Greenburgh
*Harrison
*Mamaroneck
Ossining
Pelham
Rye
Yorktown

Villages

Ardsley
Croton-on-Hudson
*Dobbs Ferry
Hastings-on-Hudson
Larchmont
Mamaroneck
North Pelham
North Tarrytown
Port Chester

*EXHIBIT 3–2*
*(continued)*
*LOCALITIES WITH ENACTED RENT REGULATIONS*

Westchester County con't

*Tarrytown
Tuckahoe

New York City

Bronx County
Kings County
Manhattan County
Queens County
Richmond County

New Jersey Notes:
(1) Original ordinance expired, not extended.
(2) Voluntary mediation board.
(3) Proposal pending.

New York Notes:
*Communities which also have enacted rent stabilization under the Emergency Tenant Protection Act of 1974 covering post-1947 buildings.

**Did not have rent regulation prior to 1974 ETPA.

## *LEGISLATIVE APPROACHES*

Legislative approaches to rent control can be defined according to two mutually exclusive issues. The first relates to the type of legislation and the governmental level from which it emanates. The second concerns the enactment of rent control vis-a-vis other housing policies and programs.

Although there is much variation in the breadth and scope of the regulatory authority provided in currently enacted rent control statutes, there are three generic types of legislation:[10]

> 1. *Home Rule Legislation*—in which the municipality (county) enacts rent control pursuant to its inherent home rule or police power authority.
> 2. *State Rent Control Statute*—in which a state enacts a rent control scheme applicable to every residential rental unit in that state except where so exempted.
> 3. *State Enabling Legislation*—in which local governments are specifically empowered by state statute to enact rent control which must follow any standards set forth in the enabling act.

An examination of the legislation and regulatory mechanisms constituting "second generation rent controls" reveals a wide disparity, not only in the definition of the need for rent control, but also in the administrative standards provided for implementation. This disparity is partially explained by variation in market characteristics and conditions in differing geographic locations. Moreover, the implementation of any one of the three general legislative approaches is a function of rent control's highly political nature, and of the differing constitutional, statutory, and common law foundations existing in the states.[11] There is no factual relationship between the scope of regulatory authority and the legislative approach utilized for enactment.

Minor civil divisions—i.e., cities and towns—are entities of state governments, and their authority to enact any legislation is derived from either the Constitution, the state, or directly from specific enabling legislation or indirectly through implied powers, i.e. the police power. Generally, the impetus for rent control has arisen from the municipal level without the benefit of state enabling legislation and, as a result, there have been a number of legal challenges on the issues of municipal authority and state preemption.

> In the leading rent control cases since World War II the courts have continually considered both state preemption and municipal

> authority. However, these cases fail to establish any definitive trend on either question. Moreover, the various state holdings based upon similar issues of law and fact have been decided in a contradictory fashion. This divergence in decision may be interpreted as arising out of an unusually close question of law, the highly political nature of rent control or differing statutory and common law foundations for rent control systems. The cases span a twenty-five year period and provide adequate precedent to support or deny municipal authority to enact rent controls.[12]

Rent control imposed as an instrument of housing policy and specifically tied to other housing programs and policies does not appear to be a generally utilized legislative approach. However, the connection between rent control and housing policy may occur via the administrative function and, thus, largely depends upon the agency delegated to administer rent control.

Rent control legislation is generally codified in the province of landlord and tenant law, and is enacted most often as an autonomous policy dealing specifically with problems resulting from a declared housing emergency. As a result, administrative authority is usually delegated to a board or administrator created through the legislation. Exceptions do exist, however. The Alaska legislation delegated administration to the commissioner of commerce who was empowered to govern the activities of appointed emergency rent review boards. The review boards, in turn, were to make recommendations to the commerce commissioner for final action. Final enforcement authority under the Maryland statute lies with the attorney general; however, routine enforcement is handled by the division of consumer protection. Rent control in Maryland is specifically tied to the broader system of landlord-tenant laws, both in terms of codification and operation. The Montgomery County, Maryland rent control statute is an article of the amended landlord-tenant code. It is under the jurisdiction of the Maryland Office of Landlord-Tenant Affairs which administers all related articles of the code. In New York State, the administration of rent control is delegated to the New York State Division of Housing and Community Renewal and within New York City it is under the Housing and Development Administration.

### *REGULATORY AUTHORITY*

The rent adjustment formulas, discussed in detail in chapter 4, are the fundamental element of rent control regulation. However, the scope and breadth of regulatory authority may extend beyond the rent adjustment function. The inclusion of eviction controls and code compliance enforcement significantly broadens the scope of regulatory authority. Although there does not appear to be a correlation between the legislative approach (the specific type of statute) and the scope of authority of the regulatory mechanism, there is a clear relationship between the stringency of the rent adjustment formula and the scope of regulatory authority, as reflected in Exhibit 3-3. The variations which exist between communities with local ordinances adopted pursuant to state enabling legislation are generally administrative in nature, since the scope of regulatory authority and the stringency of the rent adjustment mechanism are defined by the state legislation. For example, there is a great deal of difference in the formulas used to define fair net operating income in Massachusetts; however, the FNOI concept and the extraregulatory provisions are derived from the state act.

Even in the absence of state legislation, there appears to be a general similarity in the scope of authority reflected in local ordinances within a state. Although many variations exist among the New Jersey communities, the scope and stringency of the regulatory mechanisms are generally comparable. Only in Maryland are significant differences evident. The Maryland statute was enacted in 1973 and initially provided for counties and the city of Baltimore to enact superseding laws. The act was extended in 1974 and expired June 30, 1975. Montgomery and Prince Georges counties enacted their laws prior to the expiration of the act and, subsequent to expiration, Anne Arundel, Hardford, and Wicomico counties enacted ordinances based on the expired statute. All the preceding county laws allow annual rent increases of 6 percent plus pass-throughs of cost increments in designated categories. Baltimore County, however, chose to establish voluntary controls to be monitored by the Apartment Builders and Owners Council. The council attained pledges from owners that they would limit all rental increases. Howard County established a limited-jurisdiction rent control commission.

Statutes enacted through state enabling legislation may be as stringent as the Massachusetts statute or as limited in authority as the Connecticut Fair Rent Commissions. The stringency of the regulatory mechanism, chiefly a function of the rent adjustment power, is defined on the basis of the following criteria:

1. Authority to establish across-the-board controls;
2. Administrative determination of any rent increases, rather than automatic increases via a formula;
3. Authority to order rent reduction as well as rental increases;
4. Inclusion of eviction controls;
5. Inclusion of code compliance enforcement as a basis of allowable rental increments or as a basis of eviction controls; and
6. Mandatory registration of all applicable structures and units.

The most stringent regulatory mechanisms meet all these criteria, as, for example, that of Massachusetts. Intermediate regulatory mechanisms provide the

*EXHIBIT 3-3*
*SCOPE OF REGULATORY AUTHORITY*

| Locations | Number of Communities Adopted | Regulatory Mechanism: Stringent | Regulatory Mechanism: Intermediate | Regulatory Mechanism: Mild | Extraregulatory Provisions: Code[a] Compliance | Extraregulatory Provisions: Eviction[b] Controls |
|---|---|---|---|---|---|---|
| *State Legislation* | | | | | | |
| Alaska | 2 | | | X | | |
| Connecticut | 7 | | | X | X | |
| Maine | 0 | X | | | X | |
| Maryland[c] | – | | X | X | | |
| Massachusetts | 4 | X | | | X | X |
| New York (1946)[d] | 100 | X | | | | X |
| New York (1974)[e] | 25 | | X | | | |
| *Local Ordinances* | | | | | | |
| Miami Beach, Fla. | – | X | | | | X |
| N.J. (Generalized) | 100 | | X | | X[f] | X[g] |
| N.Y.C. (1962) | – | X | | | X | X |
| N.Y.C. (1969) | – | | X | | | X |
| Washington, D.C. | – | | X | | X | X |

*Notes:* (a) Code compliance is herein used in a strict sense including only those ordinances which base receipt of rent increases (or decreases) on certification of code compliance.

(b) Eviction controls are here construed to include only ordinances placing constraints on the owner's right to possession.

(c) The Maryland statewide statute was applicable to all specified rental units except those in rural counties specifically exempted. Five counties and the city of Baltimore have enacted ordinances based on the state model. Two other counties have limited jurisdiction mechanisms.

(d) Applicable to pre-1947 structures in communities outside New York City.

(e) Applicable only to communities in Nassau, Rockland and Westchester counties in extending regulation to post-1947 structures. Twenty of the twenty-five communities are also included under the 1946 act. Thus the total number of communities outside NYC is 105 (see Exhibit 3-3).

(f) A few communities include a requirement tied to the annual rent increase, however, such a provision was declared invalid in one community by a lower court decision.

(g) Some ordinances include eviction controls. However, the late 1975 New Jersey Supreme Court decision invalidated inclusion of eviction controls on grounds of state preemption.

authority to establish across-the-board controls, but include a guaranteed annual rent increment. This intermediate form of regulation may, however, invoke a code compliance requirement for additional rental increases under a capital improvement or hardship provision. The New Jersey and Maryland ordinances are representative of this type of regulatory authority.

The mildest form of regulatory authority is represented by limited jurisdiction rent review boards such as those in Alaska and Connecticut. The function of these boards, as defined in the Connecticut statute, is "to make studies and investigations, conduct hearings and receive complaints relative to rental charges on property within its jurisdiction in order to control and eliminate excessive rental charges on such property."[13] However, once the Connecticut Fair Rent Commission is involved in a complaint(s), the scope of authority is as wide as any of the more stringent regulatory mechanisms. The Connecticut law provides that

> in determining whether a rental charge is so excessive, with due regard to all the circumstances, as to be harsh and unconscionable, a fair rent commission shall consider such of the following circumstances as are applicable to the type of accommodation: (1) The rents charged for the same number of rooms in other housing accommodations in the same and in other areas of the municipality; (2) the sanitary conditions existing in the housing accommodations in question; (3) the number of bathtubs or showers, flush water closets, kitchen sinks and lavatory basins available to the occupants thereof; (4) services, furniture, furnishings and equipment supplied therein; (5) the size and number of bedrooms contained therein; (6) repairs necessary to make such accommodations reasonably livable for the occupants accommodated therein; (7) the amount of taxes and overhead expenses thereof; (8) whether the accommodations are in compliance with the ordinances of the municipality and the general statutes relating to health and safety; (9) the income of the petitioner and the availability of accommodations; (10) the availability of utilities; (11) damages done to the premises by the tenant, caused by other than ordinary wear and tear.[14]

The most unique factor included in the scope of the commission's consideration is "the income of the petitioner and the availability of accommodations." The essence of this issue—which points to the central problem in the rent control controversy—is the widening gap between tenants' ability to pay and the increased rents necessary to operate and maintain a unit. The provision of equity to landlords via rent increases commensurate with increased operating costs places a hardship on a large number of tenants.

However, the question remains whether landlords should be excpected to subsidize tenants. The establishment of a "means" test under rent control, whereby only tenants certified to be in need of controlled rents are protected, has been proposed numerous times. The problems inherent in implementing such a proposal have resulted in little besides protracted discussion–although New York City exempts senior citizens, in specific circumstances, from paying more than one-third of their incomes for rent. The proposal to control rent increases for needy tenants is closely approximated in rent supplement programs such as that provided in the federal Section 8 rental assistance program.[15] Although the tenant's income is give some consideration in Connecticut, it appears that in no case has this factor been the sole basis for rent reduction because such reductions based soley on tenants' need is viewed as unfair to the property owner.[16]

The scope of the authority of the rent control mechanism is significantly augmented, even under limited jurisdiction mechanisms, by the mediating and supportive services provided by the administrative agency. Some of the fair rent commissions in Connecticut provide social service referral and relocation assistance when it is determined that the problem confronted by the tenant is more comprehenisve than a rental dispute with the landlord. Support resources such as rent supplements and tax-relief programs for senior citizens (which are applicable to tenants as well as owners) are utilized when such needs are determined. Thus, in terms of achieving equity, administration is as important as the statutory provisions. (The administration of rent control is discussed in greater detail in chapter 6.)

## *INCREASING THE SCOPE OF REGULATORY AUTHORITY*

Provisions governing evictions and code compliance significantly broaden the scope of regulatory authority and increase its stringency.

### *Eviction Controls*

The incorporation of eviction controls in rent control statutes is not a clearcut legal issue. The inclusion of eviction controls in local ordinances has been challenged on the basis of state preemption because all states have landlord-tenant statutes which govern eviction procedures. Although the grounds for eviction may not materially conflict with state laws, a challenge may be upheld insofar as the right to recover possession is limited to grounds which are less than those provided for in state law. However, one New Jersey court's reasoning has been that the statewide statutes deal only with the remedy; therefore, the inclusion of eviction provisions in rent control legislation is acceptable to the extent that "conditioning the right to evict does not encroach upon the statutory remedies. These ordinances will not impinge upon that remedy existent in the field of landlord and tenant relationships."[17] Subsequent to this 1972 ruling, however, the New Jersey State Supreme Court has held eviction provisions in municipal rent control ordinances to be invalid: "having been preempted by state enactments."[18] The preempting state statute cited by the court was enacted in 1974 after the original 1972 ruling. The incorporation of provisions for eviction controls within statewide or state enabling rent control legislation should preclude the legal issues arising because state laws are silent on the matter.

The major purpose of including provisions for eviction in rent control legislation is to protect tenants in a time of emergency and to deter any subversion of the rent control law. The ultimate effect is to impose additional constraints and limitations on the owner's power to evict which is normally allowed under common law and established statutory eviction procedures. Under common law a tenant rents from an owner under a formal or informal agreement, but, within the guidelines of due process regarding eviction procedures, the owner has a right to reclaim his property at the end of the agreement. Under eviction controls, the tenant is granted statutory rights to continued occupancy as long as he abides by the stated regulations, i.e., he pays his rent on time and so on. Thus, he is a "statutory tenant." The following example from the Miami Beach ordinance clearly reflects the degree of increased regulatory authority provided by the inclusion of eviction controls.

> No action or proceeding to recover possession of housing accommodations shall be maintainable by any landlord against any tenant, notwithstanding that the tenant has no lease or that his lease has expired, so long as the tenant continues to pay the rent to which the landlord is entitled, unless:
>
> (1) The tenant is committing a nuisance or using the housing accommodations for an immoral or illegal purpose or for other than living or dwelling purposes; or
>
> (2) The tenant is failing to comply with any of the provisions for which eviction is permitted pursuant to Florida Statutes Chapter 83, except where this Ordinance provides otherwise.
>
> (3) The landlord seeks in good faith to recover possession of the property for his immediate and personal use or occupancy as a dwelling; or for the use and occupancy of any member of his immediate family.
>
> (4) The landlord seeks in good faith to recover possession for the immediate purpose of demolishing the property and replacing it with new construction in accordance with plans filed with and approved by the building department of the City.

(5) The landlord seeks in good faith to permanently withdraw the housing accommodations from the housing market without any intent to rent or sell all or any part of the rental unit or structure.[19]

To evict a tenant under rent control, it is often stipulated that an owner file a petition justifying the grounds for eviction, and validating proper notice and rent level compliance. After the owner has filed this petition with the rent control office, he must await issuance of a certificate from the office before eviction action can proceed. In some cases, a code compliance certificate is also required; in others however, the certificate of eviction requirement is limited to specific grounds. The Miami Beach ordinance, for example, requires no certificate for nonpayment of rent or for violations "1." and "2." as cited in the above ordinance.

The most ambiguous element in eviction controls concerns the issue of code compliance. In instances in which code compliance is required an owner must certify that there are no outstanding code violations sometimes excepting those caused by the tenants he is seeking to evict; however, as one court decision expressed it, "there may be no rational connection between a 'code violation' and the ground for evicting a tenant."[20] Essentially then, the code compliance provision invests power in a rent control board or administrator for determining whether a landlord has grounds for eviction for reasons wholly unrelated to the enforcement of rent controls. As included in the Berkeley eviction control provision, such reasoning was judged invalid by the California Court of Appeals.[21] The same court found the certificate of eviction procedure invalid.

*Code Compliance*

The determination of exactly what constitutes a code compliance provision in rent control ordinances is not easily understood because such provision may take at least three different forms. Many rent control ordinances, as a pro forma matter, recite or reference local and state legislation requiring that all units be maintained in compliance with applicable housing code standards—without specifying any relationship to other provisions in the ordinance. Other rent control ordinances include a statement to the effect that the landlords shall maintain the standards of services, maintenance, facilities, etc. previously provided (before rent control enactment) or required by law. Generally, these provisions give the rent control agency authority to order rent reductions until the deficiency is corrected. Such action, however, is only taken on the basis of a tenant's petition accompanied by a verification of the violations by the appropriate inspection department.

A third interpretation of code compliance inclusion in rent control ordinances links the receipt or amount of rental increases to the condition of the building or unit. This provision may be implemented in a number of ways. Pursuant to the Massachusetts state enabling act, the condition of the building is a factor considered in setting rent levels. Other ordinances require submitting certificates from the appropriate municipal departments stating that the building is free of code violations. To qualify for annual rent increases under the New York City Maximum Base Rent program, owners must certify to the correction of rent-impairing and other housing code violations prior to receipt of their rent increase orders. This linkage of housing code standards to the rent adjustment mechanism constitutes the strictest interpretation of code compliance provisions within rent control ordinances and is the interpretation which is herein used and was used in Exhibit 3-3.

Within the strict interpretation, code compliance provisions are included to provide incentives and inducements for owners to maintain rental structures. The existence of "code violations" seem generally accepted as relevant in determining the level of rent, particulary when such conditions are a statutory element of the rent adjustment formula as in the fair net operating income formula. However, a similar compliance provision was recently declared invalid in a New Jersey case. In denying (on the basis of code violations) receipt of the automatic 2.5 percent annual rent increase permitted in the local ordinance, the provision was determined to be an excessive penalty.[22] The court cited statutory penalty limitations and the existence of other remedies available to the tenant and municipality. Nevertheless, in other areas of the United States, code compliance has been unchallenged. For example, New Jersey ordinances which link code compliance to additional rental increases—i.e., capital improvements and hardship, rather than the automatic annual rent adjustment—have been accepted without legal controversy.

## *FACTORS OF RENT CONTROL ENACTMENT*

A number of similar interrelated factors are identifiable among those communities with enacted or proposed rent control. These factors can be broadly classified according to characteristics of the housing stock, the resident population, and the economic condition of the community.

The most obvious common element in all areas with proposed or enacted rent control statutes is a significant ratio of rental units to the total housing stock. All of the areas have rental units well in excess of the 1970 national norm of 34.5 percent with the majority of the controlled communities reflecting ratios in excess of 50 percent.

Although some common elements exist, the specific combination of variables which interact in any particular community and result in rent control imposition are unique to that community. For example, it is clear that rent control in Alaska cannot be explained by the presence of variables identical to those in Massachusetts. The rental increases of 200 and 300 percent generated by rapid population and economic expansion as a result of the Alaskan pipeline construction clearly reflects a unique emergency situation. The situation in Alaska more closely resembles wartime rather than peacetime emergency housing conditions.

Localities with significant university student populations, whether traditional "college towns" or major urban centers, are often receptive to rent control proposals. Ann Arbor, Michigan; Boulder, Colorado; Madison and Milwaukee, Wisconsin; Minneapolis, Minnesota; Palo Alto, California; and Philadelphia, Pennsylvania have all proposed rent control statutes. Berkeley, Carlifornia's rent control ordinance was enacted but overturned. Thus, the presence of a highly mobile limited-income university population and a high demand for rental units constitutes another combination of variables which may result in rent control. Of those communities with enacted, second generation rent control, Cambridge and Boston, Massachusetts as well as New Haven, Connecticut also have university populations.

In New Jersey, 97 communities with a wide variation of housing characteristics have enacted rent control regulations. The New Jersey Tenants Organization (NJTO), a statewide political force largely composed of middle class people, has been influential in promoting and supporting rent controls. Rent control proposals appear to be more successful when spurred by middle-income, highly educated tenants than when the initiative arises from a low-income segment of the population—as is apparent in the contrast between recent rent control history in New Jersey and Maine. The largely middle-class NJTO is reputed to be one of the strongest statewide tenant organizations in the country and has been credited for the widespread adoption of rent control in New Jersey. In Maine, on the other hand, the rent control movement was initiated by low-income groups. Though these groups succeeded in getting state enabling legislation passed, the legislation is inoperative because no ordinances at the local level were enacted due to a lack of local support.

In effect, rent control can and has become a political tool of a sophisticated tenant electorate which uses rent control to minimize the adverse affect of inflation upon its housing costs.

## *NOTES*

1. The Brookline Rent Review and Grievance Board was subsequently declared unconstitutional in the absence of explicit state enabling legislation. While this case was pending, however, the town filed for its own state enabling statute (Ch. 843) which passed concurrently with the statewide local option law—Chapter 842—in August 1970.

2. Boston, Massachusetts, Ch. 10 of the Acts of 1969.
3. Massachusetts General Laws, Ch. 797 (1969). In late 1970, the Boston City Council enacted over the mayor's veto Chapter 11 of the Acts of 1970, which further strengthened the regulatory powers adding eviction controls provisions and covering FHA housing previously exempted under Chapter 10.
4. Massachusetts General Laws, Ch. 842.
5. Connecticut Public Act 274, 1969.
6. New Haven, New Britain, East Norwick, Hartford, Danbury, Stamford, and Enfield.
7. Inganamort v. Borough of Fort Lee, 303, A.2d. 298.
8. "A Report By the Blue Ribbon Citizen's Commission on Rent Control," (Submitted to Mayor and Members of Council, Ann Arbor, Michigan, 1974).
9. Birkenfeld v. City of Berkeley, Cal. Super. Ct., 428971 (1972), Court of Appeals, 1 Civil 34378 (June 22, 1975). For more detailed discussion, see chapter 2.
10. Richard E. Blumberg, Brian Q. Robbins, and Kenneth K. Baar, "The Emergence of Second Generation Rent Controls," *Clearinghouse Review* 8 (August, 1974): 247.
11. The exception is the inclusion of eviction controls which have been challenged on the basis of state preemption and often invalidated. Invalidation of a specific clause does not mean that the entire legislation is necessarily invalidated.
12. Blumberg, Robbins, and Baar, p. 247.
13. Connecticut Public Act 274, 1969, Section 1.
14. Ibid., as amended by Connecticut Public Acts No. 160, 1972. Connecticut General Statutes Annotated, Sec. 7-148(h), 1972.
15. The Section 8 Housing Assistance Payment Program authorized by the Housing and Community Development Act of 1974 provides assistance to low- and moderate-income families who pay up to 25 percent of their income for rent. The subsidy is the difference between the amount paid and fair market rents prevailing in an area, as determined annually by HUD for newly constructed, rehabilitated, and existing units without code violations.
16. Telephone interviews with administrators of local fair rent commissions in Connecticut.
17. Inganamort v. Borough of Fort Lee, 120 N.J. Super 286, 293 A.2d 720, aff'd. at 303 A.2d 298.
18. Brunetti v. Borough New Milford, 68 N.J. 576 (1975). (Mimeo decision pp. 29-30). The court cites the enactment in 1974 of *N.J.S.A.* 2A:18-61.1 "which sets forth specific enumerated grounds of eviction . . . " as leaving no doubt that "the Legislature intended to preempt this area of the law."
19. Miami Beach, Florida, Ordinance 74-2018, Section 4A, adopted December 11, 1974.

20. Birkenfeld v. Berkeley, p. 22.
21. Ibid.
22. Helmsley et al. v. Borough of Fort Lee, Superior Court, Bergen County No. L-11348-74 P.W., June 30, 1975, pp. 13-14, (Unreported).

# Chapter 4
# The Substantive Provisions of Rent Control Statutes: Administrative Standards

## *THE IMPORTANCE AND FUNCTION OF ADMINISTRATIVE STANDARDS*

Contrary to World War II and 1971 Phase 1 price controls, present rent controls are not absolute freezes on rent levels. Rather, all ordinances allow for regulated increases. Further, most provide for pass-throughs or surcharges of cost increments in designated expenditure categories. It is through these provisions which define the administrative standards to be utilized that equitability for both property owners and tenants is approached. *An equitably defined ordinance does not, however, guarantee equity in its administration; however, it is clear that there is no way to equitably administer an inequitable ordinance.*

Beyond the overall objective of providing equitable regulation, administrative standards are a crucial factor in other issues. First, and foremost among these, is again a concern for the constitutional validity of the statute—which may be challenged on a number of grounds relevant to the provisions or to the absence of certain provisions within the legislation. These grounds encompass basic issues of substantive and procedural due process and specific concerns of (1) unlawful delegation of legislative powers; (2) equal protection; and (3) the taking of private property for public use without just compensation.

Recognizing that no regulatory legislation can be drafted to be self-administering, administrative authority must be delegated. When reviewing statutes challenged on grounds of unlawful delegation, "the courts generally look to see if the legislature has provided the administrator with sufficient standards for administration. If it has, the conventional wisdom holds that no delegation has occurred."[1] The courts also recognize that the inclusion of detailed rules and procedures of action within legislation is impractical if not impossible in view of complex and changing circumstances.[2] However, as a policy matter, it is apparent that the reason for the establishment of specific standards is to restrain the delegated administrative body from exercising its authority in an unbridled or arbitrary fashion. Furthermore, without objective standards agency determinations are always vulnerable to outside pressures and can "never command public respect as impartial, independent judgments rendered in accordance with the law."[3]

Given appropriate delegation and the inclusion of sufficient workable standards, the application of standards may still present substantial questions concerning the reasonableness of those standards as applied. If the standards are not universally applied, the constitutional issue of equal protection may be raised relative to any statutory provisions or subsequent regulation which unreasonably distinguishes between classes or properties. Specifically, questions arise concerning those provisions which define certain properties as subject to control or include rent adjustment formulas which make distinctions in their allowances.

The significance of the issues raised briefly here reveals the importance of the substantive provisions of rent control statutes. The specific requirements of these provisions will be discussed next. (A full analysis of the administration of these provisions is provided in chapter 6 via three case studies.)

## *DETERMINING THE RENT CONTROL UNIVERSE*

The universe of units subject to control under World War II regulations was much broader in scope than present-day regulations. World War II legislation regulated all housing accommodation–including hotels and rooming houses. Current legislation generally applies only to multi-family residential units and excludes transient units (although some residential hotels in New York City are regulated under the rent stabilization law of 1969).

The provisions that determine which units will be rent-controlled establish the scope of rent control for a given community. The definition of these provisions varies from community to community as the exigencies of the defined emergency condition vary because the imposition of controls should relate specifically and particularly to the units and population suffering the hardship of the emergency.

The final delineation of the scope of rent control for a particular community should be based on documentation derived from a community survey untertaken to validate the existence of a housing emergency. Furthermore, a provision requireing periodic surveys to determine change in emergency conditions in all or some classes of controlled housing should be included in the rent control statute. A requirement that the initial and subsequent periodic surveys be submitted to a regional or state agency for review would also be beneficial as it would provide a standardized and consistent framework of criteria from which to evaluate the emergency determination. This procedure would be particularly appropriate for states in which adjacent communities may adopt ordinances using different methods and criteria, thus generating distortions in the regional market. A provision for state review has been proposed as an amendment to the Massachusetts State Enabling Act.[4] The amendment would require all communities wishing to adopt rent control ordinances to submit documentation of the existence of an emergency to the Massachusetts State Department of Community Affairs which would be empowered to approve such documentation. Although not stipulated in the proposed amendment, it is essential that the state agency develop guidelines for conducting surveys and the documentation submission.

Present rent control provisions usually exempt one or more classes of housing from control. The following constitutes the major categories of exemption:

1. Units in structures of less than three or four units;
2. Units in owner-occupied, 1 to 3 family structures;
3. Blanket exemption of new construction after a specified date;
4. The initial rental of units in new construction which are subsequently subject to controls;
5. Luxury units, with rentals above a specified monthly contract rent, or a percentage of the highest rental units; and
6. FHA insured and/or subsidized, or other publicly assisted units.

The exemption of any one type of housing in a particular community can result in the exclusion of a significant proportion of the total number of rental units. Typically, political contingencies and administrative expediency have led to the exclusion of the small structures and small, owner-occupied structures.

### *New Construction Exemption*

In an attempt to avoid discouraging new construction in a rent-controlled community, newly constructed units are often exempted. The Massachusetts enabling act gives blanket exemption to all units constructed after January 1, 1969. However, New Jersey municipalities exempt newly-constructed units only at the initial rental; these units are then subject to control for all subsequent rent increases.

It is not apparent that even blanket exemption encourages new construction since the housing industry is often fearful that the exemption may be withdrawn at a later date. In this regard, New York City provides an example. After exempting all units constructed after February 1, 1947 in its original rent control law, twenty-three years later the city imposed rent stabilization regulations on these structures. Blanket exemptions appear to accompany stringent rent adjustments mechanisms as in the Massachusetts and Maine cases, while statutes that exampt new construction only upon initial rental appear with more flexible rent adjustment formulas as in the New Jersey ordinances.

### *Luxury Housing Exemption*

Luxury housing has often been exempted from rent control on the basis that tenants in a position to pay such rents are not in need of the protection granted by rent control. This view was held by the Federal Price Commission during Phase II control on the basis that those exempted were "only that economic strata most able to shop selectively, negotiate effectively, and move at will either into other luxury rental units or into home ownership."[5] The Massachusetts enabling legislation, however, limits exemption of luxury units to not more than 25 percent of the total number of rental units.[6]

Although not initially exempted as a class of housing in New York City, a series of three luxury decontrol orders between 1957 and 1968 has resulted in the exemption of these units. The first order issued in 1957 under state administration decontrolled units having monthly rents of $416 and $500 or more for unfurnished and furnished units, respectively. In March 1964, New York City decontrolled vacant or subsequently vacated units with monthly rents in excess of $250 unfurnished and $300 furnished effective April 1, 1960. An extension of this policy in 1968 utilized the same rent levels, but used April 1, 1965 as the base date.[7]

### *Federally Assisted Or Insured Housing Exemption*

The expansion of rent control since 1969 has resulted in controversies over the authority of rent control ordinances with regard to federally insured and assisted units. Some localities contend that tenants of FHA-insured and subsidized housing within their jurisdiction deserve the same protection afforded tenants in nonfederally assisted buildings. The federal government contends that its financial interest in properties it insures or aids warrants that those properties be exempted from local controls if their financial health is endangered by such regulations.[8] Prior to the issuance of interim regulations by HUD in February, 1975, the courts ruled in two decisions that the control of rents in FHA-insured housing was not inconsistent with the National Housing Act and thus could be subject to controls.[9]

The major distinction in the control of privately owned, federally assisted housing is made between units which are directly assisted and those which are only insured. Units owned and operated by a public authority are always exempt. Maryland exempts federally assisted units in which rents are determined as a percentage of tenants income. Cases involving indirectly publicly assisted units and federally insured structures are especially confusing in terms of regulation. For example, a structure built on an urban renewal site with a mortgage insured under Section 220 of the National Housing Act received an indirect subsidy through the urban renewal write-down of land costs and is also a recipient of government insurance.[10] To further confuse the issue, Section 220 states that the secretary of HUD "may in his (her) discretion require such mortgage to be regulated or restricted as to rents or sales, charges, etc."[11] If HUD regulates rent levels, there may be no need for further regulation. In the City of Boston Section 220 units and units insured under Section 207 are exempt.

Exemptions of one or more of the previously cited categories creates two classes of residential rental housing–controlled and noncontrolled. Whenever legislation is applied less than universally, arguments of violation of the equal protection clause may be raised. In general, however, if the classifications created by the statute bear a reasonable relationship to the purposes of the statute, it is deemed that the requirements of the equal protection clause are met.[12] In recent years the courts' attitude toward economic regulation classification has been one of a presumption of validity. It has been suggested that "only when the lack of correspondence between classification and purpose is gross or when the classification is otherwise objectionable should courts intervene on equal protection grounds."[13]

## *BASE RENT DETERMINATION: ROLLBACKS*

The invocation of rent controls requires the determination of a base rent from which future rental increases can be calculated. This determination is generally accomplished by the rollback of rents to a prior date; rents effective on that date become the base rent under rent control.

The length of time of the rollback period necessarily varies as a function of the emergency conditions and the contingencies of enactment. In the case of the 1971 Economic Stabilization Program, the date of announcement was designated as the freeze date, and it became the base for subsequent adjustments under Phase II controls. Consequently, there was no rollback period. Usually, however, a program of controls does not occur unexpectedly. Therefore, rollback periods are a normal provision, although the specific amount of time allotted varies. The Massachusetts State Enabling Act specifies that the base rent shall be that charged "for the month six months prior to the acceptance of this act by a municipality."[14]

The particular time period established in local ordinances–in the absence of a state provision defining the rollback period–is largely determined by the rationale considered to be the basis for the rollback, and the length of time ensuing between the proposed controls and their imposition. Generally, the purpose of the rollback is twofold:(1) to mitigate any speculative or anticipatory rent increases which may have taken place after the rent control proposal was announced; and (2) to set base rents at "fair" levels as determined by a normal functioning market prior to the emergency condition. On the latter point, the 1974 Miami Beach ordinance speaks explicitly: "The Director shall presume that rents for housing accommodations in this City in effect on October 16, 1974, were established at levels which yielded to owners a fair rate of return for such units."[15]

The rollback procedure has been universally upheld by the courts as constitutional.[16] Nevertheless, some iniquities result no matter how much care and consideration is given to the selection of an appropriate date. Primary among these iniquities is the reduction of rent levels below the level necessary for maintaining buildings or individual units. Also if some unwarranted rent increases were imposed prior to the period rent control considers "emergency," then the property owner who failed to exploit the emergency suffers. If the rollback date is set back too far, most rents will be inadequate and hardships will be incurred by most owners. General across-the-board adjustments or provisions for initial base rent adjustments on an individual basis are necessary to handle these inequities, as well as the inevitable exceptions which occur.[17]

In order to rectify inequities and to handle exceptional problems–such as units vacant on the rollback date–rules providing for an adjusted base rent are developed. The scope of these regulations is as broad and varied as the number of unique circumstances within the housing market. A situation which inevitably occurs, for example, is that of the unit rented on the rollback date to a relative or employee of the landlord at a level below market rents and subsequently rented to someone else. Is it fair to expect an owner to charge the same rent he may have charged a son or daughter or an employee who received a reduced rent as partial compensation? Also, variations in rents for comparable units within a building frequently occur as a function of variations in the length of the lease and base rent adjustments are necessary for leases signed during the rollback period, particularly if the rent on the rollback date was established in a two- or three-year lease expiring after the rollback date but before rent control enactment.

A housing market characterized by a significant seasonal fluctuation in demand represents a more complex situation for base rent determination and adjustment. Although this problem may be partially mitigated by the exemption of units which are clearly transient, the issue still remains with respect to units, that may, as a function of the emergency, shift back and forth from being seasonally rented units to permanent residential units. Furthermore, what provision should be made for a unit which is rented year-round to a single family or individual but is only occupied during a part of the year? Should a tenant who obviously can afford two residences be afforded the protection of rent control? Although these problems are generally confined to resort areas, they are extremely crucial in these areas, particularly given a shortage of permanent rental units. Miami Beach, Florida and Altantic City, New Jersey, for example, have adopted rent controls; and both exempt seasonally rented units.

Beyond specific base rent adjustments to handle unique circumstances, there may also be a need for a general across-the-board adjustment to counteract the impact of inflation during the rollback period. An across-the-board adjustment is particularly necessary if the rollback date has been set too far back and, as a result, incoming controlled rents are not enough to meet operating expenses. This general adjustment may also be utilized to provide pass-throughs in categories affecting all buildings, for example, an increase in the real estate tax rate.

The adoption of rent controls by a number of communities in a metropolitan region may contribute to distortions in the regional housing market. Varying rollback dates may create artificial demand in those communities with controls and particularly those with longer rollback periods. On the other hand, although regional policies would mitigate these potential distortions, they can only be politically effective if there is a regional or state agency to implement them. In the absence of such an agency, the previously-discussed requirement of state review and approval of emergency documentation will somewhat reduce potential market distortions.

### *RENT ADJUSTMENT MECHANISMS*

The method utilized to regulate rent adjustments is the most important provision of the rent control statute. Beyond the legal concerns related to the presence of an emergency and municipal authority, the adequacy of the regulating guidelines of rent adjustment provisions incur the severest constitutional challenges. Provisions which are too vague in order to provide flexibility may be judicially interpreted as insufficient and an illegal delegation of authority. On the other hand, in one court decision very specific guidelines were construed as confiscatory and as a denial of due process because of the limited flexibility available to the administrator.

One of the legal questions raised concerning rent adjustment mechanisms is whether the economic loss incurred as a result of controlled rents constitutes a "taking of private property for public use without just compensation."[18] The early federal rent control cases held that there is no constitutional requirement for assuring property owners of a fair return on their investment. In *Bowles v. Willingham,* the landmark case on the taking question, the court ruled that

> the State rent control statute was enacted to meet a passing emergency. It does not contemplate a taking of the property of any landlord. Even though it may, now and then, compel an owner to operate his real property at a loss, the statute is not for that reason to be condemned as an arbitrary use of the police power.[19]

Although this case is still relied upon, most recent decisions construe the purpose of rent control to include the provision to landlords of a fair and equitable return upon their investments.[20] The most recent decisions of the New Jersey Supreme Court, upholding the rent control ordinances of four municipalities, emphasized the necessity that rent regulation permit an owner a "just and reasonable" return.[21] The court acknowledged *Bowles v. Willingham* but noted the distinction of "surrounding circumstances" in determining what is confiscatory: "In ordinary circumstances, price controls which do not permit an *economically efficient* operator to obtain a 'just and reasonable' return on his investment are deemed confiscatory [emphasis added]."[22]

The necessity to provide a just and reasonable return was not, however, tied to the rent adjustment formula. From a procedural point of view, linkage to the rent adjustment formula was viewed by the court as "highly desirable;" but the requirement was held to be met if the ordinances provided a hardship provision allowing owners to file on the ground that they are not receiving a just and reasonable return.[23]

Most statutes allow for restircted increases and many provide for pass-throughs of increments in costs for specific categories of expenses. The difficult questions of which costs are to be considered and of how they should be treated in the regulation of rents pose additional questions of equity.

There are three general approaches to setting rent levels. The first approach is through a formula which regulates the landlord's return on investment, thus only allowing rent increases to meet increased costs once the designated rate of return is reached for a specific property. The second approach involves limiting annual rent increases from a specified base rent via a variety of methods, with or without regard for the landlord's rate of return. The third approach to setting rent levels is based on the tenant's ability to pay; this approach is used in public and publicly assisted subsidized housing and is generally found in state and federal housing finance agency laws as a mandatory condition. It is not utilized in any presently enacted rent control scheme as the primary rent adjustment mechanism; however, under New York City rent control, senior citizens are exempted from paying more than one-third of their income for rent in specific circumstances. In the following discussion only the first two approaches are treated.

*Limited Return On Investment*

Rent adjustment mechanisms devised to limit return on investment generally encompass formulas developed to yield a fair net operating income (FNOI). As indicated in chapter 1, the FNOI approach was first incorporated into federal rent control in 1949, after seven years of experimentation with rent adjustment formulas. The approach as presently used is generally based on the federal model. Cost fluctuation in all major operating categories is taken into consideration in limited return approaches to rent adjustment, but annual rent increases are in no way automatic when this mechanism is used. In fact, decreases in rent may be the end result.

The Massachusetts system is the best example of this approach. Section 7 of Chapter 842 of the General Laws of Massachusetts reads as follows:

> The board or the administration shall make such individual or general adjustments either upward or downward of the maximum rent established by Section 7 for controlled rental unit or any class of controlled rental units as may be necessary to assure that rent for controlled rental units are established at levels which yield to landlords a fair net operating income.[24]

Beyond this general statement, the legislation provides no answer to what is actually a fair net operating income. The definition of the formula is left to the municipality or the local administrative agency. As a result a wide degree of variation exists with respect to the actual formulas in use and to the overall administration and impact of rent control within each community. Appendix I summarizes the procedures and formulas used in Massachusetts and the case studies included in Chapter 6 provide an analysis of the administrative results. In addition to increases or decreases in real estate taxes, operating and maintenance expenses, and costs incurred through capital improvement, the following factors related to building maintenance and services may also be considered in the limited-return approach:

> 1. Increases or decreases in living space, services, furniture, furnishings or equipment;
> 2. Substantial deterioration (other than wear and tear);
> 3. Failure to perform ordinary repair, replacement and maintenance; and
> 4. Other relevant factors which the board of administrator may define by regulation.

As cited in chapter 3, the Massachusetts State Legislature enacted two rent control statutes concurrently. The second, Ch 843, applies only to the town of Brookline. Unlike Ch 842, the Brookline act does not list the previously cited relevant factors, but does more specifically define FNOI as:

> that income which will yield a return, after all reasonable operating expenses, on the fair market value of the property equal to the debt service rate generally available from institutional first mortgage lenders or such other rate of return as the board, on the basis of evidence presented before it, deems more appropriate to the circumstances of the case. The fair market value of the property shall be the assessed valuation of the property or such other valuation as the board, on the basis of evidence presented before it, deems more appropriate to the circumstances of the case.[25]

The constitutionality of both these statutes was upheld by the Supreme Judicial Court of Massachusetts.[26]

The degree of variation occurring under the FNOI system is evident in the following four types of formulas which are used to define fair net operating income, as a rate of return for a specific base amount.

1. *Value Formula*: FNOI is equivalent to some percentage of the value of the property; however, value can be defined by a number of approaches.
2. *Gross Rent Formula*: FNOI is equal to some percentage of the total rents charged in the building.
3. *Equity Formula*: Allows the owner a percentage rate of return on the actual cash investment in the property.
4. *Dollar Net Operating Income Formula*: This formula uses no rate of return and no base but provides the owner the same net operating income, in dollars, earned in an earlier "base year" or that amount increased by some percentage, i.e., the general rate of inflation reflected in the Consumer Price Index.

The definition of FNOI as a function of value is as varied as the range of appraisal methods. Market value may be determined by various calculations including multipliers applied to gross income or assessed value, current sale prices, and other appraisal estimates. Beyond the technical questions of developing a formula are the practical considerations of implementing the method within a reasonable period of time after rent control has been enacted. Usually, the limited time period requires utilizing available tax assessments. The potential decrease in a property's market value, based on its reduced long-term income-producing potential as a function of rent control is a long-range problem for FNOI formulas based on property values.

Gross rent formulas avoid the problems of defining and calculating value, but involve decisions as to whether current or base date gross rents should be used and how the appropriate formula percentages should be derived. Although the context is different vis-a-vis definition, conceptually this approach is similar to net operating income formulas in that either a fixed ratio or fixed dollar net operating income is established, depending on whether current or base date gross rents are used.

Formulas derived on the basis of value or investment equity often result in extreme disparities, creating a wide range of possible FNOIs within the same class of buildings. Additionally, variations in financing arrangements and methods of handling depreciation contribute significantly to the difficulty of determining actual rates of return. Only in terms of net operating income is there some comparability which is, however, limited according to variations in operation as a result of the age, size, and structure characteristics of the building. Additionally, scale of operation must be considered in addition to the economic variations in the operating pattern. Administrative allowances must be made for owner-provided management and owner-executed labor in maintenance expenses.

As a framework for rent adjustment mechanisms, the FNOI concept is generally held to be constitutional. However, specifics in the application of the resulting formulas have led to the invalidation of some ordinances. As indicated earlier, the legislative definition of the Massachusetts FNOI was upheld by the Supreme Judicial Court of Massachusetts.[27] This decision overruled arguments that the provisions in the statewide option act (842) and the specific Brookline state enabling act (843) were confiscatory or contradictory in their definitions. The court stated:

> Neither formulation of the term "fair net operating income" is inflexible enough to require a result more or less advantageous to landlords than the other . . . *The flexibility which Ch. 842 allows to each community to mold the term 'fair net operating income' to accord with its peculiar local needs is a desirable feature of the act* [emphasis added].[28]

Thus FNOI as used in both statutes was sustained, assuring to landlords a reasonable return on their investments. It should be noted that the challenges in this case were levied on the "face of the statute," that is, on the provision as drafted and not upon any specific results of its operation. The court, in conclusion, noted that no evidence had been introduced indicating "that the operation of either [statute] will necessarily be confiscatory with respect to [any landlord] individually or with respect to a general class of landlords."[29] Subsequent to this decision, the specific formula used to define FNOI in Cambridge was struck down and a new formula devised.[30]

Another example in which a specified FNOI formula was declared invalid was the formula provision included in the 1973 Miami Beach, Florida ordinance.[31] This provision allowed for a rent adjustment where "it is established that the earned income from the property does not result in a net annual return of 6% of the assessed valuation of the property in effect as of October 1, 1973."[32] Net annual return was defined as "the amount by which the earned income exceeds the operating expenses of the property, including mortgage interest, amortization, depreciation and debt service."[33]

The Supreme Court of Florida ruled that the ordinance was unconstitutional "in that its provisions and guidelines [were] arbitrary and unreasonable and would be confiscatory and a denial of due process."[34] The court further noted that "the assessed valuation of property is not necessarily the proper basis for a fair return "as it is not always current, despite a state requirement for 100 percent assessed valuation."[35] Basing its decision on expert testimony and the plaintiff's fiscal operations records, the court found the guidelines too stringent to allow an administrator to make sufficient adjustments:

> The standards and guidelines for the rent administrator are so fixed and arbitrary in this particular ordinance and in such exact percentages and amounts and terms as to prevent the administrator, even if he desired, from allowing a fair rate of return in certain situations which demanded it in order to allow the administrator leeway in specified instances. . . . These provisions remain so restrictive that the continuing spiraling costs since that date, of which we must take judicial notice, would preclude an administrator from allowing, even if he wanted, a rate of return that would be less than confiscatory at least in part. Needed in such an ordinance is a greater flexibility to take such matters into account so that the ultimate goals earlier expressed in the authorities of a fair rate of return and yet an avoidance of unfair rents would be more likely to be attained.[36]

Neither of these two cases is particularly instructive of the most appropriate approach for defining FNOI; however, one decision indicates that the uses of assessments are highly sensitive. The cases clearly reflect the vagaries of judicial interpretation and the difficulties inherent in utilizing the limited-return-on-investment mechanism. The following rent adjustment mechanisms avoid many of these problems, but present other difficulties of equal importance.

### *Maximum Base Rent Mechanisms*

Maximum base rent mechamisms are not to be confused with New York City's "Maximum Base Rents" formula.[37] They allow for an annual rent adjustment above predetermined specified base rents. The formulations for the allowable annual increment are nearly as varied as the number of ordinances represented within this category. Formulas range in complexity from a fixed-percentage maximum annual increment with allowable pass-alongs and/or surcharges to the complex MBR formula utilized for New York City's rent-controlled housing sector.

Included in this range of formulas are various price indexes. The Consumer Price Index was used in the majority of the New Jersey municipalities' initial ordinances and a specific Price Index of Operating Costs for Rent Stabilized Apartment Houses is used in New York City.[38] These indexes are used in different ways—one is used as a formula, the other as a guideline input factor. The CPI as included in many New Jersey ordinances limits the annual rent increase to the percentage increase in the CPI for the period 90 days prior to the commencement of the lease to 90 days prior to its termination. Alternative periods of 60 days to 120 days are also used. The Price Index of Operating Costs, on the other hand, is used as a guide, along with other relevant factors, by the Rent Guidelines Board in determining the maximum annual rent increases for rent-stabilized apartments in New York City. The primary thrust of these adjustment mechanisms, particularly those utilizing price indexes, is to provide rental increases commensurate with operating cost increments or the rate of inflation.

A fixed percentage to restrict the maximum allowable annual rent adjustment is frequently used because of the ease of its application; however, the logic for deriving the specific percent to be used often appears arbitrary or unclear. Because of the unexpected high rate of inflation reflected in the CPI (especially in 1974), some New Jersey communities amended their ordinances to specify a maximum fixed percentage ranging from 2.5 to 7 percent, and some apply only a portion of the CPI, for example, 50 percent. One New Jersey community has developed its own operating cost index to arrive at annual rent adjustments.[39] Any fixed percentage, however, may be construed as arbitrary and unreasonable if it does not reflect adequate rent increases to cover operating cost increments, particularly in a period of high inflation. Given a predictable, steady rate of inflation, annual fixed percentage inflators are easily established from historical trends. With recent inflationary trends, the primary issue generating controversy in the application of these maximum base rent mechanisms is the adequacy of the formulas to provide rent increases necessary to cover operation and maintenance cost increments.

Unlike the FNOI mechanism in which actual expenditures are reviewed on an individual building basis and adjustments made reflecting changes in these expenditures, maximum base rent formulas are surrogate measurements which are applied on an across-the-board basis. The fixed percentage and the CPI are surrogate estimates. The New York City operating cost index for rent stabilized buildings is also an estimating device, but it comes closer to reflecting changes in apartment operating costs than the CPI[40] (see chapter 5 for a comparison). The distinction between the application of a formula on an individual building basis and one applied across-the-board to a class of buildings is clearly significant in terms of administration but also in terms of constitutional validity. In the previously cited 1975 New Jersey Supreme Court decisions, the court, reviewed four municipal ordinances with different rent adjustment formulas and held that the regulatory mechanism need not be of a particular predetermined form—although uniform standards and procedures are desirable.

> Thus the municipality is not required to make an individual determination as to the proper rent level for each individual landlord but may adopt regulations governing rent levels of broad classes of property if fair and reasonable in application. . . . Further, if the municipality chooses to regulate by adoption of class regulations, there is no particular formula which it is constitutionally bound to employ.[41]

The major long-term issue is the erosion of the rent dollar by operating cost increments and is discussed in detail in chapter 5. This problem led to the creation of the Maximum Base Rents formula (MBR) for New York City rent-controlled housing in 1970. The MBR program was established to close the "rent gap" between existing rent revenues and the economic rents which are necessary for the operation of rental properties. The gap between market rents and actual rents was estimated by New York City's Rand Corporation to be $807 million in 1968, a result of inadequate rent adjustments over the many years of regulation.[42] Data compiled in 1973 indicated that the gap had been reduced to $362 million. The reduction was primarily a result of the MBR program; however, a portion of it was attributed to vacancy decontrol.[43]

The MBR program applies a cost-plus-profit formula to each rent-controlled apartment and building with the objective of raising rent at a rate no higher than 7.5 percent per year. In addition to cost factors, the MBR formula includes adjustment factors for non-controlled units in the building and dwelling-unit-index values, determined by location in the building. Receipt of an annual increased increment is not automatic for building owners; it is dependent upon code compliance and other requirements. In many respects the MBR formula is akin to the FNOI formulas; but unlike the FNOIs, it does not specifically limit the return on investment. Rather, the MBR formula is designed to assure an ultimate return on investment of 8.5 percent.

The annual increment allowed by the rent control agency and the number of years required to close the rent gap for a specific building depends on the existing disparity between rent revenues and costs, and particularly on the subsequent rate of inflation. Although a building's MBR formula is adjusted biannually, cost increments like those in recent years impede the gap closing process. Exhibit 4-1 indicates impact on operating costs given a 7.5 percent annual increase in rents and expenses, and the estimated results using the New York City operating cost index as a measure of actual operating cost changes.

Although the New York City example is in many ways unique, the gravity of the city's situation reveals the tremendous difficulties in providing adequate rent adjustments and closing the rent gap.

## *RENT ADJUSTMENT MECHANISM POLICY ISSUES*

Selection of a particular rent adjustment formula will to a large degree determine many of the crucial areas for which policy decisions are necessary. For example, selection of the FNOI approach necessitates the establishment of a large, formalized administrative system and a comprehensively detailed determination of administrative standards by the legislative body. Using standardized real estate accounting formats and procedures will simplify policy determinations. However, as reflected in the previous discussion of fair net operating income, many variations in formulas and policy can occur. The determination of allowable income and expenses and the application of operating expense ratios are the major administrative issues which must be addressed at some point regardless of the formula selected. Additional policy determinations are related to provisions allowing for additional increases, i.e., capital improvements, hardships and a code compliance requirement for rent adjustments.

### *Allowable Income And Expenses*

With the exception of formulas which utilize the CPI or fixed percentages as the rent adjustment standard, all other formulas require a determination of allowable income and expenses. This determination is also required in the fixed percentage and CPI formulas when a hardship provision is included in the statute.

Traditional real estate accounting practices define gross income as: the maximum gross potential rental income plus any additional commercial income or additional charges received as income (for example, parking fees) minus losses

*EXHIBIT 4–1*
*EXAMPLE OF POTENTIAL TO CATCH-UP GIVEN ALTERNATIVE RATES OF OPERATING COST INCREMENTS*

*A) Comparable Percent Increase in Rent and Expenses*

| | *Net Rental Income*[1] | *% Increase in Expenses*[2] | *Estimated Operating Expenses* | *Net Operating Income*[3] | *NOI As a Percent of Net Rental Income*[4] |
|---|---|---|---|---|---|
| 1972 | $200,000 | –– | $150,000 | $50,000 | 25.0 |
| 1973 | 215,000 | 7.5 | 161,250 | 53,750 | 25.0 |
| 1974 | 231,125 | 7.5 | 173,349 | 57,781 | 25.0 |
| 1975 | 248,459 | 7.5 | 186,345 | 62,114 | 25.0 |

*B) Assuming Increases in Expenses as Reflected in the New York City Operating Cost Index 1973-1975*

| | | | | | |
|---|---|---|---|---|---|
| 1972 | $200,000 | –– | $150,000 | $50,000 | 25.0 |
| 1973 | 215,000 | 7.9 | 161,580 | 53,420 | 24.8 |
| 1974 | 231,125 | 19.2 | 192,603 | 38,522 | 16.7 |
| 1975 | 248,459 | 6.5 | 205,122 | 43,337 | 17.4 |

*C) Assuming Rent Adjustments to Reflect Actual Dollar Increases in Expenses*

| | *Estimated Expenses* | *% Expense Increase* | *Estimated Increase* | *Adjusted Net Rental Income* | *% Increase Net Rental Income* | *Net Operating Income* | *NOI As a Percent of Net Rental Income* |
|---|---|---|---|---|---|---|---|
| 1972 | $150,000 | –– | –– | $200,000 | –– | 50,000 | 25.0 |
| 1973 | 161,580 | 7.9 | $11,580 | 211,580 | 5.8 | 50,000 | 23.6 |
| 1974 | 192,603 | 19.2 | 31,023 | 242,603 | 14.7 | 50,000 | 20.6 |
| 1975 | 205,122 | 6.5 | 12,519 | 255,122 | 5.2 | 50,000 | 19.6 |

1. Incorporates 7.5 percent annual increase in examples A and B.
2. Example A assumes 7.5 percent annual increase. Example B derives inflators from New York City Operating Cost Index for Rent Stabilized Apartments.
3. Residual from which contribution to debt, depreciation, and profit derived.
4. Assumes a marginal building in financial difficulty; an acceptable ratio is 40 to 60 percent. See chapter 5 for discussion.

due to vacancy and bad debts. For rent adjustment purposes under rent control, losses due to vacancy and bad debts are generally not deducted because the maximum potential rental income is theoretically the amount required to cover all operating expenses and yield a profit. Consequently, in making rent adjustments under rent control the maximum gross rent is calculated by determining operating expenses using limited return or investment formulas and then adding this result to the FNOI. The following examples, in which two different formulas are used, illustrate the process:

---

*EXHIBIT 4-2*
*ADJUSTMENT FORMULA EXAMPLES*

| | Bldg. A | Bldg. B |
|---|---|---|
| Value | 75,000 | 75,000 |
| Mortgage | 60,000 | 15,000 |
| Equity | 15,000 | 60,000 |
| | | |
| Expenses | 12,000 | 12,000 |
| FNOI (@ 33 percent) | 6,000 | 6,000 |
| Allowed Gross Rent | 18,000 | 18,000 |
| | | |
| FNOI | 6,000 | 6,000 |
| *Mortgage Int. @ 8% | 4,800 | 1,200 |
| **Contribution to Debt and Profit | 1,200 | 4,800 |
| | | |
| Return on Equity | 8% | 8% |

* (Additional allowable expense under Equity formula)
** From which mortgage principal and profit derived.

---

Expenditures for property taxes, fuel and utilities, insurance, and routine maintenance necessary to operate a structure are generally not contested as allowable expenses. However, in periods of rapid cost escalation the total pass-along of these costs may generate controversy, as was the case during the 1974 fuel crisis.[44] The major controversies arising relevant to allowable expenses are in the areas of administrative costs and the determination of "unavoidable" increases in operating and maintenance costs (as explicitly stated in some rent control statutes).

Administrative expenses vary widely, chiefly as a function of the scale of operation and ownership status. Management fees charged by private management firms are generally determined as a percentage of gross rents and traditional real estate accounting practices allow for imputed management expenses in the case of owner-managed properties. However, in determining rent adjustments, either administrative expenses are excluded in part or totally from allowable expenses, or a maximum fixed percentage of gross income is allowed for administrative expenses.[45] These costs may be handled in one manner for rent adjustment purposes and in a different manner for applications for additional rent increase provisions, such as hardships. The basic reason for placing limits on these expenses is that management fees are often based on the gross rent roll and their inclusion as allowable expenses unduly increases the base from which they are derived. There is further controversy regarding allowance of legal fees, particularly if such fees are used to challenge rent control. Because these expenses vary widely as a function of scale of operation, consideration must be given to allowing imputed management expenses in the case of owner-managed properties.

Ordinary maintenance and repair expenses include all maintenance, payroll, supplies, contract service, and replacement costs. The Massachusetts enabling legislation explicitly limits increases to those which are "unavoidable" leaving the definition of the term to the board or administrator. Costs for major repairs are generally amortized over the useful life of the repaired or replaced component. The primary controversy in terms of maintenance and repair expenses involves the distinction between routine maintenance and repair and extraordinary maintenance and repair, which may or may not qualify as a capital improvement and which may or may not be treated as an amortized expense with depreciation allowed. Labor costs, a significant expense item within this category, also vary as a function of scale of operation. For small-scale owners, provisions must be made to allow inclusion of self-executed labor. This consideration further necessitates determination of a reasonable cost on the basis of the type of work performed and the value of the owner's labor.

### *Application Of Operating Expense Ratio*

The purpose of the rent adjustment formula under any of the above described mechanisms is to limit rental increases to a level generally commensurate with increases in operating costs. Formulas which utilize a general across-the-board standard, whether it be the CPI or a specific price index of operating costs, avoid the detailed cost analysis of individual buildings but require determination of the proportion of the inflator to be applied in adjusting rental levels, assuming that the selected standard is an accurate reflection of true increases.

Under the FNOI formula utilized in Massachusetts and the Maximum Base Rent formula utilized in New York City, actual increases in expenditures become the standard, and gross rents are adjusted to reflect those changes in expenditures. However, in applying a percentage increment—which is assumed to reflect cost increments whether it is derived from the CPI or a price index—the issue which arises is whether the increment reflects the total inflation or only some portion of it. Generally, the operating expense ratio, or the proportion of total expenses to gross income, is used. The rationale for applying the ratio is that the portion of the rent dollar allocated to debt service, depreciation, and profit is relatively fixed over time; thus, only that portion of rental income subject to cost fluctuation should be increased.[46]

It is controversy over the operating ratio issue which to a large degree accounts for the shift from the CPI to a fixed percentage or, to a fixed proportion of the CPI increase (as in many New Jersey ordinances). As evident in Exhibit 4-3, the application of an operating expense ratio of 0.5528 to an inflator of 8 percent (derived for example from the CPI) yields the same approximate gross rent adjustment that would be achieved via a detailed cost analysis also reflecting an 8.0 percent increase in absolute expenditures. On the other hand, 8.0 percent inflator applied in total to gross rents adjusts rent levels at an economically faster pace. However, the critical problem, addressed in more detail in chapter 5, is the determination of an appropriate operating expense ratio.

## *OTHER CRITICAL STATUTORY PROVISIONS*

Other critical substantive provisions of rent control ordinances can be classified according to three major categories: (1) those which allow for rent increases in addition to the basic rent adjustment formulas; (2) those which place additional constraints and limitations on the owner's operation; and (3) those which define the administrative mechanism.

### *Rent Increases In Addition To Basic Rent Adjustment*

#### Designated Expenditure Categories

Provisions for rent increases in designated expenditure categories (in addition to the rent adjustment formula increases) are generally included in rent control statutes which provide for general across-the-board rent adjustment formulas. Provisions for increases due to property tax increases are very frequently included. Such provisions generally allow for rent reductions in the case of decreases in the property tax, after reductions in the overall rate and reductions attained through appeal have been distinguished. Increased rents granted as a result of property tax increases are generally considered surcharges

*EXHIBIT 4-3*
*EXAMPLE OF OPERATING RATIO APPLICATION TO ADJUST GROSS RENTS*

*Background data for Sample Structure:*

| | *NRI* | *Exp* | *% Inc* | *Exp/NRI* |
|---|---|---|---|---|
| Base 1973 | 500,000 | 250,000 | – | 50.00 |
| Yr. 1 1974 | 520,000 | 287,500 | 15.0 | 55.28 |
| Yr. 2 1975 | 540,000 | 310,500 | 8.0 | 57.50 |

| | *Yr. 1* | *Inflator* | *Estimated Increase* | *Yr. 2* |
|---|---|---|---|---|
| *1) Application of Total Inflator* | | | | |
| Exp. | 287,500 | 8.0% | 23,000 | 310,500 |
| NRI | 520,000 | 8.0 | 41,600 | 561,600 |
| *2) Application of Operating Expense Ratio* | | | | |
| Exp. | 287,500 | 8.00 | 23,000 | 310,500 |
| NRI | 520,000 | 4.42* | 22,984 | 542,984 |

* .5528 x 8.0 = 4.42

*Note:* NRI = Net Rental Income
Exp = Total Operating Expenses

and are not included in the base rent for calculations of future rent adjustments. Sometimes such charges are also included for excessive increases in specific expenditure categories, for example, increases in fuel and utilities, increased services, furnishing, or facilities.

### Capital Improvements

To encourage investment and preservation of the existing stock, most statutes provide for additional rent increases to cover the costs of capital improvements. Variations reflected in the definition of such improvement, and rent increase allowances are described in more detail in Appendix I.

### Hardship Provision

A hardship provision is usually necessary in the case of maximum base rent adjustment mechanisms with across-the-board formulas. The need for a hardship provision is alleviated in the case of limited-return-on-investment mechanisms since they are directed toward providing a fair net operating income. Depending upon the stringency of the requirements for application, the hardship provision may serve as a guarantee of FNOI, without limiting the return on all owners.

A 1975 New Jersey Supreme Court decision clearly established the need for a hardship provision in all New Jersey municipal ordinances by recommending that "every rent control ordinance must be deemed to intend, and will be so read, to permit property owners to apply to the local administrative agency for relief on the ground that the regulation entitles the owner to a just and reasonable rate of return."[47] Although acknowledging that the determination of methods to define "just and reasonable" returns was a legislative rather than a judicial function, the court proceeded to provide guidelines to assist in the review of future cases.

As a framework for guideline determination, the court emphasized the need to evaluate the interests of the general public as well as the interests of the consumer and the landlord. In response to the challenges raised in the case under review, the court saw no objection to the ordinance because the value of the property declined as a result of regulated rents and acknowledged that rent levels may impose hardships on landlords in atypical cases, drive inefficient operators out of the market, and preclude those owners who paid inflated purchase prices from recovering a fair return.

The court defined "just and reasonable" in broad terms, as "generally commensurate with returns on investments in other enterprises having corresponding risks," which, however, does not defeat the purpose of rent control. The specific guidelines evolving from this definition, as cited by the court and summarized in the following listing, call for rates of return high enough:

1. to encourage good management;
2. to furnish a reward for efficiency;
3. to discourage the flight of capital from the rental housing market; and
4. to enable operators to maintain and support their credit.[48]

Specifically, hardship provisions may allow an owner to maintain the same ratio of net operating income in percentage terms, or the same level of net operating income in dollars, as at some specified base period. The guidelines governing hardship provisions for rent stabilized buildings in New York City were initially aimed at maintaining the same "ratio." The guidelines were subsequently interpreted to mean net operating income dollars, since it was recognized that all owners would be eligible for hardship provisions given escalating operating costs. The ratio in percentage terms will remain constant only if gross rents increase at the same absolute percentage rate as operating costs. The requirement for eligibility under hardship provisions are often restricted to owners who are unable to meet their debt service requirements with income from rentals and who are not earning profit on their rental property.

### *Constraint Provisions*

Eviction controls and code compliance requirements place additional constraints and limitations on property owners. These provisions broaden the scope of regulatory authority and are discussed in chapter 3.

## *ADMINISTRATIVE MECHANISMS*

Thus far the discussion of rent control systems in this chapter has focused on the distinguishing features of the two principal rent adjustment mechanisms. However, these mechanisms, as well as limited jurisdiction mechanisms, must also be considered within the context of administration. (For a discussion of mechanisms within the context of regulatory authority, see chapter 3.) Because limited jurisdiction rent regulation does not include the establishment of across-the-board controls, it does not include a rent adjustment mechanism. The limited scope of these mechanisms' regulatory authority generally defines the minimal requirements for administration. However, in the case of limited mechanisms, the workload (i.e., the number of complaints received) is actually more significant in determining administrative needs than are the statutory provisions.

For rent control systems which include rent adjustment mechanisms, the statutory provisions and subsequent regulations are the significant factors in determing the type and scale of the administrative mechanism necessary. Rent control boards, consisting of appointed volunteers, are generally established; a full-time administrator may be hired. Volunteer boards usually permit a broad cross-section of the community to participate in the policymaking process and, theoretically, alleviate the possibility of partisan control. Although the Massachusetts enabling legislation provides for local determination in the appointment of a rent control board or administrator, the requirements of the legislation—utilizing a fair net operating income formula—necessitates creating a full-time staff and formalized operations. Staff size is determined by the number of structures and units to be regulated and the complexity of the regulatory system established. The case studies of chapter 6 provide insight into the administrative complexities reflected in the various rent adjustment mechanisms.

The computerized Maximum Base Rents Program, established by the New York City Council in 1970 to close the rent gap is the most sophisticated existing rent control administrative mechanism. The complexities and problems inherent in the MBR program are primarily attributable to the scale of the operation (initially over one million units) and to its function as a reform measure. It was instituted to remedy problems created by previous regulatory systems during the previous twenty-eight years.

### *Registration Requirements*

A standard administrative requirement of FNOI mechanisms is mandatory registration of all units subject to the rent control statute. Such registration usually requires submitting the number of units by type of unit, the occupancy status, base rental levels, and the facilities and services provided. Registration may also require additional information pertinent to structural characteristics, tax assessments, and purchase price. Mandatory registration is not always required under maximum base rent mechanisms; however, some New Jersey communities have recently amended their ordinances to include such a provision. Registration required on a periodic basis provides the administrative agency with the opportunity to indirectly monitor compliance. The Washington, D.C. regulations require the submission of updated data every thirty days. Registration requirements add to the administrative workload and size of staff needed.

## *ADMINISTRATIVE COSTS*

The administrative costs of rent control generally consist of the cost to support the rent control agency and property owners' costs. The level of costs for both is directly related to the type and scope of rent control mechanism utilized.

*Agency Costs*

The financial resources required to administer rent control are most often acquired from municipal budget appropriations. Government costs are determined by the scale of operation and the complexity of the regulatory system established. FNOI mechanisms are generally more expensive to administer than maximum base rent mechanisms but these costs vary substantially, as reflected in the following exhibit (Exhibit 4-4) comparing local rent control appropriations in Massachusetts communities.[49]

*EXHIBIT 4-4*
*AVERAGE 1974-75 ADMINISTRATIVE COST APPROPRIATION FOR MASSACHUSETTS COMMUNITIES**

| | 1974-1975 Rent Control Budget Appropriations | Apts. Covered By Rent Control | Cost Per Apt. |
|---|---|---|---|
| Boston ** | $1,000,000 | $118,750 | $ 8.42 |
| Brookline | 144,846 | 11,300 | 12.82 |
| Cambridge | 280,000 | 20,424 | 13.71 |
| Somerville | 43,183 | 11,388 | 3.79 |
| Average Cost Per Apartment | | | 9.07 |

* Appropriations are for fiscal year 1974-75
** Estimated

In 1968, New York City expended $7.7 million to administer rent control for 1.27 million units; the annual per unit cost was $6. Current costs are estimated to be $13.25 million for 640,000 units. Exhibit 4-5 reflects the distribution of New York City's 1968 rent control costs by type of administrative provision.[50] These provisions and cost estimates antedate the establishment of the computerized MBR program and the enactment of rent stabilization in 1969. Rent control in New York City was administered by the state until 1962, when all legislative and administrative responsibilities for cities

*EXHIBIT 4-5*
*ESTIMATED ADMINISTRATIVE COSTS OF RENT CONTROL IN NEW YORK CITY, 1967-68*

| *Rent Control Provision* | *Applications (thousands of Housing Units)* | *Total Cost ($000)* | *Cost per Application ($)* |
|---|---|---|---|
| *Increase Provisions* | | | |
| New Lease | 164.2 | 489.6 | 2.98 |
| Hardship | 20.0 | 1,222.2 | 61.11 |
| Increase Services and MCI | 102.0 | 1,863.6 | 18.27 |
| Others | 68.6 | 2,242.8 | 32.69 |
| Total | 354.8 | 5,818.2 | 16.40 |
| *Rent Reductions* | 346.3 | 1,843.3 | 5.32 |
| *Total* | 701.1 | 7,661.5 | 10.93 |

with over one million inhabitants were transferred to the locality; however, the state continued providing funds for reasonable administrative costs.

The administration of rent stabilization in New York City is almost totally supported by the real estate industry's annual $3-per-unit membership dues collected from owners of stabilized buildings. Costs to the city include overseeing the stabilization program and partially supporting the contract for the Operating Cost Index from the U.S. Bureau of Labor Statistics.

A typical New Jersey community utilizing the CPI or a fixed percentage formula for rent adjustments has a volunteer rent control board and a part-time secretary. With office space and equipment provided, the total budget for rent control frequently ranges between $3,000 to $8,000; the annual per unit costs are as low as 10¢. The administrative cost requirements for limited jurisdiction rent review boards are similar to those of the New Jersey mechanisms.

### *Owner Costs*

As in rent control agencies, the costs to the property owner vary as a function of the regulatory mechanism. Costs to the owner are incurred in meeting the statutory requirements; they are usually higher under the FNOI mechanism than under the typical maximum base rent mechanism, and primarily result in increased management expenses (i.e., additional clerical, legal, and accounting services necessitated by requirements for registration, periodic submissions of updated information, and filing petitions for rent increases). Tenant notification of any action or request which will affect rent or services is also usually mandated, and registered or certified mailings of such tenant notifications is an additional cost item. In addition to the cost for these administrative services are the less quantifiable costs incurred by legal counsel or managment representatives in attending hearings or landlord-tenant meetings.

Average costs to the property owner are difficult to determine because of variations in the scale of operation. The increment in administrative cost for a large apartment complex with a full-time professional staff is minimal. Similarly, the increment in administrative costs for a smaller building managed by a large management firm is nominal. However, for the independently managed small building, the cost impact is significant because most professional services are contracted on a fee basis.

Any owner, regardless of the scale of his operation, will incur increased management costs as a result of rent regulations. Only in the case of limited jurisdiction rent review boards can an owner avoid costs, and only then if no complaints are filed. If complaints are filed, the owner is subject to all requrirements of the board for attending hearings and submitting documents. Most owners whose buildings are handled by management firms will find it necessary to renegotiate the terms of their management agreements. Questions pertinent to these agreements have been summarized as follows:

> Should an extra fee be paid for these services [necessary to meet rent control requirements] regardless of whether the management fee is based on a percentage of operating income or set at a flat monthly per unit fee? Should the extra fee be different for those properties where there is a much higher turnover and many more code violations thereby requiring a comparably large number of submittals, hearings, and records to be maintained and processed? Should services rendered in court proceedings and commission hearings be considered as over and above the scope of normal landlord-tenant relations and therefore allow for an extra per case or unit fee?[51]

### *SUMMARY*

The following three points should be noted when considering any rent adjustment mechanism:

1. How well do the increases permitted under the law match the realities of operation? Is there a gap between legislation and real experience?
2. Are the administrative requirements which must be observed in order to secure increases based on objective or subjective standards? How much time is consumed in the process?
3. Are the requirements for securing these increases so onerous and formalized in terms of bookkeeping expense and statement recording as to mean that only large-scale owners can afford the level of detailing, of technical aid which would make even those increases which are available truly achievable?

These criteria reflect the equity problems inherent in most regulatory mechanisms, and are useful in evaluating the rent control approaches which have been discussed.

The fair net operating income approach is directed toward providing equity; it clearly recognizes the profit motive in real estate investment. This approach, however, regardless of the formula used to define rate of return, requires a large, formalized administrative system with building-by-building review, and entails the problems inherent in that scale of operation. Without adequate financial support and an efficient operation, significant time lags and some inequity are inevitable.

The range of approaches grouped under the maximum base rent programs vary in complexity and administrative requirements. The most complex approach is the computerized New York City MBR formula; less sophisticated programs use the CPI or other fixed percentage formulas. The New York City program requires a large administrative system, as does the FNOI approach.

Use of the CPI and fixed percentage ceilings have the advantage of being easier to administer, requiring a less formal system. In these approaches, most boards or administrators only have to deal with individual building or unit reviews on the basis of tenant complaints or landlord applications for additional increases, surcharges, or hardship adjustments. However, some equity is lost since these across-the-board formulas do not account for the structural variations in operations possible under the FNOI formulas which include individual building review. However, the inclusion of hardship and extraordinary cost surcharge provisions counteracts the inequity. The failure of many MBR ordinances to take the owner's rate of return into account–some MBR ordinances even lack hardship provisions–implies a lack of understanding of the real estate market and the long-term impacts on its viability; a real belief in the temporary nature of the controls; or political expedience in enacting these ordinances.

## *NOTES*

1. "The New York Rent Stabilization Law of 1969," *Columbia Law Review* 70, no. 156 (1970):164.
2. Bayonne v. Palmer, 90 N.J. Super 245, 217A.d2 141 (1966).
3. Elias, Marquette Law Review 45 (1962): 227, 332. Cited in Richard F. Arohnson and Robert Schmitt, Jr. Brief on Behalf of Amicus Curiae submitted to the New Jersey State Supreme Court in Harvey J. Cosden et al. v. Township of Wayne 68, N.J. 543 (1975).
4. Proposed amendment to Section 2 of Chapter 842 of the Acts of 1970, Massachusetts General Laws. Amended Statute reported from Local Affairs Committee to Ways and Means Committee of State Legislature pending action as of August 1975. Current statute to expire December 31, 1975.
5. Price Commission Recommendation Paper included in Agencies Packet of Rent Advisory Board, 17th meeting–August 16, 1972. The Phase II rent stabilization program exempted units renting for $400 a month or more (reduced from an initial level of $500). Typically these luxury units are defined by excluding rents above a specified level (i.e., often in the $300 to $500 per month category). Boston, however, defined its luxury exemption (under former law, Chapter 10) as monthly rents in excess of $160 for studio units; $185 for one-bedroom units; $235 for two-bedroom units and $285 for three-bedroom units.
6. Massachusetts General Laws, Ch. 842, Sec. 3(b)7.

7. New York State Rent Commission, Decontrol Order No. 51, September 16, 1957. New York City Rent and Eviction Regulations, Section 2f(14)(15). Both found in *McKinney's Unconsolidated Laws,* book 65, pp. 469-473, 476-478.
8. The U.S. Department of Housing and Urban Development in February 1975 promulgated an interim rule which asserts the exclusive jurisdiction over the maximum rentals for subsidized projects and for projects with mortgages insured or held by HUD-jurisdiction when it deems that its economic interest in the project is jeopardized by the decision of the local rent control authority or by a delay in making a decision. Chapter IV or Title 24, Part 403 "Local Rent Control "'*Federal Register,* 40, no. 34 (February 26, 1975): 8189.
9. Stoneridge Apartments v. Lindsay, 303 F. Supp. 677 (S.D.N.Y. 1969) and Helmsley v. Borough of Fort Lee, 362 F. Supp. 581 (1973).
10. National Housing Act, Sec. 220. Amended by Sec. 123 of the Housing Act of 1954.
11. Ibid., Sec. 220 (2)(A).
12. "The New York Rent Stabilization Law of 1969," 159.
13. "Developments in the Law–Equal Protection" *Harvard Law Review* 82 (1969): 1065, 1083.
14. Massachusetts General Laws, Ch. 842, Sec. 3 (6)(A).
15. City of Miami Beach, Ordinance No. 74-2018, Section 5B, Adopted December 11, 1974.
16. As stated in Marshall House Inc. v. Rent Control Board of Brookline (and three companion cases), 266 N.E. 2d 876, 886. Also see Willis, "Rent Control: The Maximum Rent Date Method," *University of Pennsylvania Law Review* (1950): 654.
17. An adjusted base rent may be necessary to provide for exception and unique circumstances. Also added to the rent on the effective date may be charges for allowable increases in designated expenses, i.e., real estate taxes, which occurred during the rollback period–after the rollback date but before the effective date of controls. In the case of units vacant on the rollback date, the late rent charged immediately preceding or following the rollback date becomes the base rent.
18. For discussion of this issue see "Residential Rent Control: Stoneridge Apartments v. Lindsay" *University of Pittsburgh Law Review* 31 (1970): 443.
19. Bowles v. Willingham, 321 U.S. 503, 516-519 (1943).
20. City of Miami Beach v. Forte Towers, Inc. 305 So 2d 764, 768 (1974). Foti v. Heller, 48 N.J. Super. 57, 137 A.2d 10 (N.J. App. 1957). Birkenfeld v. City of Berkeley, Calif. Super Ct., 428971 (1972), Court of Appeals, Civil 34378 (June 22, 1975).
21. Hutton Park Gardens v. West Orange Town Council, 68 N.J. 543 (1975); Brunetti v. Borough of New Milford, 68 N.J. 576 (1975); Cosden et al., v. Township of Wayne Council, Decision combined with Hutton Park, 68 N.J. 543

(1975); Troy Hills Village v. Parsippany-Troy Hills Township Council, 68 N.J. 604 (1975). All four cases were decided December 11, 1975. All text citations from mimeographed decisions.

22. Hutton Park v. West Orange Town Council, p. 22.
23. Troy Hills Village v. Parsippany-Troy Hills Tp. Council, p. 13.
24. Mass. General Laws, Ch. 842 (1970).
25. Mass. General Laws, Ch. 843, Sec. 3 (1970).
26. Marshall House Inc. v. Rent Control Board of Brookline et al.
27. Ibid.
28. Ibid. p. 888.
29. Ibid. p. 889.
30. Ackerman v. Corkery, Equity No. 17 (3rd District Court, 1971) aff'd at 285 N.E. 2d 449 (1972) in Cambridge v. Gifford. The formula which was overturned in this case based the fair return on current market value. Current market value was to be determined as (1) assessed valuation multiplied by a factor of 2½ to 4; or (2) annual gross income (in 1970) multiplied by a factor ranging between 5 and 7. In either case, a lower factor was to be used for better maintained buildings—on the rationale that they involved less risk and therefore warranted less return on investment.
31. City of Miami Beach, Ordinance No. 73-1978 (1973).
32. Ibid., Sec. 4(c)(4)(V).
33. Ibid.
34. City of Miami Beach v. Forte Towers, p. 769.
35. Ibid.
36. Ibid. pp 768-69.
37. Two different approaches to rent adjustments are utilized in setting rent levels in New York City. The applicable approach for a building is determined by the legislation under which that particular building falls, as described in Exhibit 3-1. As a result of the 1969 Rent Stabilization Law and the 1974 Emergency Tenant Protection Act many buildings have both rent-controlled and rent-stabilized units.
38. U.S., Department of Labor, Bureau of Labor Statistics, Middle Atlantic Regional Office, "A Price Index of Operating Costs for Rent Stabilized Apartment Houses in New York City," nos. 17, 23, 28, 33, 38, 45 (1971-1975).
39. Highland Park, New Jersey, Ordinance No. 708, adopted December 30, 1974. The Highland Park Index (HPI) utilizes regularly published Bureau of Labor Statistics data some of which is derived from the CPI; however, the HPI establishes component indexes for the major operating categories. This index is similar to that constructed for New York City under special contract; however, fewer price quotations are gathered, and the HPI relies more upon available published data.
40. Technically the index measures the changes in *prices* of goods and services

purchased by building operators. An inherent assumption of price indexes is that the same quantity of goods is purchased over time.

41. Hutton Park v. West Orange Town Council, pp. 23-24. Citations in quoted material omitted. Reference to desirability of uniform standards and procedures is found in this case at pp. 29-30 in which the attention of the state legislature is called to the "high desirability of a carefully drawn local option enabling statute on the subject of rent control."

42. Ira Lowry et al., *Rental Housing in New York City* (New York: Rand Institute, 1970-71), vol. 1, *Confronting the Crisis* (1970).

43. Frank S. Kristof, "Vacancy Decontrol in New York City: July 1971–December 1973," (New York: New York State Urban Development Corporation, January 28, 1974), (mimeo) pp. 2-3.

44. The limitations of the 1975 fuel pass-along in New York City resulted in the landlord absorbing a portion of the increased cost. It has been suggested by proponents of rent control that property tax increases be shared by the owner and tenant rather than passed along in total.

45. Boston and Brookline, Massachusetts allow a maximum of 6 percent of gross income which may be allocated to management costs. Cambridge places no limit, but requires that they meet a test of "reasonableness." The New York City CAB in reviewing hardship applications excludes administrative costs totally. The rationale for this exclusion, particularly the management fee, is that it should not input into the increase of its base (gross rents) from which it is derived, thus unjustly increasing costs.

46. The New York City Rent Guidelines Board in utilizing the Price Index of Operating Costs in making its annual rent adjustment determination has utilized a 55 percent ratio in applying the index. Recent evidence considered by the board indicated that the ratio has increased from an average of 51 percent in 1969 to approximately 65 percent in 1975.

47. Hutton Park v. West Orange Town Council, p. 27.

48. Troy Hills Village v. Parsippany-Troy Hills Tp. Council, p. 23. Citations omitted from quoted material.

49. Harbridge House, Inc., *A Study of Rent and Eviction Control in the Commonwealth,* Boston, Mass. (December, 1974); George Steinlieb et. al., *The Realities of Rent Control in the Greater Boston Area* (New Brunswick, N.J.: Rutgers University, Center for Urban Policy Research, 1975), and supplemental information obtained from the Boston Rental Housing Association.

50. G. Thomas Kingsley, *A Review of the Operations of Rent Control in New York City,* (New York: NYC Rand Working Paper, 1969), p. 14.

51. Irving M. Kriegsfield, "The Cost of Meeting Rent Control Requirements," *Journal of Property Management* 40 (March/April 1975): 70.

# Chapter 5
# The Realities of Operating Costs

## *INTRODUCTION*

An analysis of rent control is incomplete without an overview of the effect controls exert on operating costs and owners' profits, and what it portends for future real estate investment decisions.

Return on real estate investment is largely determined by net operating income. Net operating income is that amount remaining after vacancies, bad debts, and all operating costs are deducted from the estimated maximum gross income. When a real estate investor is considering possible investment, any factor—such as rent control—that affects net operating income affects the investor's ultimate decision.

The problem of maintaining a sufficient net operating income is especially difficult during inflationary periods. In such times, owners of rental properties may attempt to maintain sufficient net operating income by: (1) increasing rents; (2) decreasing or deferring expenses; or (3) absorbing short-term losses until a superior investment possibility presents itself. Rent control eliminates the option of increasing rents and minimizes the capacity to absorb short-term losses. The only option remaining is expense reduction or deferral resulting in reduced services.

In the following discussion rent control is examined primarily from the perspective of the operation and management of rental units by focussing on studies from three rent-controlled markets: the Greater Boston area; Fort Lee, New Jersey; and New York City. The methodology used to derive data for the Boston and Fort Lee studies is presented in Appendix II; a discussion of major operating components and operating ratios is necessary to an understanding of the case studies.

### *Major Operating Components*

While gross revenue may fluctuate in proportion to levels of occupancy and demand, operating expenses are relatively inflexible. The major operating expenses are: (1) real estate taxes; (2) insurance; (3) fuel and utilities; (4) management or administration; and (5) building maintenance and services. Building maintenance and services—including all maintenance and repair expenses, contract services, supplies, and ordinary replacement and labor costs—represent the primary expense category in which a minimum of flexibility is possible through a discretionary reduction or deferral of maintenance and repairs.

The relative importance of any of these components, as a proportion of total expenses, varies according to the tax rate and cost of utilities in a particular locality and the age, size, structure and tenant characteristics of rental units. The impact of changes in costs in these items also varies as a result of differences of expenditure patterns. The most widely used measure for assessing operating stability and efficiency in income-producing properties is the operating expense ratio.

### *Significance of Operating Ratios*

The operating expense ratio represents total expenses as a percentage of rental income, either gross or net. Excessively high or atypical ratios, found in the absence of restricted rent levels, generally indicate poor operational performance; they may result from poor construction or management or from neighborhood decline.

Operating ratios for apartment buildings usually fall in the following percentage ranges: for walkup buildings—40-50 percent, and for those with automatic elevators—55-65 percent.[1] Average income and expense data compiled annually by the Institute of Real Estate Management indicates a small but steady incremental increase in national average operating expense ratios. Increasing expense ratios reflect decreasing net operating income ratios. Exhibit 5-1 presents these annual averages according to building age and structure and regional variations. These averages generally represent the relatively efficient, well-managed properties which voluntarily participate in this national survey.

How do these operating ratios compare with samples in selected rent-controlled localities? The following case studies provide a basis for comparing national trends and for assessing three distinct rent adjustment and administrative mechanisms.

## *EXHIBIT 5–1*
## *COMPARISON OF OPERATING RATIO BY AGE GROUP*

*All Expenses Divided by Actual Collections*

| *Building Type* | *Year* | *1968 to Date* | *1961-1967* | *1946-1960* | *1931-1945* | *1921-1930* | *1920 to Before* |
|---|---|---|---|---|---|---|---|
| Elevator | 1974 | 51.7% | 54.6% | 58.5% | 60.4% | 65.5% | 60.3% |
| | 1973 | 49.2% | 52.4% | 57.4% | 58.0% | 58.9% | 62.3% |
| | 1972 | 49.0% | 50.6% | 55.6% | 58.1% | 62.5% | 65.8% |
| | 1971 | 45.8% | 49.4% | 53.7% | 54.9% | 60.4% | 66.4% |
| | 1970 | 46.8% | 49.3% | 52.7% | 57.4% | 60.1% | 60.8% |
| Low Rise | 1974 | 43.0% | 49.8% | 47.7% | 60.9% | 64.6% | 61.1% |
| 12 – 24 Units | 1973 | 46.5% | 49.0% | 49.6% | 55.4% | 61.6% | 61.2% |
| | 1972 | 44.2% | 47.3% | 49.8% | 54.4% | 63.2% | 67.8% |
| | 1971 | 40.3% | 45.1% | 52.7% | 58.4% | 63.9% | 64.5% |
| | 1970 | 45.4% | 46.4% | 54.2% | 56.1% | 62.6% | 62.6% |
| Low Rise | 1974 | 48.4% | 49.1% | 50.6% | 57.4% | 66.1% | 67.5% |
| 25 and over | 1973 | 44.9% | 47.2% | 52.3% | 52.5% | 61.8% | 61.6% |
| | 1972 | 45.1% | 48.2% | 49.9% | 58.0% | 65.8% | 68.4% |
| | 1971 | 45.1% | 51.3% | 52.3% | 55.7% | 66.1% | 69.7% |
| | 1970 | 43.1% | 43.9% | 50.7% | 51.8% | 62.5% | 64.9% |
| Garden | 1974 | 50.0% | 50.5% | 57.4% | 58.1% | 59.3% | 57.0% |
| | 1973 | 48.4% | 48.5% | 54.3% | 54.3% | 54.9% | 54.8% |
| | 1972 | 47.7% | 48.7% | 53.8% | 55.1% | 61.4% | 55.2% |
| | 1971 | 50.0% | 48.3% | 52.1% | 59.0% | 55.0% | 62.7% |
| | 1970 | 46.0% | 45.8% | 52.6% | 56.5% | 68.3% | 59.8% |

*EXHIBIT 5–1*
*(continued)*
*COMPARISON OF OPERATING RATIO BY REGION*

*All Expenses Divided by Actual Collections*

| *Building Type* | *Year* | *Region 1 and 2* | *Region 3* | *Region 5* | *Region 4 and 6* | *Region 9* | *Region 7, 8 and 10* | *Canada* |
|---|---|---|---|---|---|---|---|---|
| Elevator | 1974 | 60.8% | 56.7% | 53.8% | 50.2% | 58.8% | 46.6% | 53.0% |
| | 1973 | 57.3% | 52.0% | 54.7% | 42.9% | 61.9% | 47.1% | 54.5% |
| | 1972 | 56.9% | 51.9% | 53.6% | 42.9% | 51.8% | 45.0% | 49.9% |
| | 1971 | 61.6% | 50.7% | 49.1% | 63.5% | 48.6% | 47.3% | 50.6% |
| | 1970 | 55.1% | 51.3% | 49.8% | 60.3% | 54.2% | 48.0% | 44.2% |
| Low Rise 12 – 24 Units | 1974 | 64.3% | 47.1% | 58.9% | 43.8% | 45.6% | 43.5% | 54.1% |
| | 1973 | 58.8% | 49.4% | 57.8% | 47.7% | 47.3% | 45.3% | 53.5% |
| | 1972 | 50.2% | 54.3% | 58.3% | 46.4% | 48.0% | 46.7% | 49.7% |
| | 1971 | 64.5% | 58.7% | 63.3% | 43.7% | 45.6% | 46.0% | 49.7% |
| | 1970 | 63.0% | 54.6% | 62.5% | 46.5% | 49.1% | 47.5% | 46.1% |
| Low Rise 25 and over | 1974 | 57.3% | 50.4% | 53.1% | 49.6% | 47.2% | 48.5% | 45.8% |
| | 1973 | 56.7% | 48.6% | 53.1% | 43.4% | 44.4% | 48.5% | 44.3% |
| | 1972 | 54.8% | 48.8% | 55.7% | 48.9% | 45.0% | 45.6% | 41.2% |
| | 1971 | 59.0% | 47.7% | 58.1% | 60.5% | 44.0% | 43.6% | 51.7% |
| | 1970 | 50.4% | 53.4% | 58.1% | 44.9% | 43.2% | 45.7% | 41.5% |
| Garden | 1974 | 56.2% | 51.7% | 48.0% | 53.3% | 48.2% | 51.0% | 45.7% |
| | 1973 | 56.4% | 49.7% | 47.7% | 50.3% | 47.4% | 48.6% | 43.6% |
| | 1972 | 55.2% | 48.3% | 49.6% | 49.3% | 48.4% | 49.5% | 50.1% |
| | 1971 | 56.1% | 47.6% | 51.0% | 50.9% | 48.6% | 51.0% | 39.4% |
| | 1970 | 55.6% | 47.3% | 48.4% | 48.6% | 45.9% | 43.6% | 43.1% |

*Note:* Some region reports have more than one region represented. This is done to insure a large enough sample size for the above data.

*Source:* Institute of Real Estate Management, *Income/Expense Analysis,* 1975 edition.

## *THE GREATER BOSTON AREA CASE STUDY*

Data derived from a 1971-1973 study of rent control in the Greater Boston area provides insight into the realities of operating expenses for controlled and noncontrolled rental units.[2] The analyses will center around two basic sets of data. In the first set of tables expenses will be measured in dollars, not as percentages of net rent received. In this analysis changes in operating expenses, such as building maintenance and services of fuel, real estate, taxes and so on have been detailed. In order to provide a significant sample group for this data, no distinction was made between different types of rental structures. In the second set of tables expenses for controlled and noncontrolled buildings are analyzed relative to average annual contribution to debt, depreciation, and profit generated as a percentage of net rent received. This analysis measures the portion of the rent dollar which is left after all expenses are paid—excluding payments for mortgage interest, amortization, and profit charges for depreciation. The bulk sum available after all out-of-pocket costs are met is of interest here. Data in this second analysis are distinguished according to building types.

### *Average Annual Operating Results: 1971, 1972, 1973*

The following analysis focuses on the actual dollar changes and operating results for the total Greater Boston sample rent-controlled buildings which number seventy structures containing 4,834 units, and twenty noncontrolled buildings with 3,898 units.

In Exhibit 5-2 the average dollar operating results for the rent control sample are shown. In 1971, 37.5 cents out of every rent dollar remained after all operating expenses in order to meet debt service, replacement costs, and owner-profit. By 1973, the remaining amount dropped to 32.5 cents. What factors contributed to the drop in the net contribution to debt, depreciation and profit?

In the buildings under consideration during 1972 and 1973, total net rent received increased 6.7 percent, a figure representing not only increased individual apartment rents but a decline in factors such as vacancy rates and bad debts. Dollar expenditures for building maintenance services remained essentially the same during those years. Fuel expenditures, however, increased by 19.6 percent despite the fact that the eastern Massachusetts area experienced unusually warm winters during those years. The number of degree days from 1972 to 1973 declined from 6,315 to 5,367 or more than a sixth, thus indicating lower fuel use requirements. Also between 1971 and 1973, real estate taxes increased by 14.4 percent and other operating expenses by 10.4 percent. Total expenses increased 15.2 percent, generating the 7.5 percent drop in net contribution to debt, depreciation and profit.

EXHIBIT 5-2
*AVERAGE ANNUAL OPERATING RESULTS, 1971-1973 – RENT CONTROL SAMPLE*[1]
*GREATER BOSTON AREA*

| | *Net Rent Received* | *Building Maintenance & Services* | *Fuel* | *Real Estate Taxes* | *Other Operating Expenses*[2] | *Total All Expenses* | *Net Contribution to Debt, Depreciation, and Profit* |
|---|---|---|---|---|---|---|---|
| 1971 | $189,543 | $28,052 | $10,993 | $52,313 | $27,105 | $118,465 | $71,078 |
| 1972 | 201,034 | 31,160 | 10,855 | 59,908 | 29,350 | 131,273 | 69,761 |
| 1973 | 202,315 | 33,584 | 13,150 | 59,885 | 29,942 | 136,561 | 65,754 |
| | | | *AVERAGE PERCENT CHANGE* | | | | |
| 1971-72 | 6.1% | 11.1% | -1.3% | 14.5% | 8.2% | 10.8% | -1.8% |
| 1972-73 | 0.6 | 7.7 | 21.1 | 0.0[3] | 2.0 | 4.0 | -5.7 |
| 1971-73 | 6.7 | 19.7 | 19.6 | 14.4 | 10.4 | 15.2 | -7.5 |
| | | | *OPERATING RESULTS AS A PERCENTAGE OF NET RENT RECEIVED* | | | | |
| 1971 | 100.0% | 14.8% | 5.8% | 27.6% | 14.3% | 62.5% | 37.5% |
| 1972 | 100.0 | 15.5 | 5.4 | 29.8 | 14.6 | 65.3 | 34.7 |
| 1973 | 100.0 | 16.6 | 6.5 | 29.6 | 14.8 | 67.5 | 32.5 |

1. (N = 70 operating statements for 4834 units).
2. Residual of total expenses including administrative, insurance, other utility, and miscellaneous expenses.
3. Actual value = 0.03%

*Source:* CUPR Analysis of Operating Statements.

Of special note is the variation in operating results from 1971-1972 and 1972-1973, respectively. In 1972, there were still facilities from which additional rents could be extracted and the impact of inflation was still relatively insignificant. By 1973, however, possible profit earlier available in the rent rolls had been absorbed and the average dollar rent increase per sample structure was barely $1,300. This additional rent revenue was absorbed by heating fuel costs alone, leaving no dollars to cover even larger increase in real estate taxes and other operating expenses.

The cost-shift from 1971-1972 to 1972-1973 is apparent in an examination of "Operating Results as a Percentage of Net Rent Received" located at the bottom of Exhibit 5-2. It is clear that increases in taxes and fuel costs combined with fairly stable 1972-1973 rent levels meant a decrease in the dollars available for debt service, depreciation and profit.

The nature and significance of the pattern is evident when we turn to equivalent operating results for the noncontrolled sample. Here rents increased (as shown in Exhibit 5-3) 8.3 percent from 1971 to 1972 and 4.9 percent from 1972 to 1973. The buildings in question are larger than their rent-controlled equivalents; nevertheless, an examination of their expenses in dollars is useful. The combined increase in net rents received for the noncontrolled buildings totalled approximately $57,000 from 1971 to 1973. This permitted the absorption of increased heating fuel costs amounting to more than $4,000, increased real estate taxes of approximately $9,000, other operating expenses of $3,000 and, most importantly, of building maintenance services which increased from $58,000 to $71,000—an increase of $13,000. Thus total expenses increased $29,000 from 1971 to 1973; however, net contribution to debt, depreciation and profit increased by nearly the same amount (over $28,000) due to increased rent revenues. The change in net contribution to debt, depreciation and profit in percentage terms is similar to basic consumer price index shifts for the years in question, and the same holds true for the percentage change in the net rent received.

Expenditure increase patterns for the rent-controlled and noncontrolled structures are similar. Fuel costs in both cases went up approximately 20 percent; however, real estate tax increases impacted rent-controlled structures more than noncontrolled—14.4 percent versus 11 percent, respectively. And "other" operating expenses increased significantly more rapidly for the controlled group. The average owner of a controlled building in the sample had $71,078 in 1971 with which to pay debts; by 1973 this had shrunk to $65,754, a 7.5 percent decrease. The noncontrolled equivalent had an increase of net contribution to debts or profit of 13.4 percent. Exhibit 5-4 reflects the percentage increase in rent necessary to maintain the rent-controlled sector in absolute dollar terms for the years 1971-1973. However, to maintain the 1971 *percentage* contribution to debt, depreciation and profit in the rent-controlled

*EXHIBIT 5-3*

*AVERAGE ANNUAL OPERATING RESULTS, 1971-1973 – NONCONTROLLED SAMPLE*[1]

*GREATER BOSTON AREA*

| | *Net Rent Received* | *Building Maintenance & Services* | *Fuel* | *Real Estate Taxes* | *Other Operating Expenses*[2] | *Total All Expenses* | *Net Contribution to Debt, Depreciation, and Profit* |
|---|---|---|---|---|---|---|---|
| 1971 | $421,073 | $58,868 | $21,442 | $78,793 | $52,375 | $211,478 | $209,595 |
| 1972 | 455,925 | 62,475 | 23,136 | 87,611 | 57,159 | 230,381 | 225,543 |
| 1973 | 478,111 | 71,489 | 25,825 | 87,427 | 55,637 | 240,378 | 237,733 |
| | | | | *AVERAGE PERCENT CHANGE* | | | |
| 1971-72 | 8.3% | 6.1% | 7.9% | 11.2% | 9.1% | 8.9% | 7.6% |
| 1972-73 | 4.9 | 14.4 | 11.6 | -0.2 | -2.7 | 4.3 | 5.4 |
| 1971-73 | 13.5 | 21.4 | 20.4 | 11.0 | 6.2 | 13.7 | 13.4 |
| | | | | *OPERATING RESULTS AS A PERCENTAGE OF NET RENT RECEIVED*[2] | | | |
| 1971 | 100.0% | 14.0% | 5.1% | 18.7% | 12.4% | 50.2% | 49.8% |
| 1972 | 100.0 | 13.7 | 5.1 | 19.2 | 12.5 | 50.5 | 49.5 |
| 1973 | 100.0 | 15.0 | 5.4 | 18.3 | 11.6 | 50.3 | 49.7 |

1. (N = 20 operating statements for 3,898 units).
2. Residual of total expenses including administrative, insurance, other utility, and miscellaneous expenses.

*Source:* CUPR Analysis of Operating Statements.

*EXHIBIT 5-4*
*MINIMAL NET RENT REQUIREMENT TO MAINTAIN PRIOR LEVEL OF CONTRIBUTION TO DEBT, DEPRECIATION, AND PROFIT*

*GREATER BOSTON AREA*

| | |
|---|---|
| Net Rent 1971 | $189,543 |
| Net Rent 1973 | $202,315 |
| Difference | $ 12,772 |
| Plus the missing dollars of Contribution to Debt, Depreciation, and Profit | $ 5,324 |
| Two-Year Total | $ 18,096 |
| Annual Increment Required | $ 9,048 |
| Annual Percent Increase on Base Year | 4.7 |

buildings, annual rents would have had to increase by an additional 1.5 to 1.7 percent to an approximate total of 7 percent per year.

*Variation as a Function of Building Size*

Are there significant variations in expenditure patterns when these are examined as a function of the size of the building? Do large buildings or small buildings suffer most from rent control? The exhibits which are incorporated use the sample base discussed earlier with a different computational approach. The percentage data shown here was obtained by averaging the percentage results of each of the buildings within the sample. This approach alters the absolute size of the percentage results, but the basic pattern of results remains the same.

Exhibit 5-5 shows average annual contribution to debt, depreciation and profit during 1971-1973 as a percentage of net rent received. Here sample sizes are relatively small so the data should not be interpreted as absolute. Certainly, however, it seems to indicate that while the decline in debt contribution in relatively small buildings was more extreme than that for highrises—highrise debt, depreciation and profit contribution declined from 40.1 percent net contribution to 36.2, while the other buildings declined from 36.3 to 30.8 percent—there is no group that has not been adversely affected. The smaller multiple tenant structures, those in the four to forty-nine unit category, were seemingly most affected; they suffered decline from a 31.1 percent contribution to 26 percent. Noncontrolled four to forty-nine unit structures, however, were relatively stable and even experienced a slight increase, from 49.1 percent to 50.4 percent during 1971-1973. In each of the size categories the imposition of rent control had a definite, adverse impact on net contribution to debt, depreciation, and profit. Variation in the contribution figures between small and large buildings are significant because large buildings are typically newer, requiring higher debt service levels. For example, in some FHA programs the equity level may be as low as 10 or 15 percent. In small buildings, particularly older ones, sales are a relatively small multiple of the rent roll, and debt requirements are also smaller.

Exhibit 5-6 shows average annual total expenses as a percentage of net rent received by building type and number of units. It is the complement of Exhibit 5-5, but provides a clearer insight into the erosion of the rent dollar in the controlled housing stock.

*Expenditure Patterns as a Function of Building Type and Size*

Building Maintenance and Services

To determine if there were significant differences in operation as a function of the type of building and the imposition of rent control, individual

*EXHIBIT 5-5*
*AVERAGE ANNUAL CONTRIBUTION TO DEBT, DEPRECIATION, AND PROFIT AS A PERCENTAGE OF NET RENT RECEIVED BY BUILDING TYPE, SIZE, AND NUMBER OF UNITS*
*GREATER BOSTON AREA*

| | *Type of Building* | | *Number of Units* | | | |
|---|---|---|---|---|---|---|
| | *High Rise* | *Other* | *1-3* | *4-49* | *50-199* | *200+* |
| Rent Controlled | | | —[1] | | | |
| 1971 | 40.1% | 36.3% | | 31.1% | 37.1% | 57.9% |
| 1972 | 39.9 | 32.2 | | 28.8 | 35.1 | 57.4 |
| 1973 | 36.2 | 30.8 | | 26.0 | 33.4 | 49.6 |
| Noncontrolled | | | —[2] | | | |
| 1971 | 52.0 | 45.0 | | 49.1 | 45.5 | 51.6 |
| 1972 | 49.2 | 43.9 | | 49.3 | 43.0 | 48.7 |
| 1973 | 49.9 | 42.3 | | 50.4 | 42.4 | 47.6 |

1. Sample size inadequate for computation.
2. No noncontrolled units in this size category.
*Source:* CUPR Analysis of Operating Statements.

*EXHIBIT 5-6*
*AVERAGE ANNUAL TOTAL EXPENSES AS A PERCENTAGE OF NET RENT RECEIVED BY BUILDING TYPE, SIZE AND NUMBER OF UNITS*
*GREATER BOSTON AREA*

| | *Type of Building* | | *Number of Units* | | | |
|---|---|---|---|---|---|---|
| | *High-rise* | *Other* | *1-3* | *4-49* | *50-199* | *200+* |
| Rent Controlled | | | —[1] | | | |
| 1971 | 59.9% | 63.7% | | 68.9% | 62.9% | 42.1% |
| 1972 | 60.1 | 67.8 | | 71.2 | 64.9 | 42.6 |
| 1973 | 63.8 | 69.2 | | 74.0 | 66.6 | 50.4 |
| Noncontrolled | | | —[2] | | | |
| 1971 | 48.0 | 55.0 | | 50.9 | 54.5 | 48.4 |
| 1972 | 50.8 | 56.1 | | 50.7 | 57.0 | 51.3 |
| 1973 | 50.1 | 57.7 | | 49.6 | 57.6 | 52.4 |

1. Sample size inadequate for computation.
2. No noncontrolled units in this size category.
*Source:* CUPR Analysis of Operating Statements.

components of the expenditure pattern were analyzed. The analysis (Exhibit 5-7) tended to confirm our working hypothesis of a decline in maintenance in controlled buildings; subject to the limitations of size of sample, this trend seems to be relatively unaffected by the scale of the structure.

### Real Estate Tax Expense

In Exhibit 5-8 real estate tax expenses for the rent controlled stock are indicated. Note first the absolute level of taxes as a percentage of net rent received in the rent-controlled versus noncontrolled structures. While some of the variation may be a function of the manner in which particular structure types are appraised within individual communities, the real estate burden carried by the rent-controlled is evident. The tax burden for the noncontrolled structures is much smaller. For the latter group, barely 20 cents per rent dollar went to taxes in 1973, while in the controlled stock it was approximately 30 cents of the rent dollar.

It is particularly noteworthy that the controlled units are also hardest hit by increases in tax rates. For every size category in the rent-controlled group there has been an increase in the percentage of the rent dollar absorbed by taxes. This does not seem to be the case for the noncontrolled group; at least in some of the size categories, increases in rents have been adequate to support taxes as a percentage of net rent received; in a few cases even to reduce the percentage in the period of years considered here.

### Fuel Expenses

As shown in Exhibit 5-9, small buildings tend to spend a higher proportion of their rent dollar for fuel than do larger structures. The data not only reflect increases in fuel costs over time, but also indicate the relatively greater impact that fuel increases have on the rent dollar of small buildings. It is clear that even before the 1974 fuel cost increases, rent-controlled structures experienced higher proportions of fuel expenses to rent dollars than the noncontrolled structures.

## *The Data on a Per Unit Basis*

In order to gain a fuller understanding of the impact of rent control, its effect upon individual units has been analyzed. The average operating expenses for controlled and noncontrolled units are shown in Exhibit 5-10. The data representing a typical apartment in the controlled sector are for a unit in a well-maintained structure with certifiable operating characteristics. That data for the noncontrolled unit represents an average expense as derived from the

*EXHIBIT 5-7*
*AVERAGE ANNUAL BUILDING MAINTENANCE AND SERVICES EXPENSES*[1]
*AS A PERCENTAGE OF NET RENT RECEIVED BY BUILDING TYPE, SIZE AND NUMBER OF UNITS*
*GREATER BOSTON AREA*

| | *Type of Building* | | *Number of Units* | | | |
|---|---|---|---|---|---|---|
| | *High Rise* | *Other* | *1-3* | *4-49* | *50-199* | *200+* |
| Rent Controlled | | | —[2] | | | |
| 1971 | 15.2% | 14.6% | | 16.5% | 15.8% | 11.2% |
| 1972 | 13.7 | 16.3 | | 16.3 | 15.7 | 12.4 |
| 1973 | 14.4 | 17.6 | | 17.6 | 16.5 | 13.5 |
| Noncontrolled | | | —[3] | | | |
| 1971 | 11.7 | 14.1 | | 11.9 | 12.9 | 13.2 |
| 1972 | 11.8 | 14.9 | | 12.2 | 13.9 | 13.2 |
| 1973 | 12.2 | 17.7 | | 13.0 | 15.7 | 14.7 |

1. Includes payroll, contractor services, supplies and all routine maintenance expenses.
2. Sample size inadequate for computation.
3. No noncontrolled unit in this size category.
*Source:* CUPR Analysis of Operating Statements.

*EXHIBIT 5-8*
*AVERAGE ANNUAL REAL ESTATE TAX EXPENSE AS A PERCENTAGE OF NET RENT RECEIVED BY BUILDING TYPE, SIZE AND NUMBER OF UNITS*
*GREATER BOSTON AREA*

| | *Type of Building* | | *Number of Units* | | | |
|---|---|---|---|---|---|---|
| | *High Rise* | *Other* | *1-3* | *4-49* | *50-199* | *200+* |
| Rent Controlled | | | —[1] | | | |
| 1971 | 26.7% | 28.0% | | 29.9% | 28.6% | 14.8% |
| 1972 | 27.8 | 30.8 | | 32.6 | 30.6 | 14.3 |
| 1973 | 29.8 | 29.5 | | 32.6 | 30.2 | 16.7 |
| Noncontrolled | | | —[2] | | | |
| 1971 | 19.9 | 20.8 | | 23.6 | 22.0 | 16.8 |
| 1972 | 22.9 | 20.3 | | 23.5 | 23.7 | 18.9 |
| 1973 | 22.0 | 19.7 | | 22.2 | 23.1 | 18.3 |

1. Sample size inadequate for computation.
2. No noncontrolled units in this size category.
*Source:* CUPR Analysis of Operating Statements.

EXHIBIT 5-9
AVERAGE ANNUAL FUEL EXPENSES AS A PERCENTAGE OF NET RENT RECEIVED BY BUILDING TYPE, SIZE AND NUMBER OF UNITS
GREATER BOSTON AREA

| | Type of Building | | Number of Units | | | |
|---|---|---|---|---|---|---|
| | High-rise | Other | 1-3 | 4-49 | 50-199 | 200+ |
| Rent Controlled | | | —[1] | | | |
| 1971 | 4.48% | 6.2% | | 7.1% | 5.6% | 4.4% |
| 1972 | 4.6 | 5.8 | | 6.7 | 5.1 | 4.5 |
| 1973 | 4.9 | 7.2 | | 8.3 | 5.6 | 6.0 |
| Noncontrolled | | | —[2] | | | |
| 1971 | 3.6 | 6.8 | | 3.3[3] | 5.9 | 5.3 |
| 1972 | 3.2 | 7.4 | | 3.6 | 5.9 | 5.3 |
| 1973 | 3.4 | 7.3 | | 3.0 | 6.0 | 5.5 |

1. Sample size inadequate for computation.
2. No noncontrolled units in this size category.
3. Heat not provided for part of sample.

*Source:* CUPR Analysis of Operating Statements.

*EXHIBIT 5-10*

*AVERAGE OPERATING RESULTS, ANNUALLY AND MONTHLY, PER APARTMENT UNIT, 1971-1973*

*GREATER BOSTON AREA*

| | *Net Rent Received* | *Building Maintenance and Services* | *Heating Fuel* | *Real Estate Taxes* | *Total All Expenses* | *Net Contribution to Debt, Depreciation, and Profit* |
|---|---|---|---|---|---|---|
| *RENT-CONTROLLED*[1] | | | | | | |
| 1971 | $1,989 | $307 | $112 | $542 | $1,243 | $ 746 |
| 1972 | 2,067 | 323 | 109 | 605 | 1,333 | 734 |
| 1973 | 2,117 | 351 | 131 | 623 | 1,410 | 707 |
| *Average Monthly Equivalent* | | | | | | |
| 1971 | $ 166 | $ 26 | $ 9 | $ 45 | $ 104 | $ 62 |
| 1972 | 172 | 27 | 9 | 50 | 111 | 61 |
| 1973 | 176 | 29 | 11 | 52 | 118 | 58 |
| *NONCONTROLLED*[2] | | | | | | |
| 1971 | $2,552 | $318 | $116 | $524 | $1,284 | $1,268 |
| 1972 | 2,662 | 341 | 124 | 589 | 1,386 | 1,276 |
| 1973 | 2,789 | 391 | 125 | 590 | 1,443 | 1,346 |
| *Average Monthly Equivalent* | | | | | | |
| 1971 | $ 213 | $ 27 | $ 10 | $ 44 | $ 107 | $ 106 |
| 1972 | 222 | 28 | 10 | 49 | 116 | 106 |
| 1973 | 232 | 33 | 10 | 49 | 120 | 112 |

1. Selected case.
2. Noncontrolled N = 20 Operating Statements representing 3,893 units.

*Source:* CUPR Analysis of Operating Statements.

noncontrolled sample base. Our discussion focuses on annual expenses; please note that Exhibit 5-10 illustrates expenses on a per month as well as annual basis.

The typical rent-controlled unit in our Boston sample had an annual rent of $2,117 for 1973. The rent had increased approximately $10 per month since 1971 for a total increase of $128. Expenses totaled $1,410 in 1973, an increase of $167 from 1971. The key expense items included building maintenance which increased from $307 to $351, an increase of $44; heat costs which only increased $19 from 1971 to 1973; and taxes which had a substantial impact, totaling $542 in 1971 versus $623 in 1973.

Deducting all expenses for 1971, $746 remained to meet debt service, depreciation and profit; in 1973 that amount had dropped to $707. Thus, the owner of a typical controlled building in Greater Boston received $39 per unit less in 1973 than he had in 1971. *The enormous inflation in operating costs in 1974, particularly for fuel, occurred in the wake of already eroded operating profits in the rent-controlled buildings under consideration.*

For noncontrolled units, monthly expenses were $13 per unit higher in 1973 than in 1971; and whereas in 1971 noncontrolled maintenance expenses were only $1 per unit higher than those for the controlled group, in 1973 they were $4 per unit higher. Fuel costs for larger buildings did not seem to increase as much as those for smaller structures. This may be due to the prevailing use of gas heat in the newer larger buildings. In general, the smaller structures predominate in the rent-controlled group.

The actual variation in rent increases between the controlled and noncontrolled groups from 1971 to 1973 is not as great as might be anticipated. In the noncontrolled group, rent increased $19 from a $213 base; in the controlled group, the increase was $10 from a $166 base. The key factor, however, is the obvious gap in maintenance expenses between the two groups, with the controlled group providing $4 per unit less per month in maintenance.

## *THE FORT LEE, NEW JERSEY CASE STUDY*

Having examined operating expenses in the Greater Boston area we now undertake a similar analysis for Fort Lee, New Jersey. Data from 1974—the year in which fuel costs soared—is included in this analysis.

The sample consists of eleven rent-controlled structures, primarily large luxury buildings with a total of 2,769 units. Fort Lee's proximity to New York City and its many high quality apartment structures make it one of the most desirable residential communities in the New York metropolitan area, particularly for mobile, affluent renters.

### *Average Annual Operating Results: 1972, 1973, 1974*

The first portion of this section examines the sample operating results in aggregate form for the 1972 to 1974 period.

Exhibit 5-11 presents the average operating costs for the entire Fort Lee sample. Bearing in mind the significance of the "Net Contribution to Debt, Depreciation and Profit" category with respect to real estate investment decisions, notice the dramatic decrease in this category from 49.7 cents in 1972 to 41.9 cents in 1974. It is apparent that either net rental income decreased or total expenses increased during this period. As is clearly indicated by the data, however, net rental income did not decrease; rather, it increased 5.47 percent over the 1972-1974 period. Total expenses increased at a more rapid rate, eroding the amount of money available for debt, depreciation and profit. In fact, total expenses increased 21.84 percent over this period.

Throughout this analysis, total expenses are treated in five general categories: building maintenance and service; heating fuel; other utilities (including gas, water, and electricity); real estate taxes; and administrative expenses (including insurance, management fees, other management related and miscellaneous expenses). An examination of each of these categories provides additional insight into the relationship between the stated decrease in contribution to debt, depreciation and profit and the 21.84 percent increase in total expenses.

As was demonstrated in the Greater Boston case study, of the five operating expense categories which allow management the most opportunity to trim expenses, building maintenance and service is by far the most flexible expense category. However, unlike the heterogeneous Boston sample, the New Jersey sample is composed largely of luxury apartment buildings for which tenants pay well for better-than-average maintenance and services; therefore, these tenants are extremely sensitive to reductions in these areas. In general, maintenance and services are a relatively inflexible expense item in the luxury housing market. This fact is reflected in a 21.18 percent increase in the cost of building maintenance and service which parallels the overall increase in total expenses. In a relatively flexible expense category, administrative expense, one finds management more successfully stabilizing cost increases; the average increase in administrative expenses was 8.78 percent.

Of the three operating expense categories in which there is little or no flexibility, only one—real estate taxes—shows a percentage increase less than that of the increase in net rents received. The relatively insignificant 0.18 percent real estate tax increase must be qualified, however, for this figure only reflects taxes actually paid, including any and all abatements received by the sample structures. This relatively minor increase is more than compensated for by the increases experienced within the categories of heating fuel and other utilities. Heating fuel expenses increased by 114.81 percent while costs for other utilities rose 54.59 percent over the three-year period.

*EXHIBIT 5-11*
*AVERAGE ANNUAL OPERATING RESULTS*
*1972-1974*
*FORT LEE, NEW JERSEY SAMPLE*[1]

| *Year* | *Net Rent Received* | *Building Maintenance & Service* | *Fuel* | *Other Utilities* | *Real Estate Taxes* | *Administration and other expenses*[2] | *Total Expenses* | *Contribution to Debt, Depreciation, and Profit* |
|---|---|---|---|---|---|---|---|---|
| 1972 | 1,172,997 | 254,193 | 29,544 | 62,350 | 166,759 | 77,066 | 589,912 | 583,084 |
| 1973 | 1,204,887 | 264,460 | 33,037 | 68,496 | 163,667 | 79,543 | 609,203 | 595,671 |
| 1974 | 1,237,103 | 308,024 | 63,463 | 96,387 | 167,061 | 83,831 | 718,766 | 518,337 |
| | | | | *AVERAGE PERCENT CHANGE* | | | | |
| 1972-1973 | 2.72 | 4.04 | 11.82 | 9.86 | -1.85 | 3.21 | 3.27 | 2.16 |
| 1973-1974 | 2.67 | 16.47 | 92.10 | 40.72 | 2.07 | 5.39 | 17.98 | -12.98 |
| 1972-1974 | 5.47 | 21.18 | 114.81 | 54.59 | 0.18 | 8.78 | 21.84 | -11.10 |
| | | | | *OPERATING RESULTS AS A PERCENTAGE OF NET RENT RECEIVED* | | | | |
| 1972 | 100 | 21.67 | 2.52 | 5.32 | 14.22 | 6.57 | 50.29 | 49.70 |
| 1973 | 100 | 21.95 | 2.74 | 5.68 | 13.58 | 6.60 | 50.56 | 49.44 |
| 1974 | 100 | 24.90 | 5.13 | 7.79 | 13.50 | 6.78 | 58.10 | 41.90 |

1. N = 11 Operating Statements for 2,769 units.
2. Also includes insurance and miscellaneous expenses.
*Source:* CUPR Analysis of sample operating statements.

The high cost of fuel has and will continue to affect the cost of the other utilities category as a result of the recent fuel adjustment rate increases.[3]

The increases in operating costs and the absence of commensurate increases in net rents necessitates that the dollars required to cover various operating expenses, notably heating fuel and utilities, be reallocated internally from the net operating income. The "Contribution to Debt, Depreciation and Profit" category has a limited capacity to absorb these additional costs. Exhibit 5-12 indicates the increase in net rents received which would have been necessary to maintain the same overall relationship between net rents received, total expenses, and contribution to debt, depreciation and profit in 1974 as existed in 1972. Net rents received would have had to increase at a rate of 5.49 percent per year or almost exactly twice the rate at which they actually increased. The actual trend toward reduced profits not only discourages investment in the housing market but also has the long-term effect of diminishing the tax base of the community.

### *Variation by Building Type*

The first portion of this section was devoted to an analysis of operating expenses for the entire Fort Lee sample; an examination of these expenses according to building types offers additional insight into the impact of rent control. Two categories will be utilized: "Highrise," ranging in size from fifteen to twenty-nine stories and "Other," ranging in size from two to nine stories. Examining operating expenditure patterns, one observes some interesting differences between these two building types.

As evident in Exhibit 5-13, the two to nine story group fares significantly better in terms of the percentage of the net rent dollar available to meet debt service, depreciation, and profit requirements. However, in both the "Highrise" and the "Other" sample there has been a decline in the dollars available for debt, depreciation, and profit since 1972. This drop is more severe for the "Highrise" than the other group. For the highrises there was a decline from 48.47 percent in 1972 to 40.16 percent in 1974—a drop of 17.15 percent and for the "Other" group, the drop was from 57.35 percent in 1972 to 52.27 percent in 1974, a decrease of 8.86 percent.

### *Variation by Utilities Provided*

The degree to which management provides utilities such as heat, electric, gas and air conditioning affects the operating expense of a given building. For this reason, the sample buildings have been analyzed according to the utilities provided by the management (Exhibit 5-14). Because there was insufficient information to properly isolate the utility expenses for one of the structures in

*EXHIBIT 5-12*
*MINIMAL NET RENT REQUIREMENTS TO MAINTAIN PRIOR LEVEL OF CONTRIBUTION TO DEBT, DEPRECIATION, AND PROFIT*
*FORT LEE, NEW JERSEY SAMPLE*

| | |
|---|---|
| Net Rent Received 1972 | $1,172,997 |
| Net Rent Received 1974 | $1,237,103 |
| Difference | $ 64,106 |
| Plus the missing dollars of Contribution to Debt, Depreciation, and Profit | $ 64,747 |
| Two-Year Total | $ 128,853 |
| Annual Increment Required | $ 64,427 |
| Annual Percent Increase on Base Year | 5.49% |

*EXHIBIT 5-13*

*AVERAGE ANNUAL OPERATING RESULTS AS A PERCENT OF NET RENT RECEIVED BY BUILDING TYPE FORT LEE, NEW JERSEY SAMPLE*[1]

| | *Building Maintenance & Services* | *Fuel* | *Other Utilities* | *Real Estate Taxes* | *Administrative and Other Expenses*[2] | *Total Expenses* | *Contribution to Debt, Depreciation, and Profit* |
|---|---|---|---|---|---|---|---|
| High-rise | | | | | | | |
| 1972 | 22.88 | 2.11 | 5.73 | 14.09 | 6.27 | 51.53 | 48.47 |
| 1973 | 23.03 | 2.34 | 6.06 | 13.49 | 6.28 | 51.65 | 48.35 |
| 1974 | 26.45 | 4.59 | 8.36 | 13.47 | 6.61 | 59.84 | 40.16 |
| (N=6) | | | | | | | |
| Other | | | | | | | |
| 1972 | 14.20 | 5.06 | 3.06 | 14.99 | 5.01 | 42.65 | 57.35 |
| 1973 | 15.40 | 5.18 | 3.36 | 14.17 | 5.00 | 43.99 | 56.01 |
| 1974 | 15.64 | 8.34 | 4.42 | 13.69 | 5.09 | 47.73 | 52.27 |
| (N=5) | | | | | | | |

1. (N = operating statements for 2,769 units).
2. Includes insurance and miscellaneous expenses.

*Source:* CUPR analysis of sample operating statements.

*EXHIBIT 5-14*
*ANNUAL DOLLAR COST PER UNIT BY UTILITIES PACKAGE PROVIDED*

| | *1972* | *1973* | *1974* |
|---|---|---|---|
| Cost Per Unit in Buildings Providing Partial Utilities (N = 598) | | | |
| Heating Fuel | $124.38 | $136.79 | $243.39 |
| Other Utilities | 126.58 | 146.31 | 175.14 |
| Total Utilities | 250.96 | 288.10 | 418.53 |
| Cost Per Unit in Buildings Providing All Utilities (N = 2,060) | | | |
| Heating Fuel | 105.91 | 120.75 | 249.18 |
| Other Utilities | 296.85 | 321.67 | 461.37 |
| Total Utilities | 402.76 | 442.42 | 710.55 |

*Source:* CUPR analysis of operating statements.
Note: N = 2,658 units in 10 projects.

the sample, the sample size in this exhibit is ten rather than the original eleven buildings.

Those buildings in which only partial utilities are provided by the management showed an annual utilities cost of $250.96 per unit in 1972. In 1974, this figure increased to an annual cost of $418.53 per unit. The bulk of this expense consisted of outlays for heating fuel which increased from $124.38 per unit in 1972 to $243.39 per unit in 1974. Other utilities showed a far less dramatic increase, from $126.58 per unit in 1972 to $175.14 per unit in 1974. Thus, the total annual utilities expense in those structures providing only partial utilities increased by 66.77 percent from 1972 to 1974 and by 47.84 percent from 1973 to 1974.

In those structures in which the management provides all utilities, we observe a far greater annual cost per unit for utilities. Among those buildings in which all utilities are provided, those which provide "all electric" utilities experienced the greatest increase in 1974 as a function of increased electric rates. For these structures, the annual utilities cost per unit was $402.76 in 1972. By 1974, this figure had increased to an annual cost per unit of $710.55. This is an increase of 76.42 percent from 1972 to 1974 and 60.61 percent from 1973 to 1974 alone.

The difference in operating expenses between those buildings providing partial utilities and those providing all utilities is apparently attributable more to increases in electricity rates than to heating fuel costs. In the case of buildings in which only partial utilities are provided, one observes a 38.36 percent increase in the other utilities category, while in those buildings providing all utilities, the other utility category increase is 55.42 percent during the period 1972 through 1974.

## *CONTRASTS AND COMPARISONS: BOSTON AND FORT LEE*

As stated earlier, the relative importance of operating expense categories varies as a function of location, age, size, and structural characteristics of a particular building. These variations are clearly evident in the samples we have reviewed. Real estate tax expenditures, as determined by location, constitute a much larger portion of the rent dollar in the Greater Boston area than in Fort Lee, New Jersey—$2.64 per $100 valuation in Fort Lee in 1974 as compared to $196.70 per $1000 valuation in the city of Boston in 1974.

In terms of heating fuel expenditures, highrise buildings in both the Boston and Fort Lee areas paid a lower percentage of net rent received toward heating fuel than did smaller buildings. The variations in building maintenance and service expenditures are ambiguous because it is not possible to determine changes in levels of service from the data. However, in the Fort Lee sample there is a relatively large difference in maintenance and service expenditures between highrise and smaller buildings. In the rent-controlled sector of the Greater Boston sample, there is much less variation in maintenance and service expenditures between the two structural types, though the highrise buildings show a decrease in maintenance expenditures as a percentage of net rent received. In general both types of controlled structures show a decline in maintenance expenditures when compared with their noncontrolled equivalents in the Greater Boston area.

Although these locational and structural characteristics are important factors affecting the internal allocation of the rent dollar, the presence of rent control and the stringency of the rent adjustment mechanism are more important in determining "bottom-line" operating results, specifically the contribution to debt, depreciation and profit. The preceding analysis indicates that operating costs have increased substantially over the time period surveyed; however, in the rent-controlled sector, these increases have not been matched by corresponding increases in operating income.

Exhibits 5-15 and 5-16 illustrate the dramatic differences in operating results between the two case studies. In Fort Lee, only 42 cents of the 1974 rent dollar remained after expenses and only 33 cents remained from the rent dollar in the Boston area rent-controlled sample in 1973. While the Boston area sample does not include 1974 data (when significant fuel increases would presumably have had a more severe impact)[4], the trend it shows toward lower operating results is indicative of the effect of rent control over a longer period of time than in Fort Lee. Rent control was initiated in Fort Lee in 1972 under a more flexible regulatory system which utilized the CPI as the rent adjustment factor. The length of time rent controls have been in effect in the Boston area and the stringency of the rent adjustment formulas in use there account for some of the fiscal differences between the Fort Lee and Boston area sample structures (see chapters 3, 4 and 6).

## *THE NEW YORK CITY CASE STUDY: A PRICE INDEX APPROACH*

The two preceding case studies present the realities of operating multi-family rental units in recent years. As historical cost analyses, those studies represent one of the two basic approaches for obtaining reliable data on operating cost changes over time. However, the approach used for Greater Boston and Fort Lee requires detailed case data which is generally unavailable across-the-board. Research is further hampered under this method by the fact that it is difficult to measure variations in absolute patterns and in levels of service from year to year; the latter factor impacts changes in operating results as well as changes in the prices of goods and services purchased.

The primary controversy in the application of any rent adjustment formula concerns the determination of increases in operating costs; an approach facilitating the application of reasonably good indices of changes in operating

*EXHIBIT 5–15*
*CHANGE IN TOTAL EXPENSES AND CONTRIBUTION TO DEBT, DEPRECIATION, AND PROFIT AS PERCENTAGE OF NET RENT RECEIVED*
*FORT LEE, NEW JERSEY SAMPLE*

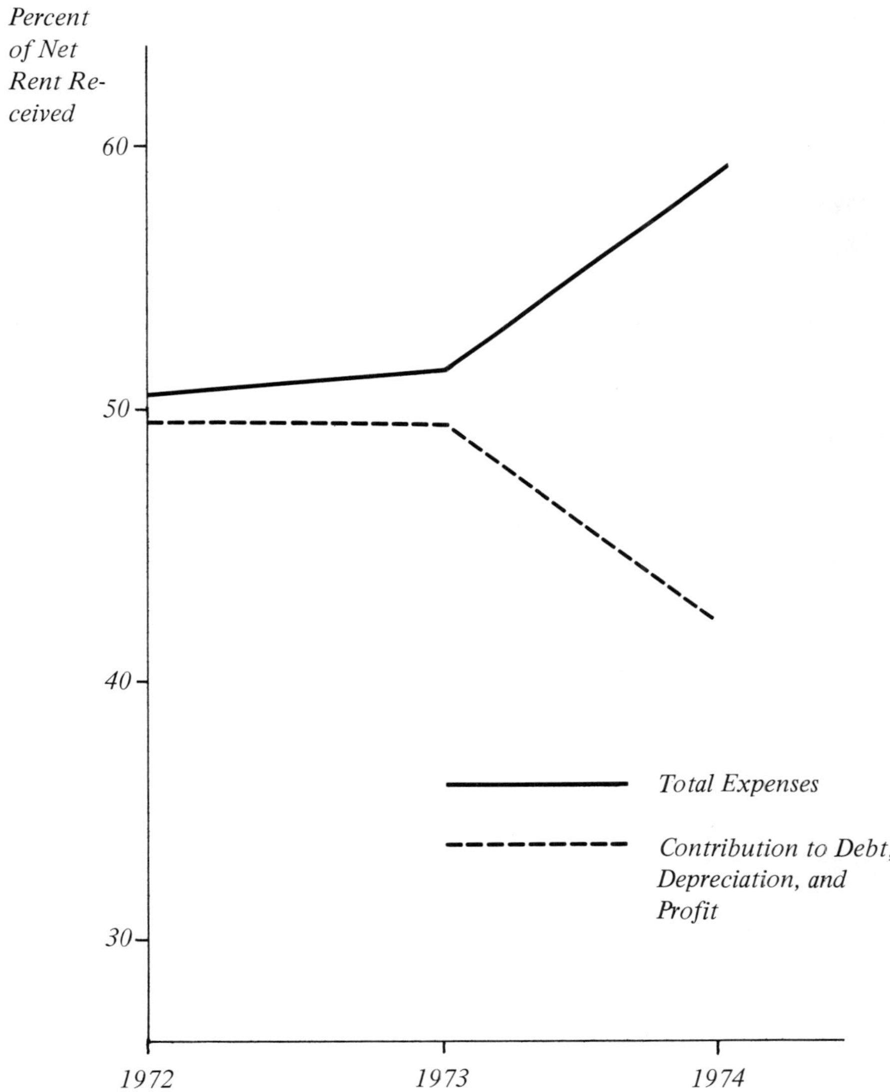


*Source:* CUPR Analysis of sample structure operating statements, 1972–1974.

*EXHIBIT 5–16*
*CHANGE IN TOTAL EXPENSES AND CONTRIBUTION TO DEBT, DEPRECIATION, AND PROFIT AS PERCENTAGE OF NET RENT RECEIVED*
*GREATER BOSTON AREA, RENT-CONTROLLED SAMPLE*

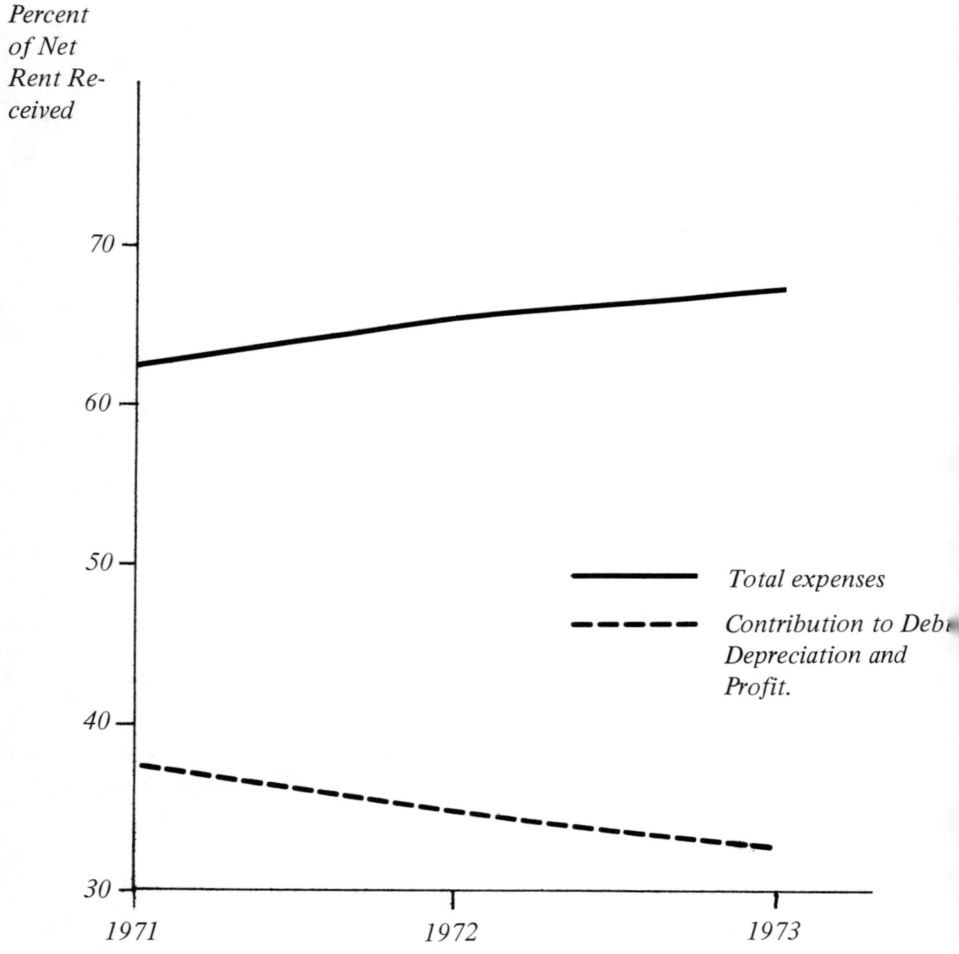


*Source:* CUPR analysis of sample operating statements, 1971-1973.

costs without unnecessary building by building calculations can resolve this problem. The approach utilized in New York City monitors such cost changes for rent-stabilized apartments in order to determine an annual adjustment index[5] (see the New York City case study in chapter 6). The method used for analyzing New York City measures changes in operating costs and reflects the realities of such costs by comparing the specifically constructed New York operating cost index to the Consumer Price Index. The latter is extensively used in many New Jersey communities as the basis for rent adjustments.

### *Comparison of CPI and New York City Operating Cost Index*

The Consumer Price Index (CPI) is a broadly used indicator of changes in the cost of living; however, it specifically reflects changes only in the purchasing power of a typical "urban wage earner and clerical worker."[6] Housing costs account for about 33 percent of the CPI. Whether in fact the CPI continues to accurately reflect changes in the cost of living is an issue of continuing debate.

It is, however, clear that the CPI can reflect changes in a building's operating expenses if changes in the items used in the CPI are comparable to those purchased by the owner or manager of the building. Exhibit 5-17 provides a comparison between changes in costs as determined by the CPI and those determined by the operating cost index for rent stabilized apartments in New York City. Examination of the exhibit reveals that beginning in 1970, apartment building cost increases surpassed increases in the cost of living index.

### *Components of the Operating Cost Index*

The "All Items Index" of the New York City operating cost index found in Exhibit 5-17 is augmented by the annual computation of eight component indexes. Exhibit 5-18 lists the component indexes with 1975 data and Exhibit 5-19 indicates the relative weight of each component and the manner in which this has fluctuated as a function of price change since 1967.

As evident in Exhibits 5-17 and 5-18, the "All Items Index" increased by 6.5 percent in 1975, the lowest increment since 1972. In 1975, the percentage increase in four of the component categories was in excess of 6.5 percent; however, these increases occurred in relatively insignificant categories (for example, "Parts and Supplies," 17.2 percent increase; and "Replacement Costs," 17 percent increase) and thus they did not substantially increase the "All Items Index." Most striking is the 345 percent increase which has occurred in fuel and utilities since 1967. Of that increase, 79.6 percent occurred between April 1973 and April 1974 when the fuel and utilities index increased from 187.0 in 1973 to 335.9 in 1974. Fuel constituted 24.0 percent of total expenses in 1975 as compared to 13.3 percent in 1967. It is clear that changes in the costs of fuel

*EXHIBIT 5-17*
*COMPARISON OF CONSUMER PRICE INDEX AND NEW YORK CITY PRICE INDEX OF OPERATING COSTS FOR RENT-STABILIZED APARTMENT HOUSES IN NEW YORK CITY*

| | *Consumer Price Index for New York-North Eastern New Jersey, 1967-1975* | | *Price Index of Operating Costs for Rent-stabilized Apartment Houses, New York City, 1967-1975* | |
|---|---|---|---|---|
| | *All Items Index* | *Percent Change* | *All Items Index* | *Percent Change* |
| 1967 | 100.0 | – | 100.0 | – |
| 1968 | 104.3 | 4.3 | 103.5 | 3.5 |
| 1969 | 110.8 | 6.2 | 107.6 | 4.0 |
| 1970 | 119.0 | 7.4 | 116.6 | 8.4 |
| 1971 | 125.9 | 5.8 | 132.2 | 13.4 |
| 1972 | 131.4 | 4.4 | 139.7 | 5.7 |
| 1973 | 139.7 | 6.3 | 150.8 | 7.9 |
| 1974 | 154.7 | 10.7 | 179.8 | 19.2 |
| 1975 | 166.6 | 7.7 | 191.3 | 6.5 |

Note: CPI represents calendar year annual average. The NYC Price Index of Operating Costs, however, is calculated from April to April, thereby resulting in lag time differentials.

*Source:* U.S., Department of Labor, Bureau of Labor Statistics, Consumer Price Index, 1967-1975; and U.S., Department of Labor, Bureau of Labor Statistics, Middle Atlantic Regional Office, *A Price Index of Operating Costs for Rent Stabilized Apartment Houses in New York City,* nos. 17, 23, 28, 38, 45 (1971-1975).

*EXHIBIT 5-18*
*PRICE INDEX OF OPERATING COSTS FOR RENT STABILIZED APARTMENT HOUSES, NEW YORK CITY, APRIL 1975*

| *Group* | *Index (April 1967=100)* | *Percent Change From April 1974* |
|---|---|---|
| All Items | 191.3 | 6.5 |
| Taxes, Fees and Permits | 153.6 | 6.4 |
| Labor Costs | 208.4 | 10.2 |
| Fuel and Utilities | 345.1 | 2.8 |
| Contractor Services | 180.3 | 8.8 |
| Administrative Costs | 142.5 | 5.7 |
| Insurance Costs | 206.8 | 1.4 |
| Parts and Supplies | 181.7 | 17.2 |
| Replacement Costs | 148.0 | 17.4 |

*Source:* U.S., Department of Labor, Bureau of Labor Statistics, Middle Atlantic Regional Office, *A Price Index of Operating Costs for Rent Stabilized Apartment Houses in New York City,* no. 45 (July 1975).

*EXHIBIT 5–19*
*CHANGES OVER TIME IN RELATIVE IMPORTANCE OF COMPONENTS IN NEW YORK CITY PRICE INDEX OF OPERATING COSTS FOR RENT-STABILIZED APARTMENT HOUSES, 1967–1975*

| | *1969 Expenditure Pattern Survey* | *Relative Importance of Components* | | | | | |
|---|---|---|---|---|---|---|---|
| | | *Percent of Operating Costs* | | | | | |
| | | *1967* | *1971* | *1972* | *1973* | *1974* | *1975* |
| All Items | 100.0 | 100.0 | 100.0 | 100.0 | 100.0 | 100.0 | 100.0 |
| Taxes, Fees and Permits | 45.6 | 46.1 | 42.8 | 41.5 | 41.7 | 37.1 | 37.0 |
| Labor | 16.2 | 15.6 | 16.9 | 17.2 | 17.6 | 16.4 | 16.9 |
| Fuel and Utilities | 12.5 | 13.3 | 15.5 | 16.4 | 16.5 | 24.8 | 24.0 |
| Contractor Services | 11.5 | 11.1 | 11.2 | 11.4 | 11.2 | 10.3 | 10.5 |
| Administrative | 8.2 | 8.3 | 7.6 | 7.5 | 7.2 | 6.2 | 6.2 |
| Insurance | 2.9 | 2.4 | 3.2 | 3.2 | 3.1 | 2.7 | 2.6 |
| Parts and Supplies | 2.1 | 2.0 | 1.8 | 1.8 | 1.8 | 1.7 | 1.9 |
| Replacement Costs | 1.0 | 1.2 | 1.0 | 1.0 | .9 | .8 | .9 |

*Note:* The relative importance of components represents their basic value weight as derived from the 1969 expenditure pattern survey adjusted for price change. Thus, the relative importance of the index value weights for 1967, 1971-1975 do not precisely indicate the respective expenditure patterns for that year, but are useful in analyzing the movement of the index because these ratios reflect adjustments as a result of different rates of price change among the various items, i.e., relative importance increases over time for an item or group having a greater than average price increase and decreases for one having a less than average price increase.

*Source:* U.S., Department of Labor, Bureau of Labor Statistics, Middle Atlantic Regional Office, *A Price Index of Operating Costs for Rent Stabilized Apartment Houses in New York City,* nos. 17, 23, 28, 38, 45 (1971-1975).

and utilities has had a significant impact upon overall operating costs, accounting for one quarter of the index movement in 1974 and 1975.

## *IMPLICATIONS OF INCREASED OPERATING COSTS*

Private investor owned and operated real estate predominates the rental housing market. Consequently, rent control has crucial significance for the future investment viability of the rental housing market. The long-term implications of the situation where operating costs exceed operating income as a result of rent control fall into three interrelated areas of concern: (1) the impact upon the physical maintenance of controlled structures; (2) the capital value of these buildings; and (3) ultimate consequences on the assessment base of local communities.

### *Deferred Maintenance*

When it is not feasible or possible to raise rents in proportion to cost increments, the only option open to owners is an internal reallocation of the rent dollar. This usually results in the reduction or deferral of maintenance expenses. The short-term impact, particularly for newer buildings, may be slight; however, the long-range effects can be disastrous. For example trends toward declining maintenance in the Greater Boston area sample compound problems in that city's many old rent-controlled buildings.

### *Capital Value*

The value of an income-producing property is substantially related to its income potential. When this potential is eroded by controlled rents and subsequent deterioration in physical conditions, the consequence is reduced capital value. Not only does the profit level decline, but the capitalization rate or gross rent multiplier—a commonly used measure for defining capital value—is also reduced. Properties purchased for six to eight times their annual rent roll are frequently sold for four to five times their rent roll under rent controls. In New York City, some rent-controlled properties are being sold at only one to one-and-one-half times the rent roll-providing a buyer can be found.[7] Furthermore, recent surveys of lending institutions indicate a trend toward lower loan-to-value ratios.[8] In the Boston area, for example, loan-to-value ratios for rent-controlled buildings are estimated at levels significantly lower than for noncontrolled buildings.[9] There the noncontrolled building loan-to-value estimates ranged from 70 to 80 percent while the rent controlled building estimates, on the other hand, ranged from 50 to 70 percent with the greatest number at the 60 percent level. Bankers indicate that they face high risks in lending under rent control because of the failure of present rent administration in providing for the recovery of expenses.

The significance of the loan-to-value ratios must be considered in terms of the larger community. On the surface, a loan-to-value ratio of 60 percent on rent-controlled properties versus 80 percent on noncontrolled may seem to be a relatively small gap; its significance, however, is evident when the loan-to-value ratio is examined in terms of the investment required to close a transaction. In the rent control situation, given equivalent property values, it takes twice as much cash to buy the rent-controlled structure than it does the noncontrolled structure. In other words, one can buy two noncontrolled buildings for the cash required for one rent-controlled structure. Under these conditions, little imagination is needed to see that enormous erosion takes place in the values of the rent-controlled properties. Again, as stated before, this problem is of significance not merely to the owners of these properties, but also to the community at large. Reduced property values result in an ever-increasing stream of tax abatement appeals which, in turn, erode the community tax base and that of the state as a whole.

### *The Community Tax Base*

The impact of rent control on the community tax base is the most crucial yet often the least understood issue in the rent control controversy. The fact that property tax is the principal source of municipal revenues needs no elaboration. In light of rising demand for and costs of municipal services, the communities' ability to secure additional revenues from their ratable stock is crucial. Because the capital value of a rental property is determined by its income-producing potential, the flow of taxes from such a structure is dependent upon the income generated by it and the value placed on this income. When the income derived from rent-controlled property is reduced, sooner or later the tax base will decline.

If real estate tax expenditures in a given locality represent, on the average, 20 percent of rental income, then for every dollar lost in lowered rents, the community foregoes 20 cents in collectable real estate taxes. For an apartment valued at $250 per month with a rent control level of $200 per month, the difference in annual rents collected is $600. Of this, the community is foregoing $120 in taxes annually. This revenue gap must be picked up by other taxpayers either through foregone tax reductions or actual tax increases; otherwise municipal services must be reduced. Furthermore, to the degree that state-aid formulas are dependent upon the ratable base of a local community, the state subsidizes the dollar gap between free market values and the actual controlled market.

The ultimate impact of rent control on the assessment base of local communities and capital values in the state can be a significant reduction in revenues, and quite possibly, significant deficits. If these negative effects are to be avoided, rent control programs must be based upon an accurate index of building operating costs and sound and reasonable formulas for measuring rent adjustments.

## *NOTES*

1. Alfred A. Ring, *The Valuation of Real Estate* (Englewood Cliffs, N.J.: Prentice-Hall, Inc. 1962), pp. 212-213.
2. The rent control sample consists of seventy structures (or multiple structure developments) containing 4,834 units and the noncontrolled sample consists of twenty structures with 3,898 units. The noncontrolled sample is derived from adjacent communities in the Boston area not subject to rent regulation. See Appendix for specific detail on methodology.
3. As obtained from Public Service Electric and Gas Company, the last approved rate increase during the study period by the Public Utilities Commission was September 23, 1974 subsequent to an increase January 7, 1974—resulting in a 4.5 percent basic minimum rate over the nine-month period. Monthly fuel adjustment charges, however, comprise an approximate additional 10 percent of the total bill as a result of an automatic "fuel adjustment clause" granted by the PUC to reflect current fuel costs.
4. At the time of the original study, 1974 operating cost estimates were made (on the basis of a price index prepared as a part of the study). A 49.5 percent increase in fuel costs and an overall increase in total expenses (excluding real estate expenditures) of 21.28 percent for highrise buildings and 24.38 percent for lowrise and other buildings in the rent-controlled sample were projected.
5. In complaince with the statutory provisions of the Rent Stabilization Law, New York City and the Rent Stabilization Association have contracted with the Middle Atlantic Regional Office of the Bureau of Labor Statistics to provide an annual review of monitoring of changes in operating costs directly applicable to rent-stabilized properties.
6. Robert Samuelsen, "How Well Does the Consumer Price Index Measure the Inflated Prices We Pay for Dog Food and Doctors, Parking Lots and Paperbacks?" *New York Times Magazine,* December 8, 1974, p. 35.
7. Frank S. Kristof, "Rent Control Within the Rental Housing Parameters of 1975" (Paper presented at meeting of the American Real Estate and Urban Economics Association, Washington, D.C., May 30, 1975), p. 11.
8. As part of the studies conducted in the Greater Boston area and Fort Lee, major New Jersey lending institutions were surveyed to ascertain their attitudes and operating policies relative to financing/refinancing rent-controlled properties. George Sternlieb et al., *The Realities of Rent Control in the Greater Boston Area; Rent Control in Fort Lee, New Jersey* (New Brunswick: Rutgers University, Center for Urban Policy Research, 1975).
9. Sternlieb, et al.

# Chapter 6
# The Potential for Equity and the Realities of Rent Control Administration

The specific impact of rent control depends upon the adequacy of the enabling legislation as well as its administration. The substantive provisions of currently enacted rent control legislation have been discussed in chapter 4. In this section, the administrative mechanisms vis-a-vis the realities of implementing rent control will be examined. The empirical data presented is derived from the previously cited studies undertaken in Fort Lee, New Jersey, New York City, and the Greater Boston Area. Description of those studies and the methodology used to derive the data is presented in Appendix III. Appendix IV contains a representative sample of the types of forms necessitated by these administrative mechanisms. The three case studies represent the range of current rent adjustment mechanisms, from complex to simple, and reflect the possibilities for achieving equity in the implementation of rent control.

## *THE GREATER BOSTON AREA CASE STUDY*

The communities of Boston, Brookline, Cambridge, and Somerville, Massachusetts have adopted local rent control ordinances under the authority of state enabling legislation passed in 1970 (see chapter 3). The Massachusetts enabling legislation provides for a rent adjustment formula by statutorily requiring that rents be established to yield a fair net operating income. The variations in formulas possible under this approach were briefly described in chapter 4 and are reflected in the approaches used by the several communities in the following analysis. In order to investigate all of these adequately, the case study of the Greater Boston area has been divided into separate sections.

Descriptions of the formal adjustment procedures in each of the communities is included in Appendix I. Also included in this appendix is a description of capital improvement procedures.

The first portion of this section is based upon a probability sampling of the total files of the several rent boards to which access was permitted.[1] The latter portions are based upon official reports of the several communities.

Although the following points were discussed in chapter 4 in general, they warrant reiteration and further discussion here as they constitute an appropriate framework for the following analyses:

1. How well do the increases permitted under the law in the several communities match the realities of operations? Is there a gap between nominal legislation and real experience?
2. Have any of the communities made significant efforts to realistically appraise costs?
3. Are the administrative requirements which must be observed in order to secure increases, matters of right or rather do they involve significant effort and lag time?
4. Are the requirements for securing these increases so onerous and formalized in terms of bookkeeping expense, statement recording, and so forth, as to mean that only large-scale owners can afford the level of detailing, of technical aid, and the like which would make even those increases which are available truly achievable?

This last point requires some elaboration. Enabling statutes which burden the applicant with high costs and numerous procedures are far from equitable. For example, if the owner of a six-family building is required to maintain audited operating statements, to detail all of his bills and to fill-out application forms of great detail and complexity in order to secure even small increases, he will bear proportionately greater costs for fulfilling these requirements than will larger scale operators. The latter can offset the costs of such procedures over a large number of units. When increase formulas are applied on an across-the-board basis they become relatively available to all. When, on the other hand, they require specific application, this is much less the case.

In order for the reader to determine how well the several rent control communities are maintaining equity in this regard, we have indicated, wherever possible, not merely the level of rent increase but also the number and structural type of units. The number of units granted rent increases in the several communities is shown in Exhibit 6-1. But what is the distribution of this unit structure class and by size of increase? And what does this tell us of the market?

*EXHIBIT 6-1*
*NUMBER OF UNITS GRANTED RENT INCREASES[a] IN SELECTED MASSACHUSETTS COMMUNITIES, 1971-1974*

| | *Boston* | *Brookline* | *Cambridge* |
|---|---|---|---|
| 1971 | – | 1,350 | – |
| 1972 | – | 1,290 | – |
| 1973 | 11,000 | 930 | 2,456 |
| 1974 | 9,500 | 1,640 | 1,656[b] |

a. Estimates by the rent control boards.

b. Cambridge Rent Control Board has estimated to June 1974 which was here doubled for an annual projection.

*Rent Adjustment Mechanisms*

The sampling procedure utilized in each of the communities to secure insight into the realities of the adjustment mechanism is described in Appendix III. The emphasis here is on the realities not merely as they are stated in the enabling or formal legislation, but in terms of their implementation. The public interest demands the determination of not merely how many adjustments are made but also who secures adjustment, for how much, and how long does it take them to do so. Unfortunately, since there is no standardization of reporting requirements under the law, the data maintained by the several rent boards varies substantially in terms of detail. The material which follows is based upon:

1. The total number of units applying for or securing rent increases. This data was secured from the individual rent boards.
2. The total number of units applying for increases is examined in light of 1970 census data to secure a picture of the total universe of buildings by size and apartment number.
3. A formula approach is used to determine the proportion of total units which normally should be under rent control. This data was checked for accuracy with the individual rent boards.

Boston

The following data represent all adjustments, general as well as individual, which have occurred in Boston under Chapter 842. At the inception of rent control under Chapter 842 on January 1, 1973, the rents of all units (with the exception of those units which had received an increase under the old Chapter 11 and those units petitioning for an increase between June 1972 and January 1, 1973) were rolled-back to the June 1972 levels. At a public hearing on February 28, 1973, a general adjustment was granted for economic hardships suffered by landlords as a result of the rollback. In order to obtain this general adjustment, the landlord was required to petition the rent control board. All other increases have been granted on a case by case basis and necessitate the filing of a petition. *Both* the individual and general adjustment petitions and the results of those petitions are reflected in the samples taken from the docket book.

Exhibits 6-2 and 6-3 illustrate the distribution of increases for Boston in 1973 and 1974. By utilizing our sampling procedures,[2] we have been able to present the data according to the scale of the structure receiving the increase. The top row of data (#1) indicates the levels of increase in rents which were granted. In general, there is indication that the one-to-four unit buildings were treated somewhat more generously than the larger structures. Increases for all buildings which received adjustments averaged 7.8 percent in 1973 and 7.2

*EXHIBIT 6-2*
*RENT INCREASES BY BUILDING CONFIGURATION GRANTED BY BOSTON RENT CONTROL ADMINISTRATION*
*1973*

| *Building Configuration by Units in Structure* | *20+* | *5-19* | *1-4* | *All* |
|---|---|---|---|---|
| Row 1<br>Percent Increase Granted | 4.8 | 5.1 | 11.5 | 7.8 |
| Row 2<br>Number of Structures in Sample Receiving an Increase | 12 | 41 | 39 | 92 |
| Row 3<br>Number of Units in Sample Receiving an Increase | 507 | 398 | 114 | 1,019 |
| Row 4<br>Percent of All Units in Sample Receiving an Increase | 49.75 | 39.06 | 11.19 | 100 |
| Row 5<br>Total Units in City Receiving Increase (Total Adjusted x Row 4) | 5,472 | 4,297 | 1,231 | 11,000 |
| Row 6<br>Percent of Total Registered Units Receiving Adjustment | 41.98 | 8.10 | 2.34 | 9.26 |
| Total Registered Units by Type | 13,034 | 53,060 | 52,656 | 118,750 |

*Source:* CUPR analysis of rent control agency files.

*EXHIBIT 6-3*
*RENT INCREASES BY BUILDING CONFIGURATION GRANTED BY BOSTON RENT CONTROL ADMINISTRATION*
*1974*

| *Building Configuration by Units in Structure* | *20+* | *5-19* | *1-4* | *All* |
|---|---|---|---|---|
| Row 1 | | | | |
| Percent Increase Granted | 6.9 | 5.9 | 8.7 | 7.2 |
| Row 2 | | | | |
| Number of Structures in Sample Receiving an Increase | 9 | 45 | 42 | 96 |
| Row 3 | | | | |
| Number of Units in Sample Receiving an Increase | 262 | 449 | 131 | 842 |
| Row 4 | | | | |
| Percent of All Units Receiving an Increase | 31.12 | 53.33 | 15.56 | 100 |
| Row 5 | | | | |
| Total Units in City Receiving Increase (Total Adjusted x Row 4) | 2,956 | 5,066 | 1,478 | 9,500 |
| Row 6 | | | | |
| Percent of Total Registered Units Receiving Adjustment | 22.68 | 9.56 | 2.81 | 8.00 |
| Total Registered Units by Type | 13,034 | 53,060 | 52,656 | 118,750 |

*Source:* CUPR analysis of rent control agency files.

percent in 1974. *However, this does not indicate that all or even a substantial portion of the rent-controlled housing stock secured an increase. The next two rows in the two exhibits detail sampling results.* "Number of Structures in Sample Receiving an Increase" (#2) presents data in terms of the size of structure. For "Number of Apartment Units in the Sample Receiving an Increase" (#3), data was secured for the actual size of each of the structures and simply multiplied the number of units by the number of structures. Row 4 in the exhibits shows the percent of all units in each size category that received increases. This percentage was multiplied by the total of all units that received an increase for the year under consideration and then prorated by the size category of structure to obtain the data for Row 5. Row 6 represents estimates of the percent of total registered units which received adjustment.

Taken as a whole the significance of the data in exhibits 6-2 and 6-3 may be summarized as follows:

1. *The levels of rent increases that were granted are relatively modest.* Certainly the 1974 average for all increases granted is far below the levels of operating cost increases.
2. *The proportion of all units which actually received increases is quite small.* In 1973, it was less than 10 percent (9.3 percent) of the total registered units which received any registered increase; while in 1974, the year of great inflationary pressures, the proportion actually declined to 8 percent. Thus, only one out of ten buildings in 1973 and one out of twelve buildings in 1974 received an increase.
3. *There is substantial indication that in Boston, the smaller the building the less its capacity to meet the costs of fulfilling rent board requirements for securing increases.* This is evident in Row 6 which indicates the proportion of structures of various size categories which received a posted increment. This pattern is repeated in the next case study of Cambridge.

## Cambridge

The Cambridge data presented here represents all increases except a 1.15 percent general adjustment made in 1973. According to the Cambridge Rent Control Board this adjustment was applied across-the-board to 100 percent of all rent control units. The general adjustment did not require any response from landlords such as the filing of a special form or petition. Instead, the rent board sent notices to all landlords informing them of their right to increase rents by 1.15 percent, and then adjusted the maximum rent levels recorded in the files. There were no other general adjustments during the 1973-1974 sample years. All other increases were the result of individual decisions based on landlord petitions.

The Cambridge Rent Control Board reports that 2,456 units received increase adjustments in 1973 (see Exhibit 6-4). This compares reasonably well with the projected total based on the CUPR sampling procedure of 2,790 units. The sample size is quite small, however, and the data should be interpreted with that fact in mind. In general, the results support the conclusions obtained from examining the Boston data. Large buildings fare better in terms of the number of increases granted; smaller buildings get fewer increases but these are proportionately larger increments when they are granted.

In 1973, less than one in eight of the city's registered units received any increase whatsoever. Unfortunately, the Cambridge Rent Control Board was able to provide 1974 data only through the month of June. For this reason an equivalent exhibit for that year is not presented. As of the end of June 1974, however, a similarly small proportion of the total controlled housing stock in the city had secured increases.

### Brookline

The basic pattern of increases granted in Brookline is quite similar to that of the other cities considered here. However, since rent control has been in effect in Brookline longer than in the other sample cities, the data for Brookline is presented from 1971 through 1974 in a composite exhibit (see Exhibit 6-5).

The data in Exhibit 6-5 indicate all individual adjustments which occurred in Brookline since the imposition of rent control. There were two additional general adjustments in 1972 and 1973 which were applied across-the-board. The 1972 adjustment was for 2.94 percent; the 1973 adjustment was for 1.2 percent. An additional 1.8 percent was granted to all owners who did not apply for an increase within the year prior to September, 1973. The full 3 percent increase was granted to 89.5 percent of all units while the remaining 1,120 units received the 1.2 percent increase. According to the Brookline Rent Control Board, 100 percent of all registered units received the 1972 increase of 2.94 percent. There were no general adjustments in 1974.

In examining the Brookline data, it is apparent that less than half of the total rent-controlled units have been granted increases. This conclusion does not allow for the possibility that the same units may be represented more than once in the Brookline files. Still, there is every indication that more than half the units in Brookline are being maintained with a maximum increase of perhaps 8 percent for the cumulative 1972-1974 period.

### *Time Lags In The Granting Of Rent Adjustment*

Administrative procedures must not merely be equitable, they must be efficient and carried out within a reasonable time period. If rent adjustments are

*EXHIBIT 6-4*
*RENT INCREASES BY BUILDING CONFIGURATION GRANTED BY CAMBRIDGE RENT CONTROL BOARD*
*1973*

| *Building Configuration by Units in Structure* | *20+* | *5-19* | *1-4* | *All* |
|---|---|---|---|---|
| Row 1 | | | | |
| Percent Increase Granted | 16.5 | 33.8 | 34.1 | 32.5 |
| Row 2 | | | | |
| Number of Structures in Sample Receiving an Increase | 7 | 17 | 24 | 48 |
| Row 3 | | | | |
| Number of Units in Sample Receiving an Increase | 352 | 140 | 66 | 558 |
| Row 4 | | | | |
| Percent of All Units in Sample Receiving an Increase | 63.08 | 25.09 | 11.83 | 100 |
| Row 5 | | | | |
| Total Units in City Receiving Increase (Total Adjusted x Row 4) | 1,549 | 616 | 291 | 2,456 |
| Row 6 | | | | |
| Percent of Total Registered Units Receiving Adjustment | 19.56 | 6.84 | 8.31 | 12.03 |
| Total Registered Units by Type | 7,918 | 9,004 | 3,502 | 20,424 |

*Source:* CUPR analysis of rent control agency files.

*EXHIBIT 6-5*
*RENT INCREASES BY BUILDING CONFIGURATION GRANTED BY BROOKLINE RENT CONTROL BOARD*
*1971-1974*

| *Building Configuration by Units in Structure* | *20+* | *5-19* | *1-4* | *All* |
|---|---|---|---|---|
| Row 1 | | | | |
| Weighted Average Percent Increase Granted | 7.6 | 7.8 | 9.5 | 8.4 |
| Row 2 | | | | |
| Number of Structures in Sample Receiving an Increase | 10 | 22 | 19 | 51 |
| Row 3 | | | | |
| Number of Units in Sample Receiving an Increase | 295 | 196 | 58 | 549 |
| Row 4 | | | | |
| Percent of All Units Receiving an Increase | 53.7 | 35.7 | 10.6 | 100 |
| Row 5 | | | | |
| Total Units in City Receiving Increase[1] (Total Adjusted x Row 4) | 3,013 | 2,003 | 592 | 5,610 |
| Row 6 | | | | |
| Percent of Total Registered Units Receiving Adjustment | 59.8 | 38.1 | 59.2 | 49.6 |
| Total Registered Units by Type | 5,037 | 5,263 | 1,000 | 11,300 |

1. The total units adjusted figure was derived by multiplying the average units per structure (10.30) from CUPR sample. This figure was confirmed as accurate by the Brookline Rent Control Board.

delayed for any significant period of time, they tend to represent past costs rather than current reality. Indeed, if they are delayed in a time of real emergency, then inequities and losses result.

Three dates are significant in the processing of petitions for adjustment. First, each petition is stampdated at the time of receipt in the rent control office. This date is recorded on the coding sheet. Each petition is then assigned to a hearing officer or examiner. In Cambridge, the officer must schedule a hearing on the petition and notify both tenant and landlord of the date and time. In Boston and Brookline, a hearing is scheduled only if one of the involved parties, landlord or tenant, specifically requests a hearing. The date of the hearing—the second sigiificant date—is then recorded in the files and is also coded. Finally, the hearing officer makes a recommendation for action to the rent board or executive director of the rent control agency. The board reviews the case and makes a final decision, usually accepting the officer's advice. The board executive director is then authorized to send a notification of decision to all parties. The date appearing on this notice is the date of decision.

Computation of average time intervals in the adjustment process was made on the basis of these three dates. The breakdown of the time intervals is as follows:

1. Date of docket entry to date of hearing.
2. Date of hearing to date of decision.
3. The overall adjustment time period, date of docket entry to date of decision.

If one or more dates was not available in the file, the particular time interval involving that date or dates was not calculated. For this reason, the total time interval for the complete process is not the same as the sum for the individual steps.

Exhibit 6-6 places some of the problems of administering rent adjustments in perspective. The total sample of 693 applications includes both landlord- and tenant-initiated petitions. A substantial proportion of the applications lack date of docket, or date of hearing, or date of decision, or a combination of these. This distortion in the data is indicated by the computations at the bottom of the exhibit.

It is evident in Exhibit 6-7 that even those owners who went through the application procedure suffered inordinately long lag times. As recently as 1974, the mean value of the lag between docket entry to date of hearing ran something over two months while the mean date of docket entry to final decision was even longer. For Boston, the mean date of docket entry to final decision was three months, for Brookline 3.7 months and for Cambridge a little less than half a year—5.5 months.

*EXHIBIT 6-6*
*DATING PROCEDURES–ALL RENT ADJUSTMENT PETITIONS SAMPLED–BOTH LANDLORD AND TENANT*[1]
*GREATER BOSTON AREA*

| | *Date of Docket Data* | *Date of Hearing Data* | *Date of Decision Data* |
|---|---|---|---|
| Total Petitions | 693 | 693 | 193 |
| Date Not Shown | 76 | 84 | 81 |
| No Hearing | – | 244 | – |
| No Decision (In Process or Withdrawn) | – | – | 152 |
| With Date | 617 | 365 | 460 |

| | *Expected Range* | *Actual* |
|---|---|---|
| Number of Petitions with Docket to Hearing Dates | 289-365 | 312 |
| Number of Petitions with Hearing to Decision Dates | 213-365 | 308 |
| Number of Petitions with Docket to Decision Dates | 384-460 | 450 |

*EXAMPLE CALCULATION OF EXPECTED RANGE: DOCKET TO HEARING DATES*

617 Petitions with Docket Dates
365 Petitions with Hearing Dates

Therefore, there is a *maximum of 365* useable petitions. If one assumes that all 76 petitions without docket dates are also missing hearing dates, there is a *minimum of 289* useable petitions (365 - 76 = 289).

1. For sampling procedures and distribution see Appendix III.
*Source:* CUPR analysis of rent control agency files.

*EXHIBIT 6-7*
*AVERAGE TIME INTERVALS IN LANDLORD PETITION RENT ADJUSTMENT PROCESS (IN MONTHS)*
*GREATER BOSTON AREA*

| | *Mean Date of Docket Entry to Date of Hearing* | *Mean Date of Hearing to Date of Final Decision* | *Mean Date of Docket Entry to Date of Final Decision* |
|---|---|---|---|
| 1971 | | | |
| Brookline | 4.7 | 1.4 | 5.4 |
| 1972 | | | |
| Brookline | 9.3 | 1.7 | 10.9 |
| 1973 | | | |
| Boston | 2.6 | 0.7 | 2.4 |
| Brookline | 4.6 | 2.5 | 7.1 |
| Cambridge | 1.8 | 2.3 | 4.1 |
| 1974 | | | |
| Boston | 2.3 | 1.5 | 3.0 |
| Brookline | 2.5 | 1.6 | 3.7 |
| Cambridge | 2.2 | 3.4 | 5.5 |

Note: The mean value of entry to hearing lag plus the equivalent lag between the latter and final decision do not add because of changes in the base. See previous exhibit.

*Source:* CUPR analysis of rent control agency files.

This kind of administrative procedural lag cannot be tolerated if real relief and equity are to be preserved within the meaning of the law. The price of administrative lag, especially in times of inflation, may well be the permanent loss of a building. By the time an increase is secured, costs may have already increased to the point that another increase is necessary—creating a cycle in which the securement of increases always lags behind the actual cost realities. Administrative lag time may well be the final economic straw for owners of small structures who lack sufficient capital reserves to compensate for the gap between income and costs. Eventually, their losses become losses for the community and the state as the capital value of the housing stock is reduced.

### *General Adjustments*

A general adjustment is an across-the-board increase applicable to all registered rent-controlled units in a community. A general adjustment may occur in one of two ways. The first type of general adjustment is a flat percentage increase based on a community or statewide operating component such as taxes. If, for example, the tax rate in the community is increased by 5 percent a year, the flat percentage adjustment provides for a parallel increase of 5 percent in all rents. The second type of general adjustment is the dollar for dollar pass-through of the increase in a specific operating component. The most current application of the dollar for dollar pass-through is best illustrated by the increase in the cost of heating fuel. Despite the fact that there has been a generally acknowledged rapid increase in the price of heating oil, the effects of this increase may vary widely among individual buildings. Thus, it may be inequitable to grant a flat across-the-board increase to all owners for this would prove to be insignificant for some and a bonus for others. The dollar for dollar pass-through provides the landlord with an opportunity to document the cost increase he has experienced for a particular operating component. He may then be permitted to increase his rent levels to compensate for the documented increase in the specific operating component. Virtually all the general adjustments in the four sample rent-controlled communities have been formulated if not implemented through one of these two techniques.

The following section is an enumeration of general adjustments which have been granted in each of the four sample communities.

#### Cambridge

To date there have been two general adjustments in Cambridge. The initial adjustment was designed to return rent levels in the city to the 1967 rates which, based upon statistical study, were presumed to be fair. To the 1967 rents a 30 percent across-the-board increase was granted to mitigate the increase in the cost of operation between September 1, 1967 and October, 1972. This, in effect, became the first general adjustment in the city of Cambridge. Landlords were required to present notarized copies either of their rent ledgers or tax filings to document the September 1, 1967 rent levels. The eventual registration date was established as November 24, 1972. Thus, for landlords whose rents were in excess of the 130 percent increment over the 1967 levels, the adjustment could effectively decrease rental levels.

The second general adjustment in Cambridge is an example of an across-the-board increase associated with a citywide increase in the tax rate. This became effective on January 1, 1974 as a result of an increase in the 1973 tax rate. The amount of the increase was 1.15 percent. The average rent increases resulting from these general adjustments and the participation in the increase is enumerated in Exhibit 6-8.

The city approved an additional general adjustment effective March 1, 1975. This increase was in the form of a modified dollar for dollar pass-through estimated to total 10 to 15 percent, depending on the expense increases documented by individual landlords. The operating cost components included within the adjustment are taxes—$1.50 for each $1.00 increase, approximately 7 percent—and a cost of living increase of 3.1 percent. As part of the adjustment, on April 1, 1975 a dollar for dollar pass-through of 3.5 to 5 percent was granted, based on expenses documented by landlords.

### Brookline

There have been three general adjustments in Brookline since rent control under the provision of Chapter 843 became effective September 29, 1970.

The Brookline Rent Control Board adopted Rent Control Regulation number 13 on July 19, 1971. The regulation was designed to provide a adjustment of rent levels of January 1, 1968 and thereby alleviate hardships caused by the initial rent rollback. The effective date for the implementation of the regulation was August 1, 1971. The implementation of the adjustment was a relatively complex procedure designed to achieve a degree of standardization of rental levels within the community.

There were basically four steps involved in determining the precise rental increase permitted by the general adjustment. The rents of January 1, 1968 were compared with the base rents of March 1970. Based upon a statistical analysis, it was determined that the rents for August 1971 should be 25 percent above those of January 1, 1968. Once the actual rent increases that had occurred prior to March 1970 were determined, it was possible to calculate the increase needed to reach a level of 25 percent above the January 1, 1968 rents. If, for example, it was determined that an individual rent had increased by 17 percent between

*EXHIBIT 6-8*
*STATISTICAL SUMMARY OF UNITS RECEIVING A GENERAL ADJUSTMENT IN CAMBRIDGE*

| *Year* | *Units Registered* | *Units Receiving General Adjustment* | *Average Adjustment* | *Units Receiving Individual Adjustment* |
|---|---|---|---|---|
| 1970 | 18,086 | 0 | 0 | 0 |
| 1971 | 18,086 | 0 | 0 | 4,564 |
| 1972 | 18,086 | 10,788 | 13.18% | 0 |
| 1973 | 20,424 | 17,100 | 1.15% | 2,456 |

*STATISTICAL SUMMARY OF UNITS RECEIVING AN INDIVIDUAL ADJUSTMENT IN CAMBRIDGE*

| *Year* | *Average Individual Adjustment* | *Number of Units Receiving an Adjustment* |
|---|---|---|
| 1970 | Not Available | Not Available |
| 1971[1] | 26.32% | 1,150 |
| 1972[1] | 0 | 0 |
| 1973 | 14.18% | 537 |

1. See Appendix I for details of 1971 and 1972 adjustments.
*Source:* Cambridge Rent Control Board, March 1974.

January 1, 1968 and March 1970, the owner was granted an additional adjustment of 8 percent to achieve the 25 percent increase. This second step was, however, conditioned by the fact that the Rent Control Board would allow no increases greater than 15 percent. Thus, if the rent levels had increased by less than 10 percent during the period between January 1, 1968 and March 1970, the owner would, in effect, be denied the full rent increase of 25 percent above the January 1, 1968 level. The inequities were obvious and the Rent Control Board remedied the situation by allowing an increase equal to the difference between the 15% limited increase and the 25 percent effective January 1, 1972. The fourth step involved those landlords who had received a hearing prior to August 1, 1971. These individuals were granted an additional 3 percent increase over and above that which the board had already granted through individual adjustment.

The following chart indicates the distribution of units with respect to the 1971 general adjustment.

| *Category* | *Number of Units* |
|---|---|
| Class I | 6,190 |
| Class II | 916 |
| Class III | 2,805 |

*Source*: Brookline Rent Control Board. Data are inconsistent, though secured from the same source. The basic proportions and scale, however, are evident.

Class I includes all units receiving an adjustment to bring rent levels up to 25 percent above the January 1, 1968 level and units receiving the 15 percent maximum adjustment. Class II refers to units which received no adjustment. And Class III includes units which had not filed the required information by the initial deadline. Thus, of a total of 10,432 units, 6,190 received an adjustment as a result of the August 1, 1971 general adjustment.

The second general adjustment, Rent Control Regulation number 14, was approved by the Rent Control Board on June 6, 1972. It was far less complex than the initial adjustment, was prompted by an increase in the tax rate and in effect, amounted to a dollar for dollar pass-through of the tax increase. The adjustment was applicable to 10,047 units in 1,007 buildings; the average increase in rents as a result of the adjustment was 2.94 percent.

The last general adjustment of the study-period, Rent Control Regulation number 17, was adopted by the Rent Control Board on June 12, 1973 and became effective September 1, 1973. It was a flat 3 percent increase composed of two parts. The first part, a 1.2 percent increase, was essentially a dollar for dollar pass-through of a citywide tax increase and was available to all landlords. The second component of the 3 percent total was intended to offset increases in operating costs and amounted to 1.8 percent. The latter increase was conditioned: if an owner had petitioned for and received an individual increase during the period from September 1, 1972 through September 1, 1973, he was not permitted the 1.8 percent increase in operating expenses. He was, however, still eligible for the 1.2 percent increase offsetting the tax increase.

In June 1974, the Rent Control Board voted not to authorize a general adjustment for the year 1974, resulting in an increase in landlord petitions for individual adjustment. As a result of the petition increase, the board ceased to perform some of its ancillary functions, including the advisory opinion procedure for capital improvements.

### Somerville

There has been a total of six general adjustments within the city of Somerville since the adoption of rent control on December 1, 1970 under the provisions of Chapter 842. Three of these have been as a direct result of tax increases, one as a result of a tax decrease, and one as a result of an increase in the cost of heating fuel. The last and perhaps most important adjustment was an attempt to equalize the effects of previous increases as well as the tremendous rise in the cost of heating fuel during the 1973-1974 winter.

The first increase was adopted in February 1971 and became effective on March 31, 1971. This was an across-the-board increase of 7 percent based on the increase in taxes in 1970; taxes in Somerville rose by 17 percent from 1969 to 1970. The increase was applied to the rolled-back rents of June 1970 for those landlords who registered with the rent control board by March 31, 1971. The second general adjustment was also based on taxes and was originally adopted in February 1972. It amounted to an increase of 2 percent and, after some delay, became effective May 1, 1972; taxes increased 1.4 percent from 1970 to 1971. The third general adjustment was not a flat percentage increase, rather it was a dollar for dollar pass-through based on the tax increase which occurred in 1972.

When this final pass-through adjustment was implemented, it resulted in adjustments amounting to only 1 to 2 percent increases; the administrative procedure necessary to comply with the terms of the adjustment made the adjustment hardly worth seeking. For example, the general adjustment of January 1973 amounted to 1 percent. In January 1974, due to a tax decrease the previous year, the Rent Control Board granted an adjustment downward to those buildings in which tenants had petitioned for the adjustment. This also was administered in the form of a dollar for dollar pass-through and amounted to a 2 percent decrease in rents.

As a result of public hearings in February 1974, the board granted a general adjustment designed to alleviate the hardships caused by the increase in the cost of heating fuel. This too was administered in the form of a dollar-for-dollar pass-through. It became effective April 1, 1974 and amounted to a 5 to 7 percent increase, depending on the fuel cost increases experienced between the periods October 1972 through March 1973 and October 1973 through March 1974. This adjustment was intended as a temporary rent surcharge to be removed the subsequent year. Instead, however, it became permanent and was increased above its initial level. The increase became effective January 1, 1975 and amounted to a 20 percent increase on all unheated units and a 30 percent increase on all heated units, as calculated from the base rent levels of June 1970. The general adjustment would appear to be an admission on the part of the board that the dollar-for-dollar pass-through was not working as intended, causing its return to the technique of the flat percentage adjustment. The adjustment will have varying effects upon landlords and tenants dependent upon the level of adjustments which have occurred on any given building prior to this most recent adjustment. According to the Somerville Rent Control Board, the previous adjustments averaged to about a 10 percent increase over the base year rents. Therefore, the January 1975 adjustment amounts to roughly a 10 to 20 percent increase over current rent levels.

Boston

There has been only one general adjustment in the city of Boston since the city adopted rent control under chapter 842 on December 1, 1972. As of January 1, 1973 the rents were rolled back to the level of June 1972. The rollback, however, did not apply to those units which had petitioned for and received rent increases (under Chapter 11) between the rollback date, June 1972, and January 1973, the effective date for chapter 842. In order to alleviate the hardships resulting from the initial rollback, it was determined on the basis of a public hearing of February 28, 1973, that a general adjustment was warranted for all units for which rents had been rolled back. Thus, the adjustment was available to all rental units subject to chapter 842 with the exception of those receiving an adjustment within the previously stated time period. It was granted as a matter of course to all who applied. The extent of the adjustment varied with the type of apartment. The maximum rents were adjusted upwards by the lesser of the following amounts: (1) 4.5 percent, rounded to the nearest dollar; or (2) the percentage necessary to establish maximum rents at the December 1972 level.

According to the Boston Rent Control Board, virtually all "luxury units," which were previously exempt from controls under Chapter 10 were permitted the 4.5 percent adjustment. A "luxury unit" included by definition all studio apartments for which rents were in excess of $160 per month, one-bedroom apartments renting in excess of $185 per month, two-bedroom apartments renting in excess of $235 per month, and three-bedroom apartments renting for more than $285 per month. The precise number of units receiving the adjustment is not available according to the Boston Rent Control Board; the board was also unable to provide information as to the average increases resulting from adjustment.

## *THE FORT LEE, NEW JERSEY CASE STUDY*

Rent control in Fort Lee has had a brief, albeit turbulent history. The requirements and regulations relating to the administration of rent control in Fort Lee have often been obscured by the controversy accompanying rent control imposition. Although an ordinance was passed in River Edge, New Jersey two weeks prior to Fort Lee's, Fort Lee is considered the birthplace of second generation rent controls in New Jersey because the impetus for subsequent ordinances emanated from Fort Lee and most New Jersey ordinances were modelled after its. The landmark second generation rent control case in New Jersey which upheld local rent control in the absence of state enabling legislation is *Inganamort v. Borough of Fort Lee*; both the Fort Lee and River Edge ordinances were challenged in this suit. After the State Supreme Court decision in 1973 temporary restraints were lifted. However, the extension of the ordinance by resolutions of the local governing body (which expired one-year from its enactment date) was declared invalid in December 1974 on the basis of the procedure used for extension. As a result, rent control imposition was invalid between February 2, 1973 and November 6, 1974, although the Fort Lee Rent Leveling Board functioned during this period.[3] This case study provides a brief description of the components and changes in the rent adjustment mechanism in Fort Lee since its inception in 1972.

### *The Rent Adjustment Mechanism*

The rent adjustment mechanism utilized in Fort Lee is much less complex than that utilized in any of the Massachusetts communities. The scope of the regulatory authority encompassed by the mechanism was described as "intermediate" in chapter 3. The Fort Lee regulatory mechanism is relatively easy to implement, requiring a less formalized system of operation than the Massachusetts mechanisms. A board generally deals with individual building or unit reviews on the basis of tenant complaints or landlord applications under the additional rent increase provisions of the ordinance. The rent adjustment mechanism is a Maximum Base Rent mechanism described in chapter 4. The primary thrust of such adjustment mechanisms is to provide rent increases commensurate with increases in operating costs as measured by the rate of inflation. As opposed to the FNOI mechanisms which limit the return on investment, the Fort Lee rent adjustment formula provides for automatic increases applied on an across-the-board basis.

Fort Lee first enacted rent control legislation in February 1972. Ordinance 72-1 was specifically designed to limit rent increases by establishing that no landlord could request or receive a percentage increase in rent greater than the percentage difference between: (1) the Consumer Price Index sixty days prior to the expiration or termination of the lease; and (2) the Consumer Price Index at the date the lease was entered into by the tenant. An amending ordinance was subsequently attached to Ordinance 72-1 (73-26, July 1973) increasing the stated time period from sixty to ninety days. These restrictions were applicable to all units occupied February 1972 and newly constructed units after the initial rent-up of the unit. Rents in newly constructed units are determined by the landlord.

As a primary result of substantial increases in the Consumer Price Index during late 1973 and early 1974, an amending ordinance was passed in May 1974 limiting the annual rent adjustment to 2.5 percent in any one year. The adoption of the 2.5 percent limit did not invalidate the previous provision but simply placed a limit on the use of the CPI in determining rent increases. In essence, an increase in the CPI below the 2.5 percent restriction would serve as the upper limit to which rents could be adjusted.

Imposition of the 2.5 percent rent adjustment ceiling inevitably provoked a legal challenge. The 2.5 percent limit was upheld although the decision is now being appealed. The decision held that Fort Lee's 2.5 percent standard is not invalid "*per se*".[4] The judge in extrapolating from the 1973 New Jersey Supreme Court decision (*Inganamort v. Borough of Fort Lee*) concluded

> that once the legislature confers an untethered grant of power, the judiciary may not thereafter insist on a particular technique for implementation. No mandate is contained which requires a fluctuating or graduated method. Rent levelling is within the untethered legislative domain . . . delegated via the police power.[5]

The established principles of judicial review, discussed in chapter 3, precluded a determination by the court as to the wisdom of the 2.5 percent ceiling, although plaintiffs argued that its imposition would have a severe adverse impact not only on the owners but on the community at large. The court did note, however, that "while it is obvious that Fort Lee landlords will suffer financially, . . . whether the particular method of rent control selected by a municipality is wise or unwise raises a question which is not our concern."[6]

The most recent (December 1975) New Jersey Supreme Court decision upheld the municipal ordinances of four communities with varying formulas and confirmed the facial validity of the rent adjustment formulas; however, it required that all ordinances provide an owner the opportunity to appeal on grounds that he is not receiving a fair and reasonable return.[7]

### *Additional Rent Increase Provisions*

In addition to the 2.5 percent annual rent adjustment now utilized the ordinance includes provisions for additional rent increase allowances for real estate tax increases, capital improvements and hardship. The real estate tax and capital improvements allowances are designated as surcharges, and thus are not included in the base rent from which annual adjustments are made.

#### Tax Surcharge

An increase in the municipal property tax means that a landlord may apply for a tax surcharge. A tax increase is not considered a component in computing annual allowable increases in rent. The surcharge is levied on each tenant in proportion to the number of square feet in the dwelling unit and was paid in the form of six monthly payments commencing July 1 of each year. In the event that the tax rate drops or the assessed valuation of an owner's structure is lowered through a successful tax appeal, the landlord must return to the tenant 50 percent of the reduction minus expenses incurred in the litigation of the appeal.

Though this method appears relatively simple, the administrative requirements necessary to its implementation are complex. In seeking a tax surcharge an owner must provide each tenant: the requested increase calculations prorated by square feet, the property tax for the unit for the previous year, the tax increase per square foot, and the number of square feet occupied by the tenant. This information must be sent to the tenant by certified mail. In a revised version of the ordinance adopted in November 1974 the provision governing the payment of the tax surcharge was deleted and replaced by a provision allowing for payment over a 3 month period if the surcharge exceeded $50 for any tenant.

It is obvious that the costs of such an administrative exercise, particularly for an owner with a large number of tenants, may well be prohibitive; he may try to absorb the tax increase rather than apply for a surcharge.

#### Capital Improvement Surcharge

Similar to the tax surcharge, the surcharge allowed for capital improvement is distinct from the annual allowable rental increases. The requirements for applying for an increase due to capital improvements include notifying each tenant by certified mail of the following: the total cost of the completed capital improvement or service; the number of years of useful life of the capital improvement determined by IRS depreciation schedules; the average cost of this improvement; the total number of square feet occupied by the tenant; and the capital improvement surcharge to be paid by the tenant. In addition, definitions of "acceptable" capital improvements are made by the rent leveling board; eligibility must be determined before a surcharge will be granted. If the rent increase is allowed, it cannot exceed 15 percent of the tenant's rent.

Subsequent amendments pertaining to capital improvements generally define what constitutes a capital improvement. Section 1(a) of Ordinance 74-32 reads:

> Capital improvements means capital which is expended by the landlord in the nature of an investment, for the improvement of a dwelling made with the expectation of its useful existence for an indefinite period into the future and which will insure in some significant degree to benefit of the tenants thereof.[8]

Furthermore, Ordinance 74-32 places additional administrative requirements upon the building owner. A complete financial disclosure of the landlord's building operation must be filed with the rent leveling board, open to public inspection for a thirty-day period. Finally, a public hearing is required to determine if in fact the improvement does warrant a rent increase under the capital improvement surcharge provision. The application the landlord must submit is included in Appendix IV.

Inadequate guidelines as to what actually constitutes a capital improvement and numerous application requirements deter landlords from applying for capital improvement increases; thus, they do not improve their properties. Representatives of the Fort Lee Rent Leveling Board revealed that only two applications for capital improvements surcharge had been filed between the inception of rent control in 1972 and May 1975.

### Hardship Provision

Like the capital improvement surcharge provision, stipulations governing hardship provisions provide owners with few definitive guidelines and require compliance with stringent regulations including public review of profit and loss statement and public hearings. The application the landlord must submit to the board is also included in Appendix IV. Section 10 of Fort Lee Ordinance 74-32 states that

> upon a finding that a landlord cannot meet his mortgage payments, taxes and current operating expenses on the dwelling, the Rent

> Leveling Board may grant the landlord a specific hardship increase for each unit of housing space in the affected dwelling.[9]

Again, increases are prorated on a square foot basis, and owners must undertake a complex administrative effort in order to take advantage of the provision. The provision quoted above was added to the ordinance in late 1974. However, a subsequent August 1975 amendment (Ordinance 75-45) modified the hardship provision—allowing an owner to file for an increase on the additional ground that he "cannot otherwise earn a fair and reasonable return upon his investment."[10] This last modification of the hardship provision, added before the December 1975 State Supreme Court decision, proved to be in full compliance with the court's ruling. However, more importantly, there is no indication how the board will determine fair and reasonable rate of return.

*Tenant Complaints*

The provisions under the Fort Lee rent leveling ordinance which allow property owners rent increases on the basis of real estate tax increases, capital improvements, or failure to meet debt requirements (hardship) include administrative regulations which make their implementation extremely difficult and, in some cases, possibly prohibitive. However, these provisions constitute a small portion of the overall regulatory mechanism. Because the rent adjustment function is primarily the responsibility of building management, the chief regulatory function of the rent control board is the handling of tenant complaints and grievances. What has been the tenants' reaction to their rent increases? The disposition of tenant complaints provides an insight into the functioning of the rent adjustment mechanism and into the overall compliance of property owners to the regulations.

Exhibit 6-9 shows the actions taken by the rent leveling board on tenant complaints. The complaint form utilized is included in Appendix IV. Tenant complaints usually originate with the levying of a rent increase above the 2.5 percent allowed or a CPI index difference lower than 2.5 percent. Thus a simple review of a specific calculation determines the validity of the complaint. (At the time of this analysis increases were based on the difference of the actual CPI).

As shown in Exhibit 6-9, 298 tenant petitions had been filed in Fort Lee since rent control became operative. Of the total filed, 14.43 percent were ruled in favor of the tenant; 18.46 percent were settled by the mutual parties without a hearing; 15.10 percent were found to have no probable cause; and 23.15 percent were still pending at the time of analysis.

In essence, of an estimated total rent control stock of 9,729 units, only 298 or 3.6 percent of the tenants in these units questioned rent increases. Additionally only 0.44 percent of total rent controlled units were found in violation, that is, were resolved by a ruling in favor of the tenants.

*EXHIBIT 6-9*
*RENT LEVELING BOARD ACTION ON TENANT PETITIONS 1973-1974*
*FORT LEE, NEW JERSEY*

| *Action Taken* | *Number* | *Percent* |
|---|---|---|
| Final Determination | 43 | 14.43 |
| Appeal | 54 | 18.12 |
| Dismissals | 9 | 3.02 |
| Settled w/o hearing | 55 | 18.46 |
| Withdrawals | 15 | 5.03 |
| No Action | 8 | 2.69 |
| No probable cause | 45 | 15.10 |
| Pending | 69 | 23.15 |
| | 298 | 100.00 |

*Source:* CUPR analysis of Fort Lee Rent Leveling Board data.

## *THE NEW YORK CITY CASE STUDY*

From a national perspective New York State's rent control history is unique because New York retained controls in many parts of the state since World War II. However, New York City has had the most active and turbulent role in rent control history. For these reasons, an analysis of currently enacted rent control would be incomplete without a New York City case study. Rent stabilization was instituted in 1969 in New York City and the concept was extended (on a limited basis) to communities in three counties outside of the city in 1974.[11] Rent stabilization constitutes a more liberal system of regulation than that of "standard" rent control which is still in operation for a portion of the New York City housing market (see chapters 1 and 3).

The implementation of rent stabilization in New York City was selected as the third case study for two reasons. First, rent stabilization in New York City represents the example of second generation rent controls (as opposed to the older form of rent control which has existed in New York City since World War II).

Second, is the apparent predisposition of New York's state and city policymakers toward rent stabilization, as evidenced in the gradual phasing-out of "rent control" through the transfer of vacant units to rent stabilization. Of the tripartite administrative structure created by the New York City Rent Stabilization law, the function of the Rent Guidelines Board (RGB) is the focus of this discussion. The RGB, appointed by the mayor, is charged with making the annual determination of rent guidelines. These guidelines are based on data reflecting current economic conditions and include, but are not limited to operating costs, financing costs, and housing supply and demand factors. The annual "Price Index of Operating Costs for Rent Stabilized Apartment Houses in New York City," discussed in chapter 5, is prepared by the U.S. Bureau of Labor Statistics under contract to the city for the express purpose of guideline determination.

Over the builk of the study period, there were three main components of rent guidelines which affected rent increase in the stabilized sector of the New York City housing market. The first and most obvious was the guideline on renewal leases. The second is the so-called stabilizer, a rent increase factor of 1 percent or less by which rents on all stabilized apartments can be increased whether or not a new lease is negotiated. The third component consists of special allowances for rent increases which may be applied to new leases and which are over and above guideline increases on renewal leases or the actual decontrol of rents on new leases for formerly vacant apartments. In the following sections, each of these guidelines will be examined in terms of how well they actually accomplish their purpose–that is, to achieve a stabilized and equitable housing market.

*Rent Guidelines: A Short History*

Guidelines on rent renewals are the most widely publicized component of the rent guidelines process. These guidelines are set largely on the basis of data provided by the Bureau of Labor Statistics (BLS) on increases in the operating costs in the stabilized housing sector. The BLS data referred to here is the operating cost index which was examined in the chapter 5 New York City case study of operating cost growth. In some instances, guidelines have been set as a function of only those cost increases which occurred in the previous year. Guidelines depend on lease term. For rent increases on renewal one-year leases, guidelines have varied since 1968 from 6 to 10 percent for annual rent increases. On renewals of two-year leases, the guidelines have suggested rent increases ranging from 8 to 10.5 percent per year; and for three-year leases, guidelines for increases have ranged from 10 to 15 percent.

The history of guidelines can be organized into three distinct periods. First, during the years 1968 to 1969, before information on changes in operating costs were available, guidelines for rent increases were set at levels which exceeded increases in operating costs by a considerable margin. When operating cost data become available for the 1970 to 1971 guidelines, rent increases were reduced on one-year leases to a fraction of the increase in operating costs. Guidelines for two- and three-year leases were set somewhat higher.

The second period in the history of guidelines began with the extremely rapid growth in costs which occurred in 1971 when operating costs were reported by the Bureau of Labor Statistics to have increased by 13.4 percent. Guideline increases for one-year leases were set at 52 percent of the level of operating cost during 1970, and even rent increases on two- and three-year leases were set below the 1971 level of operating costs. The stringency of the 1971 guidelines was replaced by more generous guidelines in 1972. However, the cumulative impact of the rent increases permitted on one-year leases in both 1971 and 1972 was barely sufficient (13 percent) to match increases in costs which occurred in 1971 alone, and fell far short of cost inflation which occurred in 1971 and 1972 (19 percent). Guidelines in 1973-1974 were set back to rent operating cost ratios quite similar to those of 1970.

The third period in the history of guidelines occurred during 1974 and 1975. The enormous fuel and utility cost increases in 1974 propelled operating costs to increase 19.2 percent (as measured by BLS). Guidelines for 1974 increases on one-year leases amounted to only 44 percent of the increase in operating costs. Even the guidelines for three-year leases amounted to only 63 percent of the operating cost increases which had occurred during 1973. The

## EXHIBIT 6-10
## GUIDELINES FOR PERCENT INCREASES IN RENTS ON LEASE RENEWALS VERSUS GROWTH IN THE BLS INDEX OF OPERATING COSTS DURING THE PREVIOUS YEAR, 1968-1975
## NEW YORK CITY RENT STABILIZED SECTOR

| Term of Lease | Guideline Increase 1975-1976 | | Guideline Increase 1974-1975 | |
|---|---|---|---|---|
| | Percent of Previous Rent | Percent of Growth in Operating Cost Index[a] | Percent of Previous Rent | Percent of Growth in Operating Cost Index[a] |
| 1 year | 7.5 | 115.4 | 8.5 | 44.3 |
| 2 years | 9.5 | 146.2 | 10.5 | 54.7 |
| 3 years | 12.5 | 192.3 | 12.0 | 62.5 |
| | Guideline Increase 1973-1974 | | Guideline Increase 1972-1973 | |
| | Percent of Previous Rent | Percent of Growth in Operating Cost Index[a] | Percent of Previous Rent | Percent of Growth in Operating Cost Index[a] |
| 1 year | 6.5 | 82.3 | 6 | 105.3 |
| 2 years | 8.5 | 107.6 | 8 | 140.4 |
| 3 years | 10.5 | 132.9 | 10 | 175.4 |

*EXHIBIT 6–10 (Continued)*

*GUIDELINES FOR PERCENT INCREASES IN RENTS ON LEASE RENEWALS VERSUS GROWTH IN THE BLS INDEX OF OPERATING COSTS DURING THE PREVIOUS YEAR, 1968-1975 NEW YORK CITY RENT STABILIZED SECTOR*

| *Term of Lease* | *Guideline Increase 1971-1972* | | *Guideline Increase 1970-1971* | |
|---|---|---|---|---|
| | *Percent of Previous Rent* | *Percent of Growth in Operating Cost Index*[a] | *Percent of Previous Rent Cost Index*[a] | *Percent of Growth in Operating* |
| 1 year | 7 | 52.2 | 6 | 71.4 |
| 2 years | 9 | 67.2 | 8 | 95.2 |
| 3 years | 12 | 89.6 | 11 | 131.0 |

| | *Guideline Increase 1969-1970* | | *Guideline Increase 1968-1969* | |
|---|---|---|---|---|
| | *Percent of Previous Rent* | *Percent of Growth in Operating Cost Index*[a] | *Percent of Previous Rent* | *Percent of Growth in Operating Cost Index*[a] |
| 1 year | 10 | 250.0 | 10 | 285.7 |
| 2 years | 10 | 250.0 | 10 | 285.7 |
| 3 years | 15 | 375.0 | 15 | 428.6 |

a. Percent cost increase during previous year, as measured by the U.S. Bureau of Labor Statistics. For a description and history of this index, see U.S., Bureau of Labor Statistics, *1975 Price Index of Operating Costs for Rent Stabilized Apartment Houses in New York City* (New York: BLS, 1975).

1975 guidelines were the most generous granted to property owners since the periods 1968-1969 and 1969-1970. The 1975-1976 guidelines, providing for rent increases of 7.5 percent for one-year lease renewals, amounted to 115 percent of the increase in operating costs of the previous year (as measured by BLS). These guidelines were a deliberate attempt to compensate for the inadequacy of the guidelines in previous years, particularly the guidelines of 1974 in which hardships were vested on owners as a result of 1974 inflation.

The variation in the guidelines over the three periods, relative to the proportion of increases in operating costs, ostensibly reflects a development trend other than the absolute fluctuations in operating costs over the period. That is, a review of the guidelines and their explanatory statements appears to indicate a change in emphasis in the guideline determinations. As initially instituted, the rent stabilization law constituted a means of limiting the rate by which rents increased to market levels in an orderly and predictable manner—thus protecting tenants from large increases at one point in time. This objective must be understood in terms of the development of market conditions during the years preceding enactment of rent stabilization in 1969.[12] A large volume of new construction occurred in New York City in the early 1960s in anticipation of the more restrictive zoning law which was enacted, effective in 1965. This surge of new construction resulted in a relative oversupply of new units for a period of time. However, as demand caught up with supply in the late 1960s, rental rates began to escalate on many of these units which had in some instances been rented at lower than market rates during the period when supply outstripped demand—thus creating a need for a mechanism to limit the progression of rent increases to market levels. Since the initiation of rent stabilization there appears to have been a subtle change in emphasis and objectives—from limiting the pattern of rent increases to "controlling" rents and limiting gross income. Although rent stabilization represents a less stringent form of rent control than other mechanisms, it is as currently constituted, in effect a control mechanism. This evolution, however, appears to be inherent in the general historical cycle of rent regulation in which the pattern of regulation has been to become more restrictive. The completion of the cycle, however, indicates that relaxation of regulations occurs in the process of phasing-out the control mechanism. This historical pattern is further confirmed in the New York City experience as rent stabilization is being used to replace the "rent control" program in the older sector of the housing stock.

Although rent guidelines on lease renewals are the most important element of the guideline process, they are by no means the whole story. In particular, until 1974, additional rent increases were permitted on apartments vacated by previous tenants and reoccupied under a new lease. From 1968 to 1971, these allowances ranged from increases of 7.5 to 25 percent, varying with lease length and from year to year. From 1972 to mid-year 1974, rents on new leases were decontrolled: landlords were permitted to move rents to market levels for the initial lease to a new tenant. Since May 1974 these units have subsequently been subjected to guidelines for lease renewals under the 1974 Emergency Tenant Protection Act which covers previously decontrolled and destabilized units (see chapters 1 and 3).

Finally, since 1970, the "stabilizer" has been permitted to owners of stabilized units. This stabilizer is a limited increase of 1 percent or less in rents charged on all existing, renewed, and new leases. The specific stabilizer is determined by the Rent Guidelines Board. The purpose of the stabilizer is to permit property owners sufficient income to pay the high interest rates currently imposed on mortgage debt. However, the stabilizer does not appear to have closely reflected fluctuation in market interest rates. It stood at 1 percent in 1970 and 1971 and since has been held at 0.5 percent.

### *Rent Guidelines And Gross Rental Income*

Analysis of the simple relationship between rent guidelines and operating cost increases does not, however, provide a comprehensive indication of the impact of the guidelines on rental incomes. Permitted rent increases depend not only on guidelines, but also on lease length (this relationship will be discussed in detail later), the number of leases being renewed or new leases negotiated in a given year, and the relative importance of lease renewal versus new leases and tenant turnover. Therefore, estimates have been made of the combined limits imposed by guidelines on lease renewals and new leases, and of the stabilizer allowance on potential gross rental income in the stabilized sector of the city's housing market. Methods used to calculate this index are presented in Appendix III.

The first variable which affects the potential rent increases permitted by the guidelines is simply the number of leases which expire each year. The more frequently leases are renegotiated, the more rapidly rent increases can be permitted. This is of obvious importance in a period of rapid inflation. The crucial variable here is lease term. In any given year, every one-year lease expires; half of the two-year leases expire, and about one-third of three-year leases expire. The proportion of leases which may be renegotiated thus depends on the number of leases in each term category.

Reliable data on the number of leases according to length of time of lease is unavailable. The data which is available suggests that the most common lease length in stabilized housing carried a term of two years, with three-year leases the next most frequent. We have assumed that one-, two- and three-year leases comprise 15, 50, and 35 percent respectively of all leases (see evidence presented in Appendix III). This assumption implies that about one-half of all leases expire in any given year.[13] It also implies that guidelines on longer term leases are relatively more important than those on one-year leases, since two- and three-year leases may comprise over 85 percent of leases renegotiated each year.

The second factor affecting rent increase guidelines is tenant turnover. Here too, there is little data available. As described in Appendix III, the data which are available suggest that new leases appear to comprise 17 percent of the total leases in any given year and one-third of all leases issued each year (because only half of all leases expire annually). As will be emphasized later, this implies that the absence of incremental allowances for new leases issued during a previous year has an extremely significant impact on the potential increase of rent income, an impact not reflected in the guidelines or the stabilizer allowance.

On the basis of these assumptions, we have estimated an index of growth in the gross potential rental incomes permitted under rent guidelines from 1968 to 1974. This index represents our indication of how average rental incomes may have changed during the period.[14]

Exhibit 6-11 represents an index of growth in rental incomes and the BLS index of housing operating costs during the 1968-1975 period. The three previously outlined periods in the history of the guidelines appear fairly clearly in the data. The index demonstrates that the guidelines permitted landlords to increase rents more rapidly than their costs were increasing in 1968 and 1969. Guidelines became more stringent in 1970 while the very rapid increase in operating costs during 1971 was not reflected in the guidelines for that year. As a result of the rapid rent increases permitted during the early years of the program, the level of the estimated index of gross potential incomes in the stabilized sector was commensurate with cost increases through 1971.

However, since 1970 rents have not been permitted to rise as rapidly as operating costs. From 1970 to 1975 gross potential rents have been allowed to increase by only 36 percent, while operating costs are indicated to have risen by 67 percent. The bulk of this discrepancy was created under the enormous cost pressures of 1971 and 1974 which were not offset in commensurate increases in rent. The disparity between increases in rents and costs was greatest in 1974. While the BLS index of operating cost increased 19.2 percent, its highest rate of increase, our index of gross potential rent income increased by only 5.7 percent, the lowest increase during the study period. This disparity highlights the importance of looking beyond the specific impact of the guidelines per se. Rent guidelines on renewal leases in 1974 were the highest ever permitted under the guidelines. However, the loss of special increases or decontrol of rents on vacated apartments meant that these guidelines resulted in the lowest level of actual increases in rent income.

*Rent Guidelines And Net Rental Income*

Rapid inflation of operating costs during 1974 and the impact of stringent guidelines on potential gross rental incomes since 1974 must have had a

*EXHIBIT 6–11*
*INDEXES OF GROWTH IN GROSS POTENTIAL RENTAL INCOMES UNDER RENT GUIDELINES AND OF HOUSING OPERATING COSTS, 1967-1975 NEW YORK CITY RENT STABILIZED SECTOR*

| | *Index of Gross Potential Rental Income*[a] | | *BLS Index of Housing Operating Costs*[b] | |
|---|---|---|---|---|
| *Year* | *Index* | *Percent Change* | *Index* | *Percent Change* |
| 1967 | 100.0 | – | 100.0 | – |
| 1968 | 108.2 | 8.2 | 103.5 | 3.5 |
| 1969 | 117.1 | 8.2 | 107.6 | 4.0 |
| 1970 | 124.6 | 6.4 | 116.6 | 8.4 |
| 1971 | 133.7 | 7.3 | 132.2 | 13.4 |
| 1972 | 141.8 | 6.1 | 139.7 | 5.7 |
| 1973 | 150.9 | 6.4 | 150.8 | 6.3 |
| 1974 | 159.5 | 5.7 | 179.7 | 19.2 |
| 1975 | – | – | 191.3 | 6.5 |

a. See text and Appendix III for descriptions of procedures used to calculate this index. The index measures gross potential rental incomes permitted under rent guidelines, incorporating the effects of vacancy allowances and the stabilizer.

b. *Source:* U.S., Department of Labor, Bureau of Labor Statistics, Middle Atlantic Regional Office, *1975 Price Index of Operating Costs for Rent Stabilized Apartment Houses in New York City* (June 1975), Table 2.

substantial and deleterious effect on levels of net rental incomes (gross income minus operating costs) in the stabilized sector. Long-term trends in levels of net rental incomes are less clear. However, there is substantial evidence that net rental income has decreased as a fraction of gross rental incomes.

Two independent sources of data suggest that actual dollar amounts of net rental income have declined in recent years. First, the Real Estate Research Corporation (RERC) reports that average net rental income per unit in the stabilized sector declined from a 1972 level of $107 to $102 in 1973 (a 5 percent drop); and continued to decline in 1974, reaching $93 (a 13 percent decline from 1972).[15] RERC further reports that financing costs for this same sample of properties held substantially constant from 1972 to 1974 and a decline in net rental income resulted in a much more precipitous decline in net cash flow, from $20 per unit in 1972 to less than $5 in 1974.[16]

Second, information on net rental incomes was available for owners who had filed for hardship rent increases with the Conciliation and Appeals Board.[17] Exhibit 6-12 indicates the change in net rental incomes which occurred between 1969 and 1974 for these owners. The exhibit presents the mean (unweighted) index of the ratio of net rental incomes for the five most recent years to net incomes earned in 1969. The only overall increase in the index of net rental income occurred in 1970. On the average, the index of net rental incomes declined in each of the subsequent years. By 1974, net rental incomes *in dollars* were 5 percent below the 1969 levels. If the costs of debt service remained constant, this implies a more rapid decrease in net cash flow.

In order to illustrate how widespread the decline in net rental income was, the number of structures experiencing rent increases and those experiencing declining net rental incomes from year to year have also been included in Exhibit 6-12. Much the same pattern emerges: between 1969 and 1971, the number of buildings with increases in net rental incomes just about equalled the number of buildings for which income declined. From 1971 to 1974, twice as many buildings suffered a decline rather than an increase in net rental income. It must be kept in mind that these sample buildings have applied for hardship rent increases. Their economic situations may be more severe than is typical. But it should also be emphasized that the economic condition of these hardship cases deteriorated less rapidly from 1972 to 1974 than did that of the sample of housing units utilized by RERC. As a result, change in the economic circumstances of the hardship buildings may well understate the severity of the economic situation in the stabilized sector.

### *Rent Guidelines In 1974: Operating Costs and Rent Growth*

As has been noted, rent guidelines in 1974 were quite stringent: first, only a relatively small portion of the increase in operating costs (as measured by BLS)

*EXHIBIT 6-12*
*INDEX OF NET RENTAL INCOMES AMONG A GROUP OF 15 SELECTED RENT-STABILIZED STRUCTURES IN NEW YORK CITY 1969-1974*
*(1969 = 100)*

| | Year | | | | | |
|---|---|---|---|---|---|---|
| | *1969* | *1970* | *1971* | *1972* | *1973* | *1974* |
| Mean Value | 100.0 | 101.9 | 101.4 | 100.1 | 97.0 | 95.0 |
| Number of Structures for which Net Rental Income: | | | | | | |
| Increased from Previous Year | – | 6 | 7 | 5 | 5 | 5 |
| Decreased from Previous Year | – | 9 | 8 | 10 | 10 | 10 |
| Total Structures | 15 | 15 | 15 | 15 | 15 | 15 |

*Source:* Tabulations of financial data for 15 selected structures which have applied for hardship rent increases with the Conciliation and Appeals Board, New York City.

was reflected in guidelines for rent increases on renewal leases—44 percent of one-year leases; second, additional increases of rent on new leases was not permitted. The justification for the latter provision was clearly stated in the debate surrounding the Emergency Tenant Protection Act of 1974. The relatively low guideline levels were the result of two assumptions made by the Rent Guidelines Board as reported in a public statement by the chairman of the board.[18] First, it was assumed that because of spectacular increases in the prices of fuel and utilities (80 percent in a single year, according to BLS), landlords would react by conserving the use of fuel, and utilities. Specifically, it was assumed that consumption would decline by 20 percent from earlier levels. Second, it was assumed that operating costs comprised 55 percent of the gross potential rental income. Therefore, by permitting landlords to increase rents by 55 percent of the increase in operating costs, it was assumed that net rental incomes and cash flow after debt service would be stabilized. Available data suggests the estimate that operating costs comprise 55 percent of gross rental income substantially understates current cost realities.

All available data suggest that the proportion of operating costs to gross potential rents has increased. Exhibit 6-13 presents a summary of recent evidence, drawn from a variety of sources by the Center for Urban Policy Research and the Real Estate Research Corporation. This data supports the assumption that operating costs comprised about 55 percent of the rent income of stabilized properties in the late 1960s. In 1970, operating costs appear to have risen more rapidly than rental incomes, and in 1974 they appear to have comprised over two-thirds of total income, rather than the 55 percent assumed by the Rent Guidelines Board. It also appears that 1974 guidelines may have been too low to maintain constant dollar levels of net rental incomes by as much as 18 percent (67 percent minus 55 percent). As a result, it is very likely that operating costs may currently comprise an even larger portion of gross potential rental incomes than in 1974.

### *Rent Guidelines And Lease Length: The Problem Of Unequal Rents*

The relative simplicity of the rent guidelines method belies the potential complexity of the effects of guidelines on the rents of individual units. Under the guidelines program, permissible *rates* of rent increases on renewal or new leases are based on the particular time a lease is issued and the length of the lease negotiated. It seems likely, however, that six years of guidelines have resulted in substantial rent disparities similar to those which exist under standard rent control for comparable units. Moreover, these disparities may increase over time unless guidelines are specifically designed to eliminate such disparities.

The basis for these hypotheses is presented in Exhibit 6-14. The exhibit shows maximum rent levels permitted under the guidelines on June 30, 1975 for

*EXHIBIT 6-13*
*OPERATING COSTS AS A PERCENT OF GROSS POTENTIAL RENTAL INCOME, 1967-1974*

| | *Sternlieb*[a] | *IREM*[b] | *RERC*[c] | *Fifteen Selected Structures* |
|---|---|---|---|---|
| 1967 | 54.1 | 51.3 | – | – |
| 1968 | – | – | – | – |
| 1969 | – | – | – | 55.4 |
| 1970 | – | – | – | 57.9 |
| 1971 | – | – | – | 59.2 |
| 1972 | – | 59.6 | 59.4 | 62.0 |
| 1973 | – | 61.0 | 63.0 | 68.8 |
| 1974 | – | – | 67.7 | 68.9 |

a. George Sternlieb, *The Urban Housing Dilemma: The Dynamics of New York City's Rent Controlled Housing,* as quoted by RERC.
b. Institute for Real Estate Management, *Income/Expense Analysis–Apartments, Condominiums and Cooperatives,* as quoted by RERC.
c. Real Estate Research Corporation.
*Source:* Real Estate Research Corporation, *A Policy Review of Rental Housing in New York City* (New York: Coalition to Save New York, April 1975), Table 8, and operating income data drawn from 15 buildings which have filed with the Conciliation and Appeals Board for hardship rent increases.

*EXHIBIT 6-14*
*MAXIMUM RENT UNDER RENT STABILIZATION GUIDELINES ON JUNE 30, 1975 FOR UNITS OCCUPIED ON JULY 1, 1967 AT A RENT OF $100*[a]

| *Lease Term and Initial Date of Occupancy* | *(A) Housing Units Occupied by Same Tenant over Period* | *(B) Housing Units with Tenant Change at Each Lease Expiration* |
|---|---|---|
| 1 year | 174 | 243 |
| 2 years | | |
| July 1, 1966 | 147 | 194 |
| July 1, 1967 | 147 | 182 |
| 3 years | | |
| July 1, 1965 | 149 | 198 |
| July 1, 1966 | 131 | 174 |
| July 1, 1967 | 128 | 149 |

a. During the period of vacancy destabilization, rents on new leases were assumed to increase by the guidelines rate for renewal leases plus 10 percent.

a stabilized apartment which was occupied on July 1, 1967 at a rent of $100. Twelve different rent levels for the apartment are presented, each calculated according to a different sequence of leases. The estimates in "Part A" of the exhibit assume the unit was occupied by the same tenant over the entire period, so that the unit was eligible for renewal increases and for the rent stabilizer. Rent levels in "Part B" assume that a change in tenants occurred on each lease renewal date. Depending on lease terms, 1975 rent levels for an apartment occupied by the same tenant over the entire period 1967 to 1975 range from $128 to $174, or a difference of $46. Even among only those units occupied under three-year leases during the period, 1975 rent levels may differ by as much as $21, depending on the initial occupancy date of the tenant.

Potential rent disparities are much more substantial among units which have frequent tenant turnover. Such turnover implies much more frequent eligibility for incremental rent increases permitted on new leases for apartments occupied under short term leases. Potential rent levels for this group of apartments differ by as much as $94.

The exhibit suggests that a systematic inequity may have resulted under rent guidelines. There is a definite tendency for apartments rented under three-year leases to bear *lower* potential rent levels than those under two-year leases; the two-year lease rent levels are in turn *lower* than potential rents charged on apartments rated under one-year leases.

Exhibit 6-15 indicates the *maximum* rent disparity which might have existed within the stabilized stock, according to the leasing assumptions used in Exhibit 6-14. It is clear that maximum potential rent disparity is increasing over time. In 1968, the maximum potential disparity amounted to $40. By 1974, this disparity had increased to $115.

Actual rent disparities are impossible to determine. The period of vacancy destabilization may have eliminated much of the random disparity. However, destabilization was permitted only upon apartment vacancy (as a result, it may have acted to *increase* rent inequality). In addition, the probability that a lease would have expired and that tenant turnover would have occurred during the period of destabilization is less for units occupied under longer term leases. As a result, destabilization is unlikely to have eliminated the tendency for longer term leases to have been more costly to property owners under the guidelines program.

## *SUMMARY*

The three case studies presented in this chapter represent the continuum of formal rent adjustment mechanisms–ranging from relatively simple to complex. The complex systems such as the Massachusetts FNOI formulas and

*EXHIBIT 6-15*
*MAXIMUM AND MINIMUM RENTS PAID BY TENANTS OF A STABILIZED APARTMENT RENTED FOR $100 ON JULY 1, 1967, AND OCCUPIED SINCE UNDER VARIOUS LEASING ARRANGEMENTS*[a]

| *Dates* | *Lowest Monthly Rent* | *Highest Monthly Rent* | *Difference Dollars Per Month* | *Percent of Lowest Monthly Rent* |
|---|---|---|---|---|
| July 1, 1967 | 100 | 100 | – | – |
| July 1, 1968 | 100 | 140 | 40 | 40 |
| July 1, 1969 | 100 | 140 | 40 | 40 |
| July 1, 1970 | 111 | 146 | 35 | 32 |
| July 1, 1971 | 113 | 174 | 61 | 54 |
| July 1, 1972 | 114 | 190 | 76 | 67 |
| July 1, 1973 | 127 | 223 | 96 | 76 |
| July 1, 1974 | 128 | 243 | 115 | 90 |

a. The leasing histories examined are those used in the previous exhibit. During the period of vacancy destabilization rents on new leases were assumed to increases by the guidelines rate for renewal leases plus 10 percent.

the Maximum Base Rent formula used in the rent-controlled sector of New York City theoretically provide optimal potential for equity in the range of factors taken into consideration, and in rent adjustments determined on an individual building basis.

Some potential for equity is lost in the simpler mechanisms which apply rent adjustments on an across-the-board basis; however, these mechanisms are easier to administer than the FNOI formula. And if adequate outlets for relief are provided (for example, through hardship provisions) relative equity may be achieved in "across-the-board" rent control programs. This is particularly true when the inherent potential for equity contained in the more complex systems is negated by the maze of administrative requirements which must be met and which often produce inordinate time lags in the granting of rent adjustments. It has been suggested in a recent New York City rent control decision that "chaos in administering a law may make it unconstitutional . . . where laws originally constitutional have collapsed in follow-through to the point that due process can no longer be said to exist."[19]

The New York City rent stabilization mechanism described in the third case study reflects a middle-range on the continuum of administrative complexity presented in the three rent control systems. This mid-range approach comes closer to providing relative equity than any other presently utilized across-the-board mechanism. The use of the operating cost index, specifically geared to measuring changes in costs to apartment house operators, significantly contributes to minimizing the problems that other across-the-board formulas incur in estimating accurate increases in operating costs. This general view should not however be construed as an endorsement. There are conceptual limitations in the stabilization program as reflected in the case study discussion, and further statutory problems in the mechanism as presently implemented. Furthermore, it is questionable whether this approach, as utilized in New York City, could be successfully or feasibly implemented in much smaller communities.

## *NOTES*

1. Specific administrative data for Somerville is not presented as access to their files was not permitted during the course of the study.
2. The sample frequency utilized in Boston was one to twenty, i.e., every twentieth adjustment claim was taken for analysis. Thus the number of structures in the sample multiplied by twenty should approximate the total number of petitions receiving an increase for both 1973 and 1974, respectively. According to the Boston Rent Board, the total number of petitions for increase in 1973 and 1974 were 2,019 and 1,900, respectively. Our sample yielded ninety-two petitions in 1973 and ninety-six for 1974. Multiplying these two figures by the sample frequency yields a total of 1,840 for 1973 and 1,920 for

1974. Thus in terms of structures (petitions), the sample data approximate the population as stated by the rent board very closely. See Appendix III for the details of the approach used in the other communities.

3. Inganamort, Helmsley-Spear et al. v. Borough of Fort Lee Council and Rent Levelling Board of the Borough of Fort Lee, Superior Court of New Jersey Chancery Division, Bergen County, Docket No. C-1696-71, L-17673-73 P.W., L-22375-73 P.W., L-31580-73 P.W. (Decided December 18, 1974), (Unreported).

4. Harry B. Helmsley and Alvin Schwartz t/a Horizon House Associates et al. v. Borough of Fort Lee Council and Rent Levelling Board, Superior Court of New Jersey Law Division, Bergen County, Docket No. L-11348-74 P.W. (Decided June 30, 1975).

5. Ibid., p. 7. See also Inganamort v. Borough of Fort Lee, 303 A.2d 298.

6. Helmsley and Schwartz et al., pp. 2, 8.

7. Hutton Park Gardens v. West Orange Town Council, 68 N.J. 543 (1975); Brunetti v. Borough of New Milford, 68 N.J. 576 (1975); Cosden et al. v. Township of Wayne Council, Decision combined with Hutton Park, 68 N.J. 543 (1975); Troy Hills Village v. Parsippany-Troy Hills Township Council, 68 N.J. 604 (1975). All four cases were decided December 11, 1975. All text citations from mimeographed decisions.

8. Borough of Fort Lee, New Jersey, Ordinance 74-32, Sec. 1(a) (1974).

9. Ibid., Sec. 10.

10. Ibid. and Ordinance 75-45, Sec. 10 (1975).

11. New York State Emergency Tenant Protection Act of 1974 (Ch. 576, Laws of 1974). Communities in the counties of Nassau, Westchester and Rockland were given the option of extending controls via the rent stabilization mechanism to structures built after February, 1947 if a vacancy rate of five percent or less was evident.

12. Edward Lukashok, "There Is a Way to Stabilize Residential Rents," *Real Estate Review,* 2, no. 1 (1972):96-99.

13. This ignores the termination of a lease before its term is completed. No data were available on the incidence of such lease termination.

14. Calculation methods are described in detail in Appendix III and the index is compared with actual increase in the gross potential rental incomes of fifteen structures which had applied for hardship rent increases. If these structures are at all representative of general trends, the comparison suggests that our index does not understate rent increases permitted under the guidelines.

15. Real Estate Research Corporation, *A Policy Review of Rental Housing in New York City* (New York: Coalition to Save New York, 1975), Table 9.

16. Ibid.

17. Criteria for selecting the buildings are described in Appendix III.

18. Emanuel Tobier, Chairman, New York City Rent Guidelines Board,

"Explanatory Statement and Findings of the Rent Guidelines Board in Relation to 1974 Lease Increase Allowances for Apartments under the Jurisdiction of the Rent Stabilization Law," February 7, 1975.

19. The Housing and Development Administration of New York City v. Community Housing Improvement Program, Inc., Civil Court of New York City, HP 186/1974. (Decided September 9, 1975). Judge Bernard Klieger initially stayed the implementation of the ruling for 60 days to allow the Housing and Development Administration time to submit a plan to correct the administrative deficiencies. Also see Max H. Siegel, "City Rules Governing Rent Are Held Unconstitutional," *New York Times,* September 12, 1975.

# Chapter 7 The Administrator's Checklist: Putting the Pieces Together

The myriad issues and topic areas important to the consideration and analysis of rent control necessitate providing the practitioner a comprehensive evaluative summary. The summary involves: (1) the consideration of proposed rent control vis-a-vis the need for such action; and (2) the implementation of a rent control mechanism.

## *THE NEED FOR RENT CONTROL*

The justification for rent control is the existence of a housing emergency for which rent control is imposed as a temporary stopgap measure. As long as the assumption of an emergency is paramount, rent control legislation will be an ad hoc approach unrelated to other housing policies and programs; it will not evolve into a comprehensive program focusing on the essence of the rent control dilemma—the widening gap between tenants' ability to pay and the increased rentals required to operate and maintain housing. Therefore, in examining proposed rent control legislation the policymaker should consider the following:

1. Is rent control an appropriate instrument to deal with the housing problems existing in a particular community?
2. If so, are the methods of regulation used appropriate and effective?
3. Of the varying methods, are some more appropriate for certain housing emergency conditions than others?

Extensive discussion of the constitutional basis of the housing emergency issue was presented in chapter 2. However, beyond this issue of constitutional validity is that of the need for appropriate application of rent regulation in the face of a housing emergency. There is widespread agreement that a housing shortage can lead to undesirable consequences such as rent gouging, but there is no consensus on the operational definition of a "low vacancy rate."[1] Furthermore, interpretations of the effectiveness of rent controls are inconclusive, particularly for the short term.[2] However, distinctions can be made between the conditions which characterized the earlier periods of rent control imposition and the housing problems which confront many communities today.

*First Generation Controls*

The initial application of rent controls was necessitated by wartime emergency housing shortages. These shortages were engendered by decreases in housing construction as resources (materials and labor) were shifted to defense production; they were further exacerbated by large and rapid shifts of population to areas of wartime defense production. As a consequence, the excess demand on the supply of housing units resulted in frequent exploitation through exorbitant and speculative rent increases. However, after the war, conditions gradually returned to normal in most communities.[3] A resurgence of new construction and a decline in the movement of the migrant population contributed to normalizing housing conditions and stabilizing rents.[4] The areas which had the most difficulty in normalizing conditions were those in which large numbers of migrants remained after the war. To counteract the housing shortages in those areas, devices such as tax exemptions which contributed to encouraging new construction were adopted following World War I.

A second point concerning wartime rent control is that it was accompanied by controls on other goods and services (particularly the formal controls of World War II). Although the problem of commodity parity was never squarely faced during World War II,[5] the existence of regulation over other goods and services did reduce the hardship faced by rental property owners. It was the decontrol of other commodities after World War II which led to several redefinitions of the rent control system and finally culminated in the introduction of the concept of "fair net operating income" in the 1949 postwar extension of federal controls. Parity must be understood within a dual context:

> Primary (direct) parity . . .mean[s], as applied to rent, that as the costs of maintaining rented property to the landlord increase, then income (rents) shall be adjusted to keep pace . . . Secondary (indirect) parity refers to the purchasing power of the income received by the landlord in relation to the price of goods and services

> he must purchase in addition to those required to maintain the premises—goods and services required for his personal living. If these goods have advanced in price, and his income is held constant by reason of rent control, there is a lack of parity in his purchasing power. *The answer to primary and secondary parity goes back to the root of price control policy. There must be control on all goods at the same time, and blanket adjustments in one line cannot be made at the expense of another or the whole price structure is placed on a wobbly foundation* [emphasis added].[6]

*Second Generation Controls*

Current rent controls are called "second generation" because they have arisen during peacetime conditions. The current cost-push inflation which characterizes the economy as a whole demands that primary as well as secondary parity be established if continued investment in the housing market is to be encouraged. Although most current rent adjustment mechanisms are geared toward the provision of direct parity, the decline in the income yielded from the investment is frequently overlooked or dismissed. The effective and equitable control of one commodity, in this case rents, without concurrent controls on other commodities is impossible. Complete parity cannot be achieved in the implementation of local rent control as long as inflation of other commodities is occurring nationwide.

*The Application Of Rent Control*

Housing shortages of emergency proportion which do occur must be confronted in order to minimize their adverse effect upon the public welfare. The most clearcut example of such a case today is the housing shortage in many Alaskan communities. In these communities excess demand generated by rapid population and economic growth as a result of the pipeline construction has led to rent increases of 200 and 300 percent. The current condition in Alaska most closely resembles that present during wartime emergencies and constitutes a unique emergency situation. Although some portion of the recent population growth in Alaska is permanent it is clear that upon completion of the pipeline many of those presently seeking housing will leave the area. This emergency therefore has definite time limits determined by the period of construction. The 1921 Supreme Court decision initially justified rent controls, holding that rent control "regulation is put and justified as a temporary measure. . . . A limit in time, to tide over a passing trouble, well may justify a law that could not be upheld as a permanent change."[7]

The end of pipeline construction in Alaska will to a large degree eliminate the housing emergency. In Alaska, unlike during the war periods, resources are available and are being deployed during the course of the emergency to meet the increased needs through new construction.[8]

However, the conditions which underlie the current imposition of rent controls in other communities are clearly different from those in Alaska. As discussed in chapter 3, there is no magic formula nor specific combination of variables which explains why some communities adopt rent control while other communities confronting similar conditions do not. Clearly, the political environment is significant. The typology presented in Exhibit 7-1 indicates in simplified form, the varieties of emergency conditions which may necessitate the application of rent control. Analyses of 1970 and 1973 vacancy rates reveal the existence of "low" ratios in many of the communities which have proposed or enacted rent control measures.[9] These vacancy ratios ranged from 2.1 to 6.0 percent in 1970 and from 1.1 to 8.8 percent in 1972. On the other hand, increased rents, as measured by the CPI rent index from 1971 to 1974, ranged from 9.9 to 20.4 percent with a national average of 13 percent over the period. Across-the-board inflation has been common to all these areas and has contributed to the increased costs of operating and maintaining existing units as well as providing new units. It is difficult to isolate the portion of rent increases which is the result of general cost-push inflation from that which reflects the forces of supply and demand in the housing market per se. Increased financing and construction costs deter new construction, even when demand for new units is great. The imposition of rent controls exacerbates rather than alleviates the housing shortage by further discouraging new investment. The imposition of rent controls *must,* therefore, be accompanied by devices and programs which encourage new investment.

Differentiation in the type and scope of regulation which may be appropriate is indicated in Exhibit 7-1. In Exhibit 7-2 this typology is carried a step further; the scheme for defining the scope of regulatory authority presented in chapter 3 is used as a framework for further differentiation.

## *IMPLEMENTING THE RENT CONTROL MECHANISM: A GUIDE FOR THE BEWILDERED POLICYMAKER*

A number of crucial issues should be considered in designing an effective and appropriate rent adjustment mechanism. These issues are outlined in Exhibit 7-3 according to: (1) the substantive elements of the legislation; and (2) the scope of regulatory authority to be invested in over-all implementation. As these elements were presented in detail in chapters 3 and 4 the focus of the

*EXHIBIT 7–1*

*A TYPOLOGY OF EMERGENCY CONDITIONS*

| *Emergency Conditions* | *Indicators* | *Projected Period of Emergency* | *Projected Resolution/ Consequences* |
|---|---|---|---|
| 1. Excess demand generated by rapid population growth and economic expansion created by unique situation, (war-production or Alaskan example). | a. A significant increase in rents.<br>b. Low vacancy rate (i.e., below 3 percent). | Determinable end of event or unique circumstances will result in decreased demand. | Rent control during period of emergency. Emergency will generally be abated via market forces as a result of decreased demand upon termination of unique conditions and increased new construction to meet increased population needs. |
| 2. Excess demand generated by rapid population growth and economic expansion, i.e., areas of the South and Southwest during the 1960s. | a. Increases in rent.<br>b. Low vacancy rate, (i.e., below 3 percent). | Indeterminate–Dependent upon rate of new construction. | Mild form of rent regulation may be required at peak of shortage. As supply catches up to demand via new construction shortage will be alleviated. |
| 3. Excess demand generated by decline in new construction created by national economic condition. | a. Increased rentals.<br>b. Low vacancy rate. | Indeterminate–Dependent upon national monetary policy and rate of new construction. | Mild form of rent regulation may be required but may necessitate accompanying inducements from national level to encourage increased investment. |

*EXHIBIT 7–1*
*(continued)*
*A TYPOLOGY OF EMERGENCY CONDITIONS*

| *Emergency Conditions* | *Indicators* | *Projected Period of Emergency* | *Projected Resolution/ Consequences* |
|---|---|---|---|
| 4. Excess demand generated by decline in new construction created by changing population characteristics which prohibit absorption of new units due to economic infeasibility. | a. Increased rents.<br>b. Declining vacancy rate, most notable in lower cost units. | Indeterminant—May be permanent emergency. | Mild form of rent regulation. May be required to minimize abuses and *must* be accompanied by publicly assisted housing programs for new construction combined with rent supplement programs. |
| 5. Excess demand generated by cost-push inflation. | a. Increased rents.<br>b. May or may not reflect low vacancy. | Indeterminant. | Mild form of regulation may be required to minimize abuses but must be accompanied by some form of rent assistance. |

*EXHIBIT 7–2*
*RELATIONSHIP OF EMERGENCY CONDITIONS AND SCOPE OF REGULATORY AUTHORITY*

| *Form of Regulation Mechanism* | *Scope of Authority* | *Conditions of Appropriate Utilization* |
|---|---|---|
| Mild | Limited jurisdiction. Fair rent boards/commissions empowered to conduct hearings and order rent reduction in cases of abuse and rent gouging. | May be appropriate under all of the conditions defined in Exhibit 7-1. |
| Intermediate | Authority to establish across-the-board controls with automatic annual increase in operating costs. Depending upon duration of period may include code enforcement provision. | Appropriate under condition no. 1 defined in Exhibit 7-1. |
| Stringent | Authority to establish across-the-board controls. With administrative determination of rent increases rather than allowable automatic increments. If long-term must include code compliance provisions. | May be appropriate under condition no. 1 defined in Exhibit 7-1 but most appropriate under national emergency when accompanied by controls on other commodities. |

*EXHIBIT 7-3*
*IMPLEMENTING THE RENT CONTROL MECHANISM: A SUMMARY GUIDE*

| *Descriptive Element* | *Significant Issues/Problems* |
|---|---|
| I. *Substantive Elements* | |
| A. *Determining the Rent Control Universe*– Designation of units subject to control and those exempted. | Controls should apply only to sector of market (class of housing) exhibiting shortage. Issue/Problem Areas: (1) new construction (2) publicly assisted units (3) luxury units. |
| B. *Base Rent Determination*– Designation of date for which extant rents become base for subsequent adjustments, generally accomplished via a rent rollback. | Rollback date should precede peak of emergency. Issue/Problem Areas: (1) rollback inequities producing base rents below economic rent; (2) regional market distortion. |
| C. *Rent Adjustment Mechanisms*– Method designed to regulate rental adjustments. | Should provide equal protection to all classes, and be easily administered with minimal procedures and lag time, and rent adjustments should match realities of operation. Issue/Problem Areas: |
| 1. Limited Return on Investment | (1) selection of formula; (2) determination of allowable income and expenses; (3) registration of all subject units; (4) formal administrative system; (5) costs of administration. |
| 2. Maximum Base Rent Mechanisms | (1) selection of formula/indicator for rent adjustment; (2) designation of pass-through categories; (3) designation of additional increase provisions–i.e., capital improvements and hardships. |

*EXHIBIT 7-3*
*(continued)*
*IMPLEMENTING THE RENT CONTROL MECHANISM: A SUMMARY GUIDE*

| *Descriptive Element* | *Significant Issues/Problems* |
|---|---|
| D. *Administrative Mechanism*– Entity to which regulatory authority delegated. May be new entity or existent agency. | Scope of responsibility determined by rent adjustment mechanism. More complex systems require fulltime staffs. Issue/Problem Areas: |
| 1. Rent Control Board | (1) generally appointed volunteers; (2) may incur significant lag time in decisions due to infrequent meetings; (3) necessitates at minimum parttime staff positions. |
| 2. Rent Administrator | (1) compensated staff position and support staff. |
| 3. Existent Agency | (1) can facilitate coordination of support services and achievement of rent control objective if agency is of related concern. |

*EXHIBIT 7–3*
*(continued)*
*IMPLEMENTING THE RENT CONTROL MECHANISM:*
*A SUMMARY GUIDE*

| *Descriptive Element* | *Significant Issues/Problems* |
|---|---|
| *II. Scope of Regulatory Authority* | |
| A. *Extant Housing Shortage*—See Exhibits 7–1 and 7–2. | Statutorily delineated via legislation which defines substantive elements cited in I above. |
| B. *Determining the Purpose/Focus of Control*—Delineation of protection of either (1) the unit or (2) the tenant. | Will affect Base Rent Determination in I above. Issues/problem areas: (1) vacancy decontrol; (2) statutory tenantry; (3) standard vs. variable lease length. |
| C. *Eviction Controls*—Places limitation on grounds allowed owner to dispossess tenant. | Included to protect existing tenants. Legislative approach (state/local) may determine validity of inclusion. Issues/Problem Areas: (1) enforcement; (2) linkage to code enforcement. |
| D. *Code Enforcement Compliance*—Requires code compliance for rent increase or eviction certification. | Inclusion to encourage maintenance and investment in property and discourage maintenance deferral/abandonment. Issues/Problem Areas: (1) rent reductions or absence of required increases may impede objective of provision; (2) may require expansion of appropriate municipal department. |

following discussion is on the relative significance and issue/problem areas accompanying consideration and adoption.

*Substantive Elements*

Effective rent control administration depends upon clear statutory guidelines. Experience indicates that legislative definition, to the extent feasible, of administrative standards minimizes the number of subsequent legal challenges which occur when legislative intent or interpretation is ambiguous.

Determing The Rent Control Universe

The number of units to be controlled necessarily varies from community to community as a function of the housing stock characteristics. Beyond the exemption of transient and institutional dwelling units the major exemption categories are: (1) new construction; (2) publicly assisted or financed units; and (3) luxury housing. To encourage continued investment in a rent-controlled community, new construction is exempted either via a blanket exemption or on the initial rental. Blanket exemption, of course, provides a greater incentive; however, investors may fear that the units will be subjected to controls at a later date and, therefore, still hesitate to invest.

Rent levels in publicly assisted housing projects are controlled as a function of the requirements for assistance, particularly government "public housing" and subsidized units for which the rents are determined as a percentage of the tenant's income. Thus, to subject these directly assisted units to further controls is unnecessary and may lead to conflicts between the governmental agency providing the assistance and the rent control agency. Such conflicts have already arisen over directly publicly assisted units and government insured structures; court challenges are presently pending as a result of HUD interim regulations promulgated in February 1975.[10]

The primary argument for exemption of luxury units is that affluent tenants have the resources and mobility to attain alternative housing and thus are not in need of the same protection as their less wealthy counterparts. Further, the rent levels in such housing reflect the amenities provided. The major problem concerning control of luxury housing is the definition of what constitutes luxury housing, particularly as rent level, not amenities, is the criterion used for definition.

Base Rent Determination

Initial base rents are generally determined via a rollback of rents to a date preceding rent control enactment.[11] The rent on that date becomes the base from which subsequent rent adjustments are made.

Although the rollback constitutes a relatively objective method for establishing base rents, some inequities result no matter how much care and consideration is given to the selection of an appropriate date. Among these inequities is the reduction of rent below the level necessary to meet operating costs.

### Rent Adjustment Mechanisms

If the rent control statute provides for across-the-board controls, the mechanism utilized to regulate rents is the most important provision in defining the potential for equity. The mechanism should be easy to understand and administer with a minimum of "red-tape" and lag time. Rent adjustments should be made on the basis of actual operating costs. The determination of allowable income and expense categories is necessary for any selected mechanism either as an element of the mechanism itself or as an element in the consideration of additional rent increase provisions, for example, hardship.

The particular rent adjustment formula selected determines many of the crucial issues for which policy decisions will be necessary. Using the classification described in chapter 4, the policy areas may be summarized according to two broad approaches to rent adjustments: limited return on investment and maximum base rent mechanisms.

### Limited Return On Investment

The wide degree of variation possible under this approach is indicated in the case study of the Greater Boston area included in chapter 6 and Appendix I. Representing the most stringent form of regulation, the limited return on investment mechanism requires a large formalized administrative system and comprehensive administrative standards determined by the legislative body. The most crucial component of this method is the selection of the formula used to define fair net operating income. Although the FNOI approach theoretically considers each case on an individual basis, the definition of FNOI as a function of value or investment may produce extreme disparities because the parameters utilized may provide for a wide range of possible FNOIs within the same class of buildings.

### Maximum Base Rent Mechanisms

Formulas utilized under this approach allow for limited annual rent increments with or without regard for the landlord's rate of return. Generally applied on an across-the-board basis, this approach is easier to administer and requires a less formal system of implementation than does the FNOI method. However, any across-the-board formula needs accompanying provisions for relief in the inevitable cases in which hardship is encountered.

Since the primary thrust of this adjustment mechanism is the provision of rental increases commensurate with the increments in operating costs or the rate of inflation, an adequate measure of operating costs must be determined. As discussed in chapter 4, these formulas may include a fixed percentage, a price index (either specifically of operating costs or the more general CPI), or a complex MBR formula such as that used in New York City which assesses a unit's value according to a wide range of factors including location in the building.

A fixed percentage formula to restrict annual rent increases is perhaps the easiest method to implement, but it does not take changes in operating costs into account. In order to consider these costs, a price index is needed. The CPI is a broad index of changes in the cost of living, but it does not always reflect the specific expense items or increases incurred by landlords in operating their buildings. Therefore, a specific price index of operating costs is recommended. A further issue in the application of an operating cost index is the determination of the proportion of the rent dollar subject to cost increments—thus the operating expense ratio which is applied to the price index.

Regardless of the formula or indicator selected, further decisions must be made concerning real estate tax pass-throughs, capital improvements, and hardship provisions. Policy decisions pertinent to increases or decreases in services or facilities provided to tenants must be made with reductions in rent levels considered.

### Administrative Mechanisms

The extent of regulatory responsibility and the scale of administration required in any community will be dictated by the legislative provisions defining the rent adjustment mechanism and scope of regulatory authority. The more stringent and complex the regulatory authority, the larger and more formal the system of administration required and the greater the expense of implementation.

The selection of a volunteer rent control board is most appropriate in conjunction with the "mild" or "intermediate" forms of regulation in which across-the-board determinations constitute the major adjustment method with designated provisions for relief. Staff needs depend on the type of mechanism and the number of units subject to control. A volunteer board theoretically minimizes political partisanship in the administration of rent control. However, the fact that the boards are voluntary means that time lags for decisions will occur. Adoption of a stringent rent adjustment mechanism necessitates a fulltime staff and an administrator who is empowered to make day-to-day decisions. It is obviously a more expensive administration system than that which utilizes the volunteer boards.

Delegation of administrative responsibility to an existing governmental agency has certain political disadvantages but has the potential to facilitate efficient implementation and coordination of support services and facilities. If the scope of regulatory authority includes a code compliance provision, implementation may be facilitated if the rent control responsibility is delegated to a department which coordinates building inspection.

### *Scope Of Regulatory Authority*

Exhibit 7-2 presents a typology which links the form of the regulatory mechanism to the severity of existing housing conditons. The selection of a particular rent adjustment mechanism implicitly defines the extent of the authority of the mechanism. There are, however, two additional regulatory issues for which policy decisions must be made. The first concerns the focus of rent control protection, and the second concerns whether eviction and code compliance controls will be included in the provisions.

#### Determining The Purpose/Focus Of The Control Mechanism

Given our basic premise—that rent control is imposed as a temporary stop-gap measure for the purpose of stabilizing rents during a housing emergency—the question which tests and serves to focus the basic philosophy underlying specific administrative procedures is whether one is "protecting the tenant in residence or controlling the apartment unit." As described by two students of rent control:

> If we wish to protect the present occupants of apartments from inordinate rent increases, we decontrol the unit when they leave that apartment.
> If we are stabilizing the apartment unit, we go beyond the immediate occupants' rights to reordering the market itself.[12]

In order to provide a compromise between controlling rents and protecting tenants several administrative approaches have been used. For example, it is possible to permit the first rent on a vacated unit to be established by the tenant and landlord with subsequent rent increases controlled by the rent control agency. It is also possible to provide for an extra rent increase upon vacancy although the unit would still be subject to control.

Further questions are pertinent to the issue of tenants rights: (1) when is a unit deemed vacant? (2) are sublessees granted the protection of controls? (3) do children inherit the right of continued occupancy? (4) will leases be required? (5) if so, will leases be restricted to single terms of one year or are variable lease lengths allowed?

### Eviction Controls

Eviction controls limit a property owner's right to recover possession of his property. There has been considerable controversy over the constitutionality of this provision especially when it is included in local ordinances in the absence of state enabling legislation or in the absence of such a provision in the state enabling act (for further discussion of this issue, see chapter 3).

Enforcement of eviction controls has led to requirements for certification of rent level and proper notice to the rent control agency prior to court proceedings. Code compliance certification to ensure that the building is free of any building or health code violations is sometimes included as an additional requirement for evictions. However, the connection between the grounds for eviction and the condition of the building is often tenuous. In some cases, however, the conditions of the building may be a direct result of the actions of the tenants who are to be evicted, for example, nonpayment of rent or destruction of the premises.

### Code Compliance

Code compliance enforcement is an approach which encourages maintenance and investment. However, excessive penalties may counteract this objective since adequate rental income is necessary to maintain code compliance. If code compliance is required for rent adjustments or eviction certification, the rent control agency will have a greater than normal workload and will probably require an expanded staff.

## *CONCLUSIONS*

The previous discussion has addressed the major issues and problems involved in implementing rent control. Given the premise that rent control is intended to be a *temporary* stop-gap measure to minimize the adverse effects of a housing emergency, the following criteria are presented as guidelines for maximizing the potential for equity:

1. Ordinance provisions and administrative regulations should be easy to understand and administer.

2. Administrative requirements and procedures should be kept to a minimum.
3. Stipulated requirements for processing times should be strictly adhered to.
4. Rent adjustments should correspond to the realities of operating costs.
5. Unavoidable cost increases should be retrievable through rent adjustments.
6. Ordinances should be objective in their application, that is, issues of equal protection and due process should be carefully considered to avoid unnecessary legal challenges.
7. Ordinances should also be flexible in acknowledging variations between properties and operations as a result of differences in
   - age, i.e., the generally more expensive maintenance requirements of older buildings
   - configuration of structure, i.e., size, type
   - debt service requirement variations
   - level of services provided, i.e., provision of all utilities, partial utilities or the provision of extra services and amenities.
8. Finally, ordinances should be "self-liquidating"–geared toward phase-out, via
   - companion programs directly focused on eliminating the cause of the emergency through incentive programs to encourage new construction or the provision of housing allowances (as determined by the nature of the emergency)
   - vacancy decontrol.

The questions which should be raised prior to the enactment of any rent control statute are: (1) does the ordinance encourage building maintenance and improvements, or does it lend itself to deferred maintenance which must ultimately result in a deteriorating housing stock? (2) how does the ordinance affect the mortgageability of properties? (3) and finally, how is the community tax base affected?

The rent control issue is not simply a conflict between tenants and landlords. Rather, the impact of rent control extends to the viability of the housing stock, and the capital resources of the entire rent controlled community. In the long term, rent control policies and practices may even affect state revenues, as a result of widespread reductions in property tax. Thus, it is of vital importance that rent control programs be viewed comprehensively. Ideally, they should only be initiated in conjunction with control on other commodities as well as housing. If not, equity in a rent-controlled housing market will probably be a concept only, not a reality.

## *NOTES*

1. As indicated in chapter 2, only two of the currently enacted state rent control statutes define the vacancy criteria: New York at 5 percent and Alaska at 3 percent. Additionally, seven New Jersey communities use the 5 percent standard. Furthermore, the definition of "low" or "critical" is relative as determined by a number of variables characterizing the housing stock (See footnote 44 in chapter 2).

2. Analyses of the effectiveness and value of rent regulation during World Wars I and II are inconclusive and often contradictory. These differences in interpretation reflect biases inherent in the data analysis but also reflect varying market conditions in different parts of the country. External market forces in some regions appeared to refute the argument that rent control deterred new construction, while in other locales the absence of these forces or presence of other forces appeared to support the allegation. The important point is that national, or sometimes even regional housing data, does not reflect the range of situations existent in individual localities. For a summary of the arguments, data, and interpretations of the effectiveness of World War I controls, see Edith Drellich and Andrée Emery, *Rent Control In War and Peace* (New York: National Municipal League, 1939), pp. 52-65. Also see Friedman and Stigler, "Roofs or Ceilings?" in *Verdict On Rent Control,* ed. F.A. Hayek (London: Institute of Economic Affairs, 1972); for critique of this analysis, see Lawrence Bloomberg, "Rent Control and the Housing Shortage," *Journal of Land and Public Utility Economics* 33 (May 1947):214-218; Karl Borders, "The Problem of Determing Fair Rents," *Journal of the American Statistical Association* 57 (March 1942): 34-40; Leo Grebler, "Implications of Rent Control Experience In the United States," *International Labor Review* 65 (1952): 462-485; and Ernest M. Fisher, "Twenty Years of Rent Control In New York City," in *Essays On Urban Land Economics* (Los Angeles: University of California, Real Estate Research Program, 1966), pp. 31-66. See chapter 1, note 49, for further references of analyses of New York City experience.

3. "Normal" is here defined to mean restoration of equilibrium in the housing market forces of supply and demand and not necessarily a return to conditions or uses existent before the war.

4. It should be recognized that rents generally did not decline to prewar levels, primarily as a result of cost-push inflation pervasive in all sectors of the economy as a result of the war. The failure of rents to decline to prewar levels and the projected impact of decontrol on the economy were used as arguments during the post-World War I extension period when the U.S. Supreme Court ruled that inflation was not sufficient justification for extending rent control. Chastleton v. Sinclair 264, U.S. 543 (1924).

5. See Daniel D. Gage, "Wartime Experiment in Federal Rent Control," *Journal*

*of Land and Public Utility Economics* 23 (1947): 50-58. Under the Emergency Price Control Act of 1942, prices on certain commodities were allowed to move up before coming under price controls and, subsequent to controls, blanket upward adjustments were made on other commodities, but never on rent. Adjustments in rents were only made during this period on an individual case-by-case basis (See chapter 1).

6. Gage, p. 55.

7. Block v. Hirsh, 256 U.S. 135, 157 (1921).

8. The construction costs of many of these units may well make rent levels prohibitive as the emergency recedes and concurrent inflated wage rates decrease.

9. U.S., Bureau of the Census, 1970 Census of Housing, United States Summary, *Detailed Housing Characteristics,* Tables 22 and 39. 1973 metropolitan vacancy figures derived from Postal Service surveys conducted for HUD, *Real Estate Analyst* 42 no. 31 (September 1973).

10. Pursuant to the promulgation of the interim regulation, a nationwide challenge to its effectuation was initiated by the New Jersey Tenants Organization, see *New York Times,* April 20, 1975. A legal battle between HUD and the Newark, New Jersey Rent Commission subsequently ensued relative to the HUD-ordered rent increases by the local rent commission in two subsidized buildings.

11. This method is also known as the "freeze date" method utilized during World War II controls. Although other methods may subsequently be used, as in the New York City Maximum Base Rent Program which is a cost-plus-profit formula, the starting point is usually via a rollback. See chapter 1 for discussion of methods considered prior to enactment of controls during World War II.

12. George Sternlieb and Elizabeth Brody, "The Pitfalls in Rent Control," *Real Estate Review* 4 (Spring, 1974): 124.

# Appendix I
# Formal Rent Adjustment Procedures in the Greater Boston Area

*INTRODUCTION*

Exhibit AI–1 shows the procedures under which the four Massachusetts communities evaluated landlord petitions for rent adjustments. Each community chose a base year for which to establish fair net operating income as well as a rent rollback date in compliance with Section 6(a) of Chapter 842. The state Enabling Act prescribes a six-month rollback of rents prior to the acceptance of rent control by a municipality. Exhibit AI-1 also shows the varying techniques used to determine fair net operating income (FNOI) adopted by the four municipalities. The following brief presentation describes and analyzes each formula and suggests possible impacts, particularly on the application of a pass-along system. Examples of income/expenses statements, depreciation schedules, and other administrative forms are presented in Appendix IV.

*Boston*

The formula under use in Boston fixes a structure's dollar NOI as of the end of December 1971. The method assumes that the rents charged as of this date yielded the landlord a fair net operating income. Thus, in theory, to retain the same net operating income (NOI) in dollars subsequent to December 1971, landlords simply must be given rent increases commensurate with increases in operating costs.

Yet, the Boston system prohibits the operation of a pass-along system by limiting fair NOI to parameters arrived at by a private market survey

*EXHIBIT AI-1*
*RENT ADJUSTMENT PROCEDURE*
*(LANDLORD PETITIONS)*

| *City or Town* | *Rent Roll-Back Date* | *Formula (NOI)** | *FNOI Derivation*** | *Comments* |
|---|---|---|---|---|
| Boston | June, 1972 or earliest subsequent month if unit unoccupied as of 6/72. | $NOI-year end December, 1971. | A) NOI base year 12/71 adjusted by the following parameters based on building type and measured as a percent of 1971 gross income:<br>1) Buildings constructed after January 1, 1960, 35-50 percent of GOI.<br>2) Any building containing more than 6 controlled units, 20-35 percent of GOI.<br>3) Any building containing 6 controlled units or less 20-40 percent of GOI<br>B) NOI 12/71 adjusted by 1971 property taxes as a percent of gross income<br>1) Less than 30 percent<br>2) More than 35 percent | Unlike Cambridge, no CPI is applied to NOI.<br><br>NOI as a percent of property taxes is no longer utilized. |
| Cambridge | March, 1970 | $ net operating income for 1967 x Consumer Price Index (General) for adjusted year (CPI base year 1967). | Base year $NOI 1967 or where data not available next following year. With base year subsequent to 1967 1.8 x expenses is utilized as check in arriving at allowable maximum rents.*** | General Consumer Price Index applied to base year net operating income to retain buying power of NOI. |

*Net Operating Income
**Fair Net Operating Income

***1.8 multiplier represents expenses to NOI ratio of 55-45 found to be average ratio in 1970. Its use is predicated upon the belief that NOI after 1967 cannot be assumed "fair."

*(continued)*
*RENT ADJUSTMENT PROCEDURE*
*(LANDLORD PETITIONS)*

| *City or Town* | *Rent Roll-Back Date* | *Formula (NOI)** | *FNOI Derivation*** | *Comments* |
|---|---|---|---|---|
| Brookline | March, 1970 | Return (percent of NOI to current market value) equals 6-11 percent of property value. Formerly, allowable return equal to return in 1970 subject to 6-11 percent parameter. | A) Methods of determining current market value:<br>1) Current purchase price.<br>2) Estimate of certified appraiser.<br>3) Landlord testimony.<br>4) 5.5 gross income multiplier.<br>5) 1.45 x assessed value.<br><br>B) Rate of return contingent upon condition of property<br>1) 6-7 percent poor properties.<br>2) 8-9 percent fair properties.<br>3) 10-11 percent good to excellent properties. | The 11 percent maximum rate of return is assumed to be the upper limit necessary to retire mortgage debt.<br><br>5.5 gross multiplier based on statistical study of selling price and 1970-1972. It will be soon updated. |
| Somerville | June, 1970 | 4-10 percent return on market value determined as adjusted purchase price. | FNOI closest year available pre-rent control 1970. Original purchase price adjusted by Consumer Price Index for Housing. FNOI subject to 4-10 percent parameter. Purchases subsequent to 1970—yield based on first mortgage interest rate. | Unlike Brookline, the 4-10 percent return on market value is not tied to the condition of the property. |

*Net Operating Income
**Fair Net Operating Income

commissioned by the Boston Rent Control Board. The parameters are based on varying percentages of 1971 gross income based on building type.

Net operating income for buildings constructed after January 1, 1960 are allowed a NOI ranging from 35 to 50 percent of gross operating income (GOI); buildings of more than six uncontrolled units, 25 to 40 percent of GOI; buildings containing six or less units, 20 to 35 percent of GOI.

Property taxes as a percent of gross income have been utilized occasionally to determine NOI. The rationale for this approach is that since real estate taxes are calculated as a percentage of GOI, property taxes as a percentage of gross income should fall within a range of 30 to 35 percent. This method was restricted to situations for which the landlord had no operating experience due to a recent sale or for which operating cost data was inadequate or unavailable. The property tax device is, however, no longer utilized.

Additionally, the Boston administration has analyzed the return to accumulated equity in order to determine if a landlord is receiving a fair return on equity. The formula operates as follows: net operating income is calculated as total expenses subtracted from gross potential income. Expenses include vacancies (the lesser of actual or 5 percent of gross income), operating costs, property taxes, annual permissable amortization charge for capital improvements, and the mortgage interest. Next, accumulated equity is calculated as equity (downpayment) plus accumulated principal. Using this base, net operating income is divided by accumulated equity, giving the percentage return on equity. If return on equity is less than 6 percent, accumulated equity is simply multiplied by .06 to arrive at a net income needed to provide a 6 percent return.

These procedures for arriving at FNOI present some inequities. The parameters utilized in determining the allowable net operating income for a structure provide landlords within the same class of buildings with a wide range of possible FNOIs. Potentially, one landlord could be receiving a FNOI 15 percent lower than another counterpart. Furthermore, a report prepared by the Real Estate Research Corporation in 1972 for the Boston Rent Control Administration indicated that the range of operating income ratios was probably 28.9 percent to 53.7 percent in Boston for 1969. The parameters for properties of six units or more hold that a property with a net income of over 40 percent is receiving excessive income. In essence, the Rent Control Board contends that a potentially large number of rental housing structures are receiving excessive income, and reasonable increases in operating expenses will not be reflected in increased rental income until the property is first adjusted to the 40 percent maximum without supplemental data to substantiate expenses on the part of the landlords.

What does this 40 percent maximum remainder of the rent dollar mean? Current mortgage rates for large-scale buildings are around the 9 to 10 percent mark. Given this maximum, a building's rent roll can support a value at a maximum of four times the rent roll. But typical multipliers that are used for modern buildings run six to eight times the gross rent roll. The enormous markdown in real market value is evident. The impact on the city's tax base is inevitable.

Also note that the interest rates shown do not include amortization. In the example cited, the actual *cash flow* would be negative. There would not be enough actual monies derived from operations to meet the requirements of annual payments on the mortgage principals.

Other inequities are evident in the procedures. Landlords with operating data for 1971 are subject to two review processes, both the parameters defining allowable NOI and the return on accumulated equity analysis. Yet, landlords who purchase property subsequent to 1971 and possibly lack cost data for the base year 1971 are only evaluated on an equity basis. A case in point would be a landlord who purchased a property in 1973 and experienced operating cost increase in the following year. Under these circumstances he would not be allowed to pass along those increases if return on equity was calculated to be 6 percent or more. This procedure may also adversely affect small property owners unfamiliar with bookkeeping and accounting procedures. Finally, in deriving accumulated equity as accumulated principal plus the downpayment, the Boston Rent Control Board has failed to recognize the impact of inflation on the book value of equity or the stream of payments derived from it.

### *Cambridge*

After a brief and limited use of two formulas based on 10 to 15 percent of value and 8 to 12 percent of value, the Cambridge Rent Control Board adopted a formula similar to the Boston method. For Cambridge, like Boston, FNOI equals NOI dollars earned at a 1967 base year. The determination of a base year was developed by a 1971 planning staff survey of rents in Cambridge from 1960 through 1970. The study showed that rents remained fairly stable between 1960 and 1967, while rising drastically after 1968; therefore, the Rent Control Board assumed that the rents charged in 1967 offered the landlord a FNOI. The study was based not on the realities of rents for occupied units but rather on newspaper listings. The results are summarized in Exhibit AI-2.

With increases in operating costs the landlord is given a "dollar for dollar" pass-along of "reasonable" expenses. Next, net operating income is adjusted by using the Consumer Price Index (base year 1967). Increasing NOI income by the CPI allows the landlord to retain buying power over time.

Cambridge deviates from this procedure when considering increases on structures for which 1967 data are not available or built subsequent to 1967 and not exempted by Chapter 842.[1] In these instances the Cambridge administration

*EXHIBIT AI–2*
*INCREASE IN RENTS*
*AS REFLECTED IN APARTMENT ADVERTISEMENTS*[1]
*(Percentages are percent increase over previous year)*

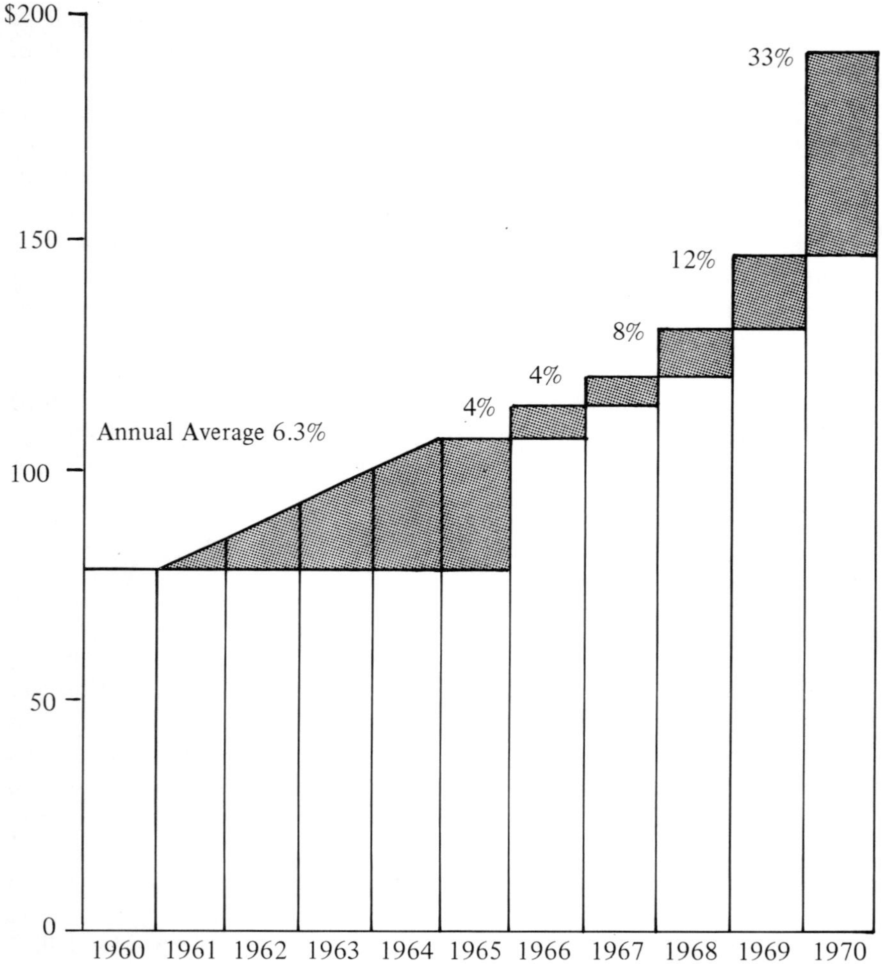


1. Rents asked for apartments advertised in first Boston *Sunday Globe and first* Cambridge *Chronicle* in September of indicated year.

*Source:* Department of Planning and Development, City of Cambridge.

applies a multiplier of 1.8 to actual expenses in the available annual expense base in order to derive maximum rents. The multiplier provides an expense base in order to derive maximum rents. The multiplier represents an expense to NOI ration of 55 percent to 45 percent, found to be the average ratio in 1970 through inspection of the Cambridge files. In essence, the 1.8 multiplier retains the 55 to 45 percent expenses to net operating income ratio in evaluating each application for rent adjustment. In structures with a rent greater than 1.8 times expenses, the NOI would be adjusted downward until it meets the required ratio.

The Cambridge formula offers some advantages compared to that of Boston. Cambridge's 1967 base year for determining FNOI is based on a more objective foundation than Boston's and the use of the CPI allows the landlord an increase in NOI which reflects the lower purchasing power of the dollar. Yet the use of the 1.8 multiplier places landlords who recently purchased a structure or are unable to provide 1967 data at a disadvantage. The FNOI of owners operating under the 1967 base year is not questioned while, in contrast, a NOI subsequent to 1967 is subject to the 1.8 multiplier.

The validity of the multiplier also must be questioned. As indicated previously, the 1.8 multiplier represents an average ratio of expenses to NOI. Therefore, reasonable increase in operating expenses will not necessarily bring commensurate increases in net income since the rent will be subject to the 1.8 multiplier limitation. The use of an average multiplier does not take into account that costs vary by the age and configuration of buildings. The impact of this limitation of the multiplier on the housing market is evident.

### *Brookline*

Brookline departs from the fixed NOI approach of both Boston and Cambridge by utilizing a return on current value method. The formula provides for 6 to 11 percent return on estimated property value (NOI as a percentage of property value). The 11 percent maximum rate of return is based on the Brookline board's decision as to the upper limit necessary to meet debt retirement. For recently purchased properties the interest rate on the first mortgage is allowed.

Market value has been determined by various calculations including multipliers applied to gross income and assessed value, current purchase price, appraisal estimates, and landlord testimony. Recently, the administration has turned away from using multipliers and has moved to current prices based on comparable sales and individual appraisal estimates.

Brookline has also placed greater emphasis upon current rate of return on market value as the ultimate rent limitation rather than referring to a rate assumed to yield a FNOI to the landlord as of the base year (March 1970). Furthermore, the fair rate of return formula has now been based upon the condition of the property: a poor property is allowed 6 to 7 percent; a fair property, 8 to 9 percent; and a good to excellent rental property, 10 to 11 percent.

Before the recent changes, a landlord was allowed a rate of return (NOI as a percentage of value) equal to his 1970 return. The new NOI computed by increasing rents commensurate with cost increases would only be adjusted if it fell outside of the parameters (6 to 11 percent) allowed by the board. Presently, current market value as a percentage of the new adjusted NOI (as determined after expenses are passed along) is conditioned by the quality of the property and adjusted appropriately.

The Brookline method offers some advantages. The market value approach allows increase in NOI as property appreciates in value. The recent emphasis upon appraisal practices in determining market value provides a more accurate estimate of value on individual buildings, as compared to a flat multiplier approach applied similarly to all structures. But, like Boston and Cambridge, limits on FNOI will mean that many structures will have to forego increases in rents directly proportionate to increases in operating costs. Theoretically, the approach is somewhat appealing; landlords who maintain a fair level of services and maintenance will receive higher rates of return on their properties. However, investors determine the rate of return expected from a building upon the risk involved. Poorer and older properties thus would be expected to yield a higher rate of return while higher quality buildings would be expected to yield lower return as a function of investment risk. In effect, some buildings would be denied a dollar-for-dollar pass-along of increased operating costs if their rate of return surpassed the levels designated "fair" by the board. This may actually serve to reduce the flow of funds available for improvement and maintenance.

*Somerville*

Somerville has also adopted a return on market value method but it differs from the Brookline approach in several important ways. Somerville allows a 4 to 10 percent rate of return on an adjusted purchase price. The rate of return earned in precontrolled 1970 is considered the base FNOI, and the purchase price is adjusted for inflation by the Consumer Price Index for housing.

Thus, in Somerville, methods for determining value are limited to an adjusted purchase price, while Brookline provides the option of several formulas. Furthermore, purchase price is adjusted by the CPI for housing as a surrogate for determining current value. In contrast, current purchase price in Brookline is determined by recent comparable sales. Also unlike Brookline, Somerville has established a base year FNOI. Finally, Somerville uses a wider range of allowable rates of return (4 to 10 percent), unconditioned by the quality of a property.

One of the few similarities between the two municipalities concerns properties purchased after 1970. In both Brookline and Somerville, the first mortgage interest rate is assumed to yield a fair rate of return. However, comparable properties may be receiving far different rates of return depending upon financing patterns and the wide range of allowable rates of return. Assuming, as in Brookline, that the 10 percent maximum return is the upper limit necessary to meet debt requirements, the board has failed to adjust the mortgage interest rates commensurate with increasing mortgage rates.

## *FACTORS AFFECTING FAIR NET OPERATING INCOME (FNOI)*

As enumerated in Chapter 842, each rent control board and administration considers a similar range of factors effecting FNOI.[2] Briefly they include: property taxes; operating and maintenance costs; capital improvements; living space; services or equipment; deterioration of structures and units; and failure to perform ordinary maintenance and repair. Generally, each administration treats these categories in a similar manner, but variations exist.

General operating and maintenance costs encompass utilities, fuel, insurance, labor and supplies, payroll, and management fees. Landlords and operators are allowed increases for reasonable expenses. The boards depend on verification of expenses by landlords through actual bills or invoices. Boston also relies heavily upon consistency of costs over time, demanding an analysis of expenses over a three-year period.

Beyond the operating costs mentioned above, other cost components are normally included in expenses; these other costs may include brokerage, legal, and audit fees. Audit and brokerage fees, if they meet the requirements of consistency and verification, are normally allowed. Legal fees, which have taken on greater significance since the inception of rent control, are allowed but with limitations. In Boston and Cambridge, legal fees incurred for rent adjustments or eviction purposes are not permitted. Similarly, Brookline does not permit legal fees for rent adjustments; but unlike the other municipalities, Brookline does allow legal expenses for eviction purposes. The Brookline board's rationale for this policy is that eviction of a tenant for failure to pay rent or destruction of the unit is directly tied to the operation of a building, while the need for a rent increase is not.

Labor costs can constitute a substantial amount of the operating costs. For landlords, particularly small-scale owners who perform their own maintenance and repairs, the boards have made provisions to allow pass-alongs for self-executed labor.

The Brookline administration requires documentation on estimates of hours worked by the landlord. The permissible hourly wage will vary with the type of maintenance and repair performed (painting, carpentry, plumbing, etc.).

The wage rate is normally what a nonunion wage earner would earn. The executive director of the Brookline administration indicated that the rate is generally around $5 per hour. Cambridge differs from Brookline in that it attempts to determine the competency of the landlord and the length of time normally needed to reasonably perform the specific repair in question.

It is evident that few reliable measurements exist with which to determine the value of the landlord's labor and a great deal of discretion is left to the staff person evaluating the audit. In contrast, Boston utilizes costs derived and documented by the Community Improvement Project (CIP)—an organization which has compiled figures detailing the average costs and time spans necessary to perform a full range of housing related repairs.

A crucial element in determining what costs the landlord will be permitted is the time period covering the expenses. Cambridge and Boston allow the landlord to submit data representing the last fiscal year. Brookline grants the owner the choice of submitting expenses for the twelve-month period, giving the landlord the advantage of presenting the most recent increases. This is particularly important in a period of rapid inflation.

Property taxes are perhaps the easiest cost to determine and evaluate. Documentation of actual taxes incurred is readily available from the local tax assessor and anticipated increases are public knowledge. The Brookline board goes beyond incurred property tax expenses and permits anticipated property taxes, not yet actually paid by the landlord, to be considered in determining FNOI.

Management fees are becoming a normal part of operating expenses as an increasing number of apartment owners are turning management responsibilities over to private management firms. Boston and Brookline allow a maximum of 6 percent of gross income to be allocated to management costs. Cambridge does not place a ceiling on management fees, but simply requires that they have been incurred and meet the test of "reasonableness."

### *Nonallowable Costs*

Expenses excluded from the allowable expense categories include depreciation for capital expenditures (prior to the base year date) and debt service (principal and interest). Each is considered part of a building's FNOI.

In addition, other costs not regarded as allowable expenses are vacancies and bad debts. It is difficult to allow for vacancies since the apartment may soon become occupied and an argument can be made that with vacancies expenses are not incurred. Yet, more often than not, operating costs do not stem from the unit but rather are incurred in upkeep of the building as a whole—for example, the heating, lighting, and cleaning of common areas. The computation of FNOI upon 100 percent occupancy instead of an average vacancy percentage results in a reduction of the FNOI to the landlord.

Brookline's policy of permitting nonincurred property taxes as allowable expense resembles a contingency allowance. None of the other boards allow increases for projected or anticipated costs. In Cambridge, the assumption is made that the rent charged as of the base year by the landlord included provision for contingencies which will remain in effect in subsequent years.

*Code Compliance, Decreases in Services, Deterioration of Unit*

In each community, the quality and level of services of a structure are inspected by the staff or the local housing inspector or tenant testimony is received if a hearing is requested. Where problems are detected, rents are decreased until defects are corrected. In the event that an increase is warranted, the adjusted rent becomes active, contingent on repairs or on the return of service previously terminated.

Decreases in rent vary with the type of service, repair needed, and the level of deterioration. However, no definitive criteria is utilized in determining the level of rent decreases; the final decision is left solely to the discretion of the board. More importantly, this practice places many owners within a vicious cycle. Repairs are economically prohibitive without increased rentals; yet, increases will not be granted until the ruling of the board is met—the result: a stalemate. The impact on older sections of the city, areas which have been subject to neglect, gradual deterioration, and the onus of institutional disinvestment in many instances predating the enactment of rent control, may well be the loss of entire neighborhoods.

*Hardship and Inequity Provisions*

Hardship and inequity provisions are usually included in approaches which use an FNOI formula. The Boston regulations cite specific factors which may override the FNOI allotment. These include capital improvements, taxes, and operating and maintenance costs not reflected in the base year rents. The hardship and inequity provisions can also be applied to individual units. These provisions relate to both landlords' and tenants' petitions for adjustment. The provisions are ineffectual for a landlord who surpasses the limits set by the board as FNOI.

The Cambridge and Brookline boards, unlike Boston, do not cite capital improvements or actual operating expense not reflected in the base year rent as grounds for contesting the validity of FNOI. The Cambridge board simply provides for adjustments of the base year rent if the rent was materially affected by family or special relationship other than family, and as a result the rent was substantially different from the rent generally prevailing for comparable housing.

In response to rapid increases in fuel costs in 1974 and mounting protests from landlords, the Boston and Brookline boards allowed pass-alongs by application of cost increases (in Boston, a proportion of total projected increases) under a claim of gross equity and extreme hardship. Boston allowed a 50 percent pass-along for projected increases in 1974 fuel costs over 1973 levels.

A provision operating in Brookline, as well as Cambridge and Boston, states that the board may dismiss any landlord petition if a hearing before the board regarding the same building or unit occurred within twelve months. However, in the face of rising fuel costs Brookline allowed landlords to submit petitions within the twelve-month period.

### *CAPITAL IMPROVEMENTS*

Each community has developed a different approach toward extraordinary repairs and capital improvements. In the following section these approaches will be examined in detail. One must bear in mind that if rent control is to accomplish the objective of alleviating the problems arising out of the housing emergency, maintenance and improvement of the existing housing stock should be encouraged.

#### *Brookline*

Of the four communities, Brookline has perhaps the most clearly defined approach to capital improvements. All repairs and replacements of items enumerated in the depreciation schedule entailing an expenditure of more than $150 may be amortized as a capital expenditure. Capital improvements are classified according to six general categories: (1) exterior renovation and construction; (2) landscaping; (3) interior renovation and construction; (4) utility and service systems; (5) appliances; and (6) furnishings. The amortization periods are set forth for both total as well as partial replacement of an item.[3] If, for example, the improvement is determined to be a repair rather than a total replacement, an abbreviated amortization period is applied.

In an effort to maintain the housing stock and specifically encourage capital improvements, Brookline has established a procedure known as the "Advisory Opinion." This procedure was initiated on an informal basis applicable to vacant apartments only. As of September 1973, however, it has been incorporated as a formal procedure. The advisory opinion procedure may be utilized by any landlord or management firm contemplating a capital improvement. The landlord may submit his proposed plan of improvements to the rent control board with an estimate of all relevant expenses. The rent control board will then proceed to amortize the proposed expenses in accordance with the time framework outlined in the "Depreciation Schedule" to arrive at an annual expense figure. This permits an estimate of the rent increase attributable to the capital improvement. If this figure is satisfactory to the landlord, he will proceed with the improvement. Once the improvement has been completed, the owner must submit all bills and invoices to document his expenditures which are then audited by the rent control board. If the actual expenditure associated with the capital improvement is equal to the original estimate, he is then granted the estimated rent increase. If the actual expenses are greater than the original estimate, the rent increase allowed will be adjusted upward to reflect the difference. If the actual expenses are less than the original estimate, the rent increase may be adjusted downward. In every instance but one for which a landlord utilized the advisory opinion procedure, the capital improvement was in fact executed.

In 1973 the advisory opinion procedure was modified to the extent that, if in order to execute the capital improvement, it became necessary to obtain a property improvement loan, the rent control board would allow "reasonable" financing costs to be included in the depreciation cost of the improvement.

Closely related to the area of capital improvements is the question of when large-scale rehabilitation becomes de facto new construction thereby qualifying for an exemption from rent control under the provisions of Chapter 842. Investment in deteriorated property by way of total rehabilitation should be encouraged as it is of significant benefit to the community. Rehabilitation serves the dual purpose of returning the property to the tax rolls as well as removing a potential blight from the community.

The town of Brookline currently approaches this problem by considering the merits of each individual case. If the cost of the renovation is in excess of the assessed value, or the purchase price of the structure, then these factors weigh heavily in favor of an exemption from rent control. Additional considerations, such as the replacement of the entire mechanical or electrical system, will also effect the board's decision. The underlying criterion in the decision is an assessment of the value of the property to the town prior to the renovation as opposed to the value of the property to the town after the renovation has been completed.

### *Boston*

In Boston, capital improvement is defined within Rent Regulation 6 (2/1/74) Section 2. The regulation states:

> Capital improvement includes any substantial rehabilitation, addition or improvement which adds to the value of the property and has a useful life of more than one year but does not include ordinary repair replacement or maintenance. Amortization of capital improvements shall be limited to the

annual amount necessary to amortize a level payment loan in the amount of the reasonable cost of such improvements at 8½ percent interest per year over the useful life of such improvements.

Section 4, "The Method of Adjustment," sets forth the manner in which capital improvements may be reflected in terms of increased rent levels. Once the initial adjustments have been made in accordance with the regulation, the amortization of capital improvements made after January 1, 1972 may be added either:

1) to the full extent of such amortization in the case of units vacant at the time the improvements are made or occupied by tenants consenting to such improvements, or
2) to the extent that such amortization does not result in increasing the rent charged by more than 10 percent of the rent charged for December 1971 in any one year in the case of all other units.

The 10 percent limitation appears counterproductive in terms of encouraging capital improvements. In those instances in which the 10 percent limitation on rent increases is applied, the landlord is in effect penalized for improving his property. In many instances, he is placed in the position of carrying the cost of the improvement without a sufficient increase in rent income to offset the expenditure associated with improvement. This arrangement is detrimental not only to individual owners seeking to recoup their investments, but also to the housing stock in general as it fosters a negative approach to capital improvements of the existing housing stock.

In Exhibit AI-3, "Boston Capital Improvements Limitation," the computation of the maximum investment which can be financed at 10 percent for eight years, given an apartment renting for $175 per month in Boston is outlined. Even if the landlord is willing to accept these terms, the maximum investment would be limited to merely $1,121.07, a figure hardly sufficient in a city of aging structures.

Several procedures are conspicuously absent from the Boston rent regulations. For example, there is no procedure paralleling that of the "Advisory Opinion" in Brookline. Thus, there is no formal means for a landlord to ascertain the results, as reflected in rent levels, of a capital expenditure. With respect to the related issue of distinguishing new construction from rehabilitation, one finds a less flexible approach in Boston as compared to Brookline; Boston's approach relies primarily on the per unit cost of rehabilitation. If costs are in excess of $10,000 per unit, the structure is permitted an exemption from Chapter 842. Although the regulation allows for administrative discretion, it is apparent that the $10,000 per unit costs serves as the yardstick against which renovation is measured.

## *EXHIBIT AI-3*
## *BOSTON*
## *CAPITAL IMPROVEMENTS*
## *LIMITATION*

---

*Illustration of Effects of 10% Increase Limit on Capital Improvements in Boston (Boston Rent Regulations, Section 4[e] [2]).*

---

*Assume:* (1) Monthly Rental = \$175.00 for typical 1-bedroom unit.
(2) Financed at 10% interest rate per annum.
(3) Amortization period of 8 years.

*Formula:* Present Value of an Investment $V = \sum_{i=1}^{n} \frac{Ri}{(1 + r)}$

V = Present Value of the investment
R = Dollar Return from investment in a given year
r = Rate at which returns are discounted for maturity
Σ = Refers to summation of discounted returns over all years in which investment will pay
*i* = 1 for first year, 2 for second . . .

The 10% limitation allows additional rental income of \$210/year or \$17.50/month.

$$V = \frac{\$210}{(1+.10)^1} + \frac{\$210}{(1+.10)^2} + \frac{\$210}{(1+.10)^3} + \frac{\$210}{(1+.10)^4} +$$

$$\frac{\$210}{(1+.10)^5} + \frac{\$210}{(1+.10)^6} + \frac{\$210}{(1+.10)^7} + \frac{\$210}{(1+.10)^8}$$

$$V = \frac{\$210}{1.10} + \frac{\$210}{1.21} + \frac{\$210}{1.33} + \frac{\$210}{1.46} +$$

$$\frac{210}{1.61} + \frac{210}{1.77} + \frac{210}{1.95} + \frac{210}{2.14} =$$

$$V = \$190.91 + \$173.55 + \$157.89 + \$143.83$$

$$\$130.43 + \$118.64 + \$107.69 + 98.13$$

$$V = \$1{,}121.07$$

This is the maximum capital improvement expenditure per unit without an allowance for a return on investment that is warranted given the foregoing set of assumptions.

On the whole, one must conclude that these factors work against substantial capital improvements in the Boston housing stock subject to rent control.

*Cambridge*

Cambridge Regulation, Series no. 72 (Individual Adjustments), Section 04 states:

> In determining Fair Net Operating Income the following adjustments shall be made for:
>
> (c) Capital improvements not necessary to comply with state or city housing and health codes and ordinances in an amount per dollar of capital expenditure equal to level payments required to amortize a loan to finance such improvements during the useful life thereof, provided that such adjustment shall terminate at the end of the useful life of such improvement and *provided* that tenant approval of such improvements shall be required for any improvement commenced after the date of this regulation.

If interpreted literally, the regulation would preclude reimbursing any investment in a capital improvement associated with a code violation. This apparently is not the case; rather the regulation is directed at blatantly deferred maintenance and basic amenities which should be present and are not. In the opinion of the Cambridge Rent Control Board, the owner should not be entitled to a rent increase for simply satisfying code standards.

The application of the regulation in the case of the replacement of an inadequate roof, for example, allows the landlord to recover his investment. There is no doubt that there are problems attendant to the application of a regulation of this type. Inevitably the rent control board makes the determination as to what is or is not a recoverable improvement. The problem would seem to be that in order to encourage capital investment, any improvement should be recoverable by the landlord. To deny the landlord an opportunity to recover investments in those areas related to code standards is to ignore the economics of real estate investment.

Major repairs and replacements amounting to more than $200 are to be considered capital expenditures. For all such capital expenditures, the Cambridge Rent Control Board allows an interest rate of 9.5 percent on capital improvements. The Cambridge approach to capital improvements is to view such improvements within the overall context of operating costs. Although this is a logical approach in an administrative sense, it does not take into account the importance of, and rather unique role played by, capital improvements with respect to the existing housing stock. There is no formal procedure whereby a landlord can petition for an increase based solely on capital improvements. Nor is there a formal procedure whereby the landlord may submit his proposed plan for capital expenditures to obtain an estimate as to postimprovement rent levels. The absence of such a mechanism deprives the smaller and less sophisticated investor of a means to evaluate the effect of a capital expenditure on future rent levels. The problems of the small owner are particularly evident in Cambridge because the depreciation schedule is considerably more complicated than the straightforward schedule utilized in Brookline. The most important shortcoming, however, is Cambridge's failure to recognize capital improvement as a significant, indeed critical, aspect of maintaining the existing housing stock.

With respect to making a determination of new construction as opposed to repairs, and thereby qualifying for the new construction exemption of Chapter 842, the Cambridge approach closely resembles that of Brookline; that is, there are no objective criteria upon which to base the decision. The general criterion used is to determine whether the building is "substantially new" after repairs are made. More specifically, the board looks for improvements such as a new roof, new plumbing, new electrical system, and the like. These criteria, according to the Cambridge Rent Control Board, are extremely difficult to apply, yet have been upheld in the courts.[4] The case of *Roos and Morley* v. *Allan Lefkowitz, et al.* serves as the precedent for upholding the criteria and involves two buildings in which the dollar amounts expended were approximately equal. One structure qualified for an exemption based on the improvements while the other was subject to rent controls.

## *NOTES*

1. Chapter 842, Sec. 1(b)(2) exempts rental units constructed on or after January 1, 1969.
2. This portion of the analysis will exclude practices in Somerville due to the unavailability of data.
3. Brookline Depreciation Schedule Form 27 (6/5/73) included in Appendix IV.
4. Roos and Morley v. Allan Lefkowitz, et al., Equity No. 9, Third District Court of Eastern Middlesex.

# Appendix II Summary of Operating Results Methodology

The empirical data which constitute the basis of analysis in chapter 5 were derived from two independent studies of the Greater Boston Area and Fort Lee, New Jersey conducted in 1974-75 by the Center for Urban Policy Research. Data included in chapter 5 for the New York City case study were derived from a variety of published sources as cited in the text.

## *THE GREATER BOSTON AREA CASE STUDY*

In analyzing the realities of rent control, one of the criticisms heard most frequently from the private sector is that the control mechanisms are administered in such a fashion as to leave rents far behind the inflationary increases in operating costs. To determine the validity of this claim, as well as the extent of the operating expense increases that the private sector has in fact experienced, it was necessary to examine operating statements from private landlords and management firms. This examination was then expanded to include audited operating data for limited dividend projects submitted to the U.S. Department of Housing and Urban Development and government-certified operating data for nonprofit operations such as the Boston Housing Authority. The methodological design consisted of a three-phase certification of the increases in operating costs.

### *Implementation*

The first phase of the process consisted of acquiring data in the private sector. The target areas were defined as those within the Route 128 perimeter (which encircles communities to the north, west, and south of Boston), thereby including the four rent-controlled communities as well as a significant number of noncontrolled communities.

The information obtained included operating income and expenses as well as pertinent descriptive information (see Exhibit AII-1). The data was organized on a project-by-project basis to facilitate internal analysis over time as well as comparison between projects of similar type.

The second phase focused on the operating expenses of the nonprofit sector. These data were obtained from the Boston Housing Authority and included federally subsidized units, state-assisted family public housing and state-assisted units for the elderly. The operating data for these 14,564 governmental nonprofit units generally confirmed the pattern of expenditures and increases reflected by the private sector. However, the data for this housing sector are not included in the analysis of chapter 5.

The third phase of certification of operating costs consisted of an analysis of audited operating statements submitted to the Department of Housing and Urban Development for limited dividend projects. In some cases, data were also procured directly from the management firms responsible for operating and maintaining limited dividend projects.

The final data base utilized includes audited operating statements for 4,520 limited dividend units and 7,548 units within the private sector, for a total sample size of 12,068 units in these two categories.

### *Methodological Procedures*

The data for both the private sector and limited dividend projects were then posted on a standard coding form (Exhibit AII-2). Initially the data had been recorded according to varied accounting procedures, ranging from hand-entered ledger books to sophisticated computer print-outs with five-digit expense accounts. In the process of coding and standardizing the data, additional units were eliminated from the sample.[1] The coding procedure provided an opportunity to review all the data on a year-by-year, project-by-project, and entry-by-entry basis. This proved to be valuable in locating inconsistencies from year to year, missing data, incorrect entries and a host of other problems attendant to the standardization of sixteen different accounting systems encompassing 124 projects and 12,068 units. Each of these problems was followed up with the management firm and landlord and corrections were made wherever possible. In those instances for which missing information was not available, the project was discarded from the sample. It was essential that unusual expenditures be distinguished from the normal level of repairs to obtain a conservative picture of the cost increases experienced in the operation of

*EXHIBIT AII-1*
*RENT CONTROL STUDY*
*BUILDING INFORMATION SHEET*

---

Facesheet Information: Operating Experience

1. Project Number: __________

2. Location: (Town/City) ____________________

3. Bedroom Mix
   - Efficiency _____
   - 1 – Bedroom _____
   - 2 – Bedroom _____
   - 3 – Bedroom _____
   - 4 – Bedroom or more _____
   - Total Number Units _____

4. Configuration:
   1. High Rise (4 story or more, with Elevator) _____
   2. Garden Apartment _____
   3. Misc. _____

5. Rent Control: Yes Or No

6. Type of Construction Brick Frame Concrete Other

7. Age of Structure _____Yrs.

8. Type of Heating Fuel, Oil _____ Gas _____ Electric _____ Steam _____

9. Incinerator Yes – No

Date ______________

*EXHIBIT AII-2*
*STANDARD CODING FORM*
*#1 CLASSIFICATION CARD*

---

| | | | |
|---|---|---|---|
| 1. Our Code No. of Bldg. | | | (1,2,3) |
| 2. Town Located (Write in name) ________ | | | (5,6) |
| 3. Rent Controlled | [1] yes [2] no | | (7) |
| 4. Type of Building | High Rise Elevator | [1] | |
| | Low Rise Under 25 Units | [2] | |
| | Low Rise 25 or more Units | [3] | |
| | Garden Type | [4] | (9) |
| 5. Type of Ownership | [1] Investor | [1] | |
| | [2] F.H.A. | [2] | |
| | [3] Mass. Hous. Auth. | [3] | |
| | | [4] | |
| | | [5] | |
| | | [6] | (11) |
| 6. Heating Fuel Type | Coal | [1] | |
| | Oil | [2] | |
| | Gas | [3] | |
| | Combination | [4] | |
| | Electricity | [5] | |
| | | [6] | |
| | | [7] | (13) |
| 7. Utilities Included in Rent: | | | |
| | Electricity yes [1] | no [2] | (14) |
| | Heat yes [1] | no [2] | (15) |
| | Gas-cooking yes [1] | no [2] | (16) |
| | Air Cond. yes [1] | no [2] | (17) |
| | Window wash yes [1] | no [2] | (18) |
| | Water yes [1] | no [2] | (19) |
| Other ________ | | | (20) |
| 8. Total No. of Apts. | | ________ | (22-25) |
| 9. No. of Efficiency | | ________ | (27-29) |
| 10. No. of One Bedroom | | ________ | (31-33) |
| 11. No. of Two Bedroom | | ________ | (35-37) |
| 12. No. of Three Bedroom | | ________ | (39-41) |
| 13. No. of Four of More Bedroom | | ________ | (43-45) |

*EXHIBIT AII–2*
*(Continued)*

| | | | |
|---|---|---|---|
| 14. Type of Documentation | Audited Statement | [1] | |
| | Certified to Gov't Agency | [2] | |
| | Rent Appeal | [3] | |
| | | [4] | |
| | | [5] | (47) |
| 15. Fiscal Year End | First Quarter | [1] | |
| | Second Quarter | [2] | |
| | Third Quarter | [3] | |
| | Fourth Quarter | [4] | (49) |
| 16. Number of Years Oper. Date Available ______ | | | (50) |
| 17. Do we have '74 date | Yes [1] | No [2] | (52) |
| '73 | Yes [1] | No [2] | (53) |
| '72 | Yes [1] | No [2] | (54) |
| '71 | Yes [1] | No [2] | (55) |
| '70 | Yes [1] | No [2] | (56) |
| '69 | Yes [1] | No [2] | (57) |
| Other | Yes [1] | No [2] | (58) |
| End of Card No. 1 | | | (80) |

*EXHIBIT AII-2*
*(continued)*
*CARD 2*

| | | | |
|---|---|---|---|
| 18. Bldg. No. | | | (1,2,3) |
| 19. Fiscal Year | '74=[1], 73=[2], 72=[3], 71=[4], 70=[5], 69=[6], 68=[7], 67=[8] | | (4) |
| Quarter Ended | First [1], Second [2], Third [3], Fourth [4] | | (5) |
| 20. Apartment Rentals @ 100% [Include Employees Apt.] | | ________ | (6-12) |
| 21. Total Fees for Garages | | ________ | (13-17) |
| 22. Total Store and Office Income | | ________ | (19-23) |
| 23. Losses Due to Vacancies | | ________ | (25-29) |
| 24. Losses Due to Rent Non Payment | | ________ | (30-34) |
| 25. Total Rent Loss | | ________ | (36-40) |
| 26. Net Rent Received | | ________ | (42-48) |
| 27-28. Total Payroll Expenses, Supplies, Interior Paint, Mtnce. & Reprs, Services Exterminating etc. | | ________ | (50-55) |
| 29. Miscellaneous Oper. Expenses- See Explanation | | ________ | (57-61) |
| 30. Electricity | | ________ | (63-67) |
| 31. Water | | ________ | (69-72) |
| End of Card No. 2 | | | (80) |

*EXHIBIT AII-2*
*(continued)*
*CARD 3*

| | | |
|---|---|---|
| 32. Bldg. No. | ________ | (1,2,3) |
| 33. Gas Excluding Heating Fuel | ________ | (5-8) |
| 34. Heating Fuel | ________ | (10-14) |
| 35. Management Fee (Including Wages) | ________ | (16-20) |
| 36. Leasing Fee (Including Wages) | ________ | (22-25) |
| 37. Other Admin. Costs | ________ | (27-30) |
| 38. Insurance (Exclusive of FHA Mtge and Employee Group Insurance) | ________ | (32-36) |
| 39. Real Estate Taxes | ________ | (38-42) |
| 40. Other Taxes, Fees, Permits, Franchise Personal Property, etc. | ________ | (44-48) |
| 41. *Total All Expenses* | ________ | (50-56) |
| 42. *Net Operating Income* | ________ | (58-63) |
| 43. Negative [1] Positive [2] | | (65) |
| End of Card No. 3 | | (80) |

multifamily structures. However, it became evident during the coding process that frequently this distinction was not made by the individual landlords and management firms. Thus, it became necessary to establish criteria for the amortization of extraordinary repairs and expensive improvements to provide an accurate portrayal of operating costs. If an item within the general category of repair and maintenance represented more than 5 percent of the net rent received, and if the cost for this item increased by more than 100 percent, it was considered to be an unusual expenditure, and was therefore amortized. The amortization process consisted of calculating the average operating costs for the particular account excluding those years in which an extraordinary expense had been incurred. The average obtained was then deducted from the extraordinary expenditures to determine the amount to be amortized. A five-year depreciation schedule was adopted to represent the amortization period. This procedure permitted a conservative reflection of typical maintenance and repair costs. In general, however, it tends to understate increases in operating costs.

The data were then submitted to a computer analysis for consistency. For each of the twenty-one variables on the standard coding sheet, the percent of increase or decrease was calculated from one year to the next. In the case of increases, any year-to-year increase or decrease greater than the median for the group was printed for review. These increases and decreases were then rechecked by the coding staff to determine their validity. In all cases for which the data were questionable, the variable was checked with the original source for an explanation of the increase or decrease. If an explanation was not available, the project was discarded from the sample. This process yielded a standardized sample that was considered to be virtually free of error. This sample constitutes the basis for the analysis of those cost increases experienced by both the private sector and those operating limited dividend projects.[2]

The total sample size of private and audited operating costs consists of 12,068 units. The data base represents a relatively good cross-section of both large and small structures as well as rent-controlled and noncontrolled properties. As the analysis presented in chapter 5 focuses on average annual operating results over the 1971-73 period, the data subset utilized was that for which a minimum of three consecutive years of data (ending in 1973) was included. This data subset consists of seventy rent-controlled properties of 4,834 units and twenty noncontrolled properties of 3,898 units (see Exhibit AII-3). For the distribution of the total sample by structure type and ownership status, see Exhibits AII-4 and AII-5.

## *THE FORT LEE CASE STUDY*

Constituting a smaller geographical area with a much more homogeneous housing stock than the Greater Boston area, the Fort Lee sample could be

*EXHIBIT AII–3*
*SAMPLE DISTRIBUTION OF UNITS AND CASES BY DATA SUBSETS*
*(As Determined by Consecutive Years of Operating Statements for Reporting Establishments)*
*GREATER BOSTON AREA*

| | *Five Year Data Subset* | *Three to Five Year Data Subset* | *1973 Data Subset* | *Total Sample* |
|---|---|---|---|---|
| Rent-controlled | | | | |
| Number of Cases | 31 | 70 | 86 | 94 |
| Number of Units | 2,070 | 4,834 | 5,526 | 6,363 |
| Noncontrolled | | | | |
| Number of Cases | 7 | 20 | 28 | 30 |
| Number of Units | 1,474 | 3,893 | 5,509 | 5,705 |
| Total Sample | | | | |
| Number of Cases | 38 | 90 | 114 | 124 |
| Number of Units | 3,544 | 8,727 | 11,035 | 12,068 |

*Note:* Number of cases reflects number of operators for which operating statements are included. Operating statements may represent individual or multiple structures. Total sample includes total number of buildings for which data was available for one or more years. Not all in the total sample contained consecutive years, nor was 1973 data available for all.

*Source:* CUPR sample of operating statements.

*EXHIBIT AII–4*
*SAMPLE DISTRIBUTION OF UNITS*
*BY TYPE OF STRUCTURE AND CONTROL STATUS*
*GREATER BOSTON AREA*

| | *High-rise Elevator* | *Low-rise (<25 Units)* | *Low-rise (>25 Units)* | *Garden* | *Total* |
|---|---|---|---|---|---|
| Rent-controlled | 3,792 | 448 | 1,515 | 608 | 6,363 |
| % Rent-controlled | 59.6 | 7.0 | 23.8 | 9.6 | 100.0 (52.7) |
| Noncontrolled | 2,664 | 0 | 1,016 | 2,025 | 5,705 |
| % Noncontrolled | 46.7 | – | 17.8 | 35.5 | 100.0 (47.3) |
| Total | 6,456 | 448 | 2,531 | 2,633 | 12,068 |

*Source:* CUPR sample of operating statements.

*EXHIBIT AII–5*
*SAMPLE DISTRIBUTION OF UNITS*
*BY TYPE OF OWNERSHIP AND CONTROL STATUS*
*GREATER BOSTON AREA*

| | *FHA*[1] | *FHA*[2] | *Private Investor* | *MHFA*[3] | *Total* |
|---|---|---|---|---|---|
| Rent-controlled | 1,819 | 1,445 | 3,099 | – | 6,363 |
| Nonrent-controlled | 2,587 | – | 2,904 | 214 | 5,705 |
| Total | 4,406 | 1,445 | 6,003 | 214 | 12,068 |

1. Operation including rent levels subject to regulation of the Department of Housing and Urban Development.
2. Not under HUD regulation.
3. Massachusetts Housing Finance Agency.

*Source:* CUPR analysis of operating statements.

smaller and still retain validity because it represented less variation. C primarily of structures built since 1960, the sample generally reflects the distribution of units within the community. The borough of Fort Lee experienced a 175.3 percent increase in rental units (in structures with 10 or more units) between 1960 and 1970. The sample also represents the various structure-type characteristics of the Fort Lee rental stock of which 59.9 percent of existing units in 1975 were in the highrise category. All properties were subject to rent control as described in chapter 6. The majority of these buildings, as reflective of the community, are in the luxury housing market and provide a high level of amenities. Exhibit AII-6 reflects the median distribution of rents according to bedroom configuration and class of unit. Although other factors such as view, security provisions, recreation facilities, and apartment extras (number of bathrooms, dishwashers, and so forth) determine luxury class, rent levels are a significant measure of the presence of these amenities.

The inclusion of a luxury class sample in this study provides an opportunity to compare the operating expenses of buildings which assumedly have a more flexible budget. However, as discussed in chapter 5 and reflected in a resident survey included in the original study, the tenants in these units pay a premium for better-than-average maintenance and services and therefore are extremely sensitive to reductions in these areas.

### *Implementation*

The data utilized in the Fort Lee study were derived from eleven properties containing 2,769 units. Because the sample was smaller in size, the process of coding and checking the data was a far less complex task than that necessary for the Boston data; however, the same methodological procedures were utilized (see Exhibits AII-1 and AII-2). The original Fort Lee sample consisted of thirteen properties. Two buildings were discarded from the sample on the basis of insufficient operating experience, as they were in rent-up years during the period of analysis.

Exhibit AII-7 reflects the distribution of units included in the Fort Lee sample according to bedroom configuration and structure type.

*EXHIBIT AII-6*
*AVERAGE AND MEDIAN RENTS FROM A SAMPLE OF FORT LEE LUXURY BUILDINGS BY LUXURY CLASS AND BY BEDROOM CONFIGURATION**

| *Building* | *Studio/ Efficiency* | *One Bedroom* | *Two Bedroom* | *Three Bedroom* | *Weighted Average* |
|---|---|---|---|---|---|
| Class I | $302 | $402 | $495 | $590 | $439 |
| 1 | $330 | $435 | $514 | $632 | $468 |
| 2 | $253 | $335 | $475 | – | $388 |
| 3 | $345 | $475 | $645 | – | $482 |
| 4 | $280 | $428 | $563 | $693 | $490 |
| 5 | – | $369 | $475 | – | $411 |
| 6 | – | $314 | $418 | $521 | $398 |
| 7 | – | $460 | $425 | $515 | $458 |
| Class II | $232 | $295 | $385 | $414 | $329 |
| 8 | $212 | $286 | $350 | $360 | $294 |
| 9 | $244 | $298 | $392 | $468 | $356 |
| 10 | $280 | $307 | – | – | $288 |
| 11 | – | $302 | $356 | – | $316 |
| 12 | – | $280 | $440 | – | $335 |
| Class III | $190 | $214 | $228 | – | $212 |

*Rents by bedroom type are median figures; however, aggregate data per building reflects average weighted in proportion to number of units within category.

*Source:* CUPR survey of Fort Lee, New Jersey, Spring 1975.

*EXHIBIT AII–7*
*DISTRIBUTION OF SAMPLE UNITS BY BEDROOM CONFIGURATION AND BUILDING TYPE*
*FORT LEE CASE STUDY*

| | *High-rise* | *Low-rise* | *Total* |
|---|---|---|---|
| Efficiency/Studio | 278 | 75 | 353 |
| One Bedroom Units | 948 | 280 | 1,228 |
| Two Bedroom Units | 686 | 161 | 847 |
| Three+ Bedroom Units* | 292 | 49 | 341 |
| Total | 2,204 | 565 | 2,769 |

*Note:* High-rise = 14 stories or more, N=6 structures. Low-rise includes one garden apartment, N=5 structures.

* Three+ bedroom units include small number of professional apartments (8) and penthouse apartments (20).

*Source:* CUPR survey, Fort Lee, New Jersey, spring 1975.

*NOTES*

1. Of the original 16,945 units provided by the private sector, a total of 7,103 units were eliminated due to data problems. Of the 2,436 units provided by HUD, 210 were eliminated due to data problems. Of the remaining 9,842 units of private operating cost statements, 2,264 were actually audited operating statements for privately managed, limited dividend projects and they were thus reclassified resulting in a final sample breakdown of 4,520 units of audited operating costs and 7,548 units of private operating costs for a total sample size of 12,068 units in both categories.

There were a total of sixty-two projects discarded from the original data secured from both the private sector and the audited statements submitted to HUD. These projects were discarded for a multitude of reasons including: insufficient operating experience (minimum 3 years); failure to provide the necessary supplemental descriptive information; missing operating cost data for one or more of the twenty-one variables on the coding sheet; inconsistencies in the reporting of the data; prepayments and past payments of accounts when the year an item was to be attributed could not be determined; and all rent-up years were discarded as they were deemed unrepresentative of normal operating experience.

2. Consistency checks were run of operating data based on government audited and privately secured data. The variations, allowing for building types, were minor.

# Appendix III Summary of Rent Control Administration Methodology

The material included in this appendix summarizes the methodology and data sources from which the three case studies included in chapter 6 were derived.

## *GREATER BOSTON AREA CASE STUDY*

The information presented in chapter 6 was derived from a study conducted by the Center for Urban Policy Research in 1974. The data on the rent adjustment process were obtained through a random sampling of adjustment petitions submitted to rent control agencies (Exhibit AIII-1). Due to variances in the administration of rent control in each community, a separate methodology was used for each community. Through the cooperation of the Boston Rent Control Administration and the executive directors of the rent control boards in Cambridge and Brookline, project staff members adapted a sampling technique for each agency and searched the files for specified data. These data were coded and processed by computer into the format presented here. Somerville is not included because access to the rent control files was denied.

The data gathered from all three communities included: the origin of the petition, either tenant or landlord; the nature of ownership, either an investor or a subsidized housing agency (FHA); the dates of docket entry (receipt by the agency), hearing, and decision; the total number of units in the structure involved in the petition; and the type and scale of structure and the type of construction (masonry/brick, frame, concrete, or other). If any of this information was not available in the files, it was coded as "unknown." A separate listing was maintained for responses coded as "other."

*EXHIBIT AIII–1*
*RENT CONTROL AGENCIES*
*CODING FORM*

---

1. Petition Code No. ___ [1-3]
   Study Code 9 [4]
2. Town – _ [5]
   - Boston [1]
   - Brookline [2]
   - Cambridge [3]
   - Somerville [4]

3. Type of Ownership –
   - Investor [1]
   - FHA [2]
   - Other [3]

4. Adjustment Petition Submitted by _ [9]
   - Landlord for Increase [1]
   - Tenant for Reduction [2]

5. Date of Docket Entry
   Month – Jan. [01] through Dec. [12]
   Data not available [99] _ [11-12]

   Year -1974 [1]
   1973 [2]
   1972 [3]
   1971 [4]
   1970 [5]
   1969 [6]
   1968 [7]
   1967 [8]
   Data not available [9]

6. Date of Hearing
   Month __ [14-15]
   Year _ [16]
   No Hearing Held [0]

7. Date of Decision
   Month __ [17-18]
   Year _ [19]
   No Decision Date [0]

*EXHIBIT AIII–1*
*(continued)*

| Item | Code | Field | Columns |
|---|---|---|---|
| 8. Present Rent Roll (dollars) | | ________ | [21-28] |
| Not Applicable | [77777777] | | |
| Not Available | [99999999] | | |
| 9. Present Rent of Unit | | ___ | [30-32] |
| Not Applicable | [777] | | |
| Not Available | [999] | | |
| 10. Requested Rental Increase (dollars) | | _____ | [34-38] |
| Not Applicable | [77777] | | |
| Not Available | [99999] | | |
| 11. Requested Rental Reduction (dollars) – Unit | | ___ | [40-42] |
| Not Applicable Use | [777] | | |
| Not Available | [999] | | |
| No Specific Amount Requested | [888] | | |
| 12. Rental Increase Approved (dollars) (Structure) | | _____ | [44-48] |
| Not Applicable | [77777] | | |
| Not Available | [99999] | | |
| 13. Rental Reduction Approved – Unit | | ___ | [50-52] |
| Not Applicable | [777] | | |
| Not Available | [999] | | |
| 14. Approved Maximum Rental (dollars) (Structure) | | ________ | [54-61] |
| Not Applicable | [77777777] | | |
| Not Available | [99999999] | | |
| 15. Approved Maximum Rent (dollars) – Unit | | ___ | [63-65] |
| Not Applicable | [777] | | |
| Not Available | [999] | | |
| 16. Total Units in Structure | | ____ | [67-70] |
| Unknown | [9999] | | |
| 17. Type of Structure | | _ | [72] |
| 1 to 4 units | [1] | | |
| 5 to 19 units | [2] | | |
| 20 or more units | [3] | | |
| Unknown | [9] | | |

*EXHIBIT AIII–1*
*(Continued)*

18. Type of Construction _ [74]
    - Masonry/Brick [1]
    - Frame [2]
    - Concrete [3]
    - Other [4]
    - Unknown [5]

19. Decision _ [76]
    - Approved [1]
    - Disapproved [2]
    - Petition Withdrawn [3]
    - Petition Dismissed [4]
    - Petition Not in File [5]
    - File Not Available [6]
    - Petition Still Pending [7]

20. Reason for Request _ [78]
    - Increase in Operating Costs or Taxes [1] or [3]
    - Capital Improvements [2]
    - Decrease in Maintenance and Repair [4]
    - Decrease in Services [5]
    - Decrease in Operating Costs [6]
    - Other [7]
    - Not Available/No Answer [9]

21. Reason for Decision _ [80]
    - Increase in Operating Costs or Taxes [1]
    - Capital Improvements [2]
    - Decrease in Maintenance and Repair [3]
    - Decrease in Services [4]
    - Decrease in Operating Costs [5]
    - Tenant Failed to Justify Decrease [6]
    - Landlord Failed to Justify Increase [7]
    - Other [8]
    - Not Available/No Answer [9]

Petitions submitted by landlords were generally for an increase in the maximum rent for all units in a particular structure. Information was, therefore, gathered on the basis of the rental income of the structure and included: rental income of structure at time of petition; the requested rental increase for the structure; the rent increase actually approved; and the approved maximum rental income for the structure. Any information not available in the petition file was coded as "not available."

In contrast, tenant petitions typically involved only one unit and were requests for rent reductions. The information gathered included: rent of unit at the time of petition; the requested rent reduction; rent reduction actually approved; and the approved maximum rent of the unit. Again, missing information was coded as "not available." However, many tenants did not request a specific amount for a reduction; instead, they requested particular structural improvements or an increase in general maintenance and repairs. In these cases, the code "no specific amount requested" was used and a separate listing of individual cases was maintained.

In a few instances, a landlord actually received a decrease in maximum rent levels after requesting an increase or a tenant petitioning for a reduction would actually receive an increase in rent. Since the coding sheet was not geared for this reversal, the increase or reduction "amount approved" column for these cases was coded as "zero" and the agency's action was reflected in the approved maximum rent column.

The outcome of the petition was classified in one of five ways: (1) approved by the rent control agency; (2) disapproved; (3) petition withdrawn; (4) petition dismissed by the agency; or (5) petition still pending. Problems in locating the petition were noted either as "petition not in file" or "file not available."

Reasons for request were also noted. The landlord petitions typically were either based on general operating cost increases including taxes or on capital improvements. Tenant petitions claimed a decrease in maintenance or services. The particular reasons for the final decision were coded with the same categories plus "tenant failed to justify decrease" and "landlord failed to justify increase." If the reason given for either the request or the decision was significantly different from any of these previously stated, it was coded as "other" and recorded on a separate listing. Surprisingly, many petitions did not specify any particular reason for the adjustment request. These cases were coded as "no answer" as were many cases under the reasons for decision column. In part, this was because strict application of an adjustment formula often leaves no single factor as dominant in the determination of the decision.

### *Boston*

There are approximately 232,000 residential units in the city of Boston. Of these, an estimated 150,000 to 175,000 or 65 to 76 percent are classified as falling under the provisions of rent control legislation and the jurisdiction of the Boston Rent Control Board (Chapter 19) or the Rent Control Administration (Chapter 842). A single staff and executive director manage the daily operations of both agencies though separate files are maintained. Since the most recent form of rent control began in January 1973, the staff estimates that 6,750 rent-controlled structures have been involved in adjustment proceedings.

By regulation, all adjustment petitions are stamp-dated, numbered, and placed in a general docket in the order received. This chronological docket is initially kept by hand and later entered into a computer system which is set up to print out the docket number, property address, owner, and dates of entry, hearing, inspection, and decision. The dollar amounts of the request, present rent, and final approved rent can also be included. Unfortunately, the information for any one property is rarely complete and errors are not removed from the print-out. In practice, therefore, the information is available only through the files.

A systematic random sample was taken from the chronological computer print-out docket by noting every twentieth property address. As a landlord may place more than one property on a single petition, the sample is not based on every twentieth petition received. Instead it is based on the total number of properties (or units when they have a separate petition in the file).

Once the sample properties were identified, a search of the files began. The file system lists every property that has been registered with the rent control agency in alphabetical order by street address. In each individual file, a pink folder contains registration information (building type, base rents), white folders contain individual adjustment petitions and all associated papers including a decision statement, and blue folders contain individual eviction cases. All data were gathered from the registration and petition files.

Few problems were encountered in the search with the exception of properties falling under Chapter 19. A separate file is maintained for these structures. Registration forms are filed by street address but petitions are filed by owner. Staff members freely admitted the files were confusing and, unfortunately, several sample properties could not be located.

### *Cambridge*

The present rent control adjustment process has been operated by the Cambridge Rent Control Board since January 1972. In 1974, 20,424 of the 37,600 units in the city (54 percent) were registered with the board. Case-by-case adjustments were begun in December 1972 and by December 1974 over 750 petitions representing either individual structures (usually landlord) or individual units (typically tenant pleas) had been received by the board.

When petitions are received at the board's office, they are entered in the order of receipt in a master docket and numbered in progression from the effective data of rent control. A systematic random sample of every fifth petition received was made from this chronological docket. Generally, there is only one property included on a petition for adjustment.

Once the properties in the sample were identified, the files were consulted. There are three sets of files each arranged alphabetically by street address: "live petitions," decision not yet made; "dead petitions," decisions made; and registration materials. In addition, there is a computer-printed card for each property under rent control which has information on building type and, in the future, will also show rent adjustments and current maximum legal rent. To gather the required information, all four information sources were consulted.

Petitions designated "live" were not available to the researchers. The only information coded on these properties were the dates of docket entry and hearing, if any. Interestingly, total rent figures were rarely calculated on any of the forms in the file. Also, very few tenant petitions survived the adjustment process. The director of the board's office indicated that petitioning tenants were cautioned that their petition could well result in an increase in their rent rather than any decrease. With this advice, many petitions were withdrawn. As in Boston, most dismissals resulted from failure of the petitioner to appear at a scheduled hearing or to sustain the burden of proof.

In addition to the standard information gathered, researchers took note of rent as of March 1970 for all properties and whether heat, hot water, or electricity are included in the rent.

### *Brookline*

Half of Brookline's 23,000 dwelling units are considered to fall under the regulation of the Brookline Rent Control Board. Since rent control began in this city in December 1970, approximately 2,000 adjustment petitions have been received by the board. Unlike Boston and Cambridge, Brookline maintains separate docket books for different categories of business brought before the board. Of nine dockets, two were of concern to this study—tenant petitions received and landlord petitions received.

Two random samples were taken. Every third petition was included from the chronologically listed tenant docket while every fifteenth petition was taken from the similar landlord docket. Petition and all registration forms are filed alphabetically by street address. All data were gathered from the files.

It was discovered through the sampling process that approximately 40 percent of all landlord petitions were withdrawn before completion of the adjustment process. This can be attributed to the comparative frequency of general adjustments in Brookline. Any petition for an increase on file before a final decision at the time of a general adjustment is considered withdrawn unless the landlord returns a special form indicating his intent to pursue his requested increase.

### *A Note on Computation: Statistical Summary of Rent Board Data*

The sampling procedures used to gather data from the rent control board files were designed to facilitate a projection to the total population of rent-controlled units in each of these three communities. The data procured were then classified by number of units according to the standard census categories of building size: twenty or more units, five through nineteen units, and one through four. The last category is an aggregate of three census categories (1 unit, 2 units, and 3 and 4 units) to facilitate the presentation of the data.

The sample data were submitted for computer analysis and cross tabulation. Thus, it was possible to determine the average annual percent increase granted structures by number of units. The average percent increase granted was based on the number of petitions in the sample requesting an increase and resulting in an administrative decision by the individual rent control board. The sample includes those increase petitions for which only partial increase was permitted as well as those that were disallowed. It does not include those that had not yet been acted upon at the time of the sampling or those that were withdrawn. In addition to determining the average annual percent increase granted by census category, the sample yielded the number of structures as well as the number of units receiving an increase by census category based on number of units. It was, therefore, possible to calculate the number of sampled units receiving an increase in each of the three building configurations as a percentage of the total number of sample units receiving an increase.

The next step was to obtain from each of the three rent control boards the actual number of units granted an increase in each of the sample years. Using this figure as a base, the percent distribution of the sample units by building configuration was applied to the total number of units receiving an increase, as a means of determining the relative distribution of the increases granted by the rent control board.

As it was not possible to obtain from the various rent control boards a distribution of the number of rent-controlled units in each of the three building configurations, it was necessary to utilize a surrogate figure based on the 1970 Census data. It was assumed that there would be a greater probability of a unit in the lower end of the building configuration spectrum escaping registration.

Therefore, the number of units in both the twenty or more unit and the five through nineteen categories of the 1970 Census were determined. From these totals, the number of units in each category exempt from control (i.e., public housing) was deleted. The resulting figures were assumed to be the actual number of rent-controlled units in the twenty or more and five through nineteen categories. Thus, the difference between this total and the census total for the one through four unit category was assumed to be the number of unregistered or exempt units. Only in Brookline was it possible to obtain an estimate of the number of one through four units under rent control (1,000 units).

As it was not possible to obtain an equivalent estimate in either Cambridge or Boston, the one through four unit category was calculated as a residual. The total number of rent-controlled units was available from the various rent control boards, therefore it was simply a matter of subtracting the number of units in the twenty or more and the five through nineteen categories and assigning the remaining controlled units to the one through four unit category as indicated by the census and the residual calculation was determined to be the number of unregistered or exempt units.

## *THE FORT LEE CASE STUDY*

As discussed in chapter 6, administrative responsibilities of the Fort Lee Rent Leveling Board are only occasioned on the basis of tenant complaints or landlord applications for additional rent increases under the provisions of the rent control ordinance. The first phase of the analysis of Fort Lee procedures consisted of reviewing the provisions of the rent control ordinance and subsequent amendments. This information was supplemented by visits to the rent leveling board office and interviews with the board secretary regarding board procedures. Various forms and applications utilized by the board were also obtained. Borough council and rent levelling board minutes and transcripts were also reviewed. The summary of board dispositions for the period of administration included in chapter 6 was obtained from the secretary's disposition book and includes all, rather than only a sample of board activities.

Forms utilized by the Fort Lee Rent Leveling Board in its administration are included in Appendix IV as follows: Landlord Application For Capital Improvements; Landlord Application For Hardship Increase; and Tenant Complaint Form.

## *NEW YORK CITY CASE STUDY*

The case study of New York City in chapter 6 is derived from a report prepared in mid-1975.[1] The empirical data included were primarily derived from an analysis of published annual rent guidelines for rent-stabilized apartment buildings for the years 1969 through 1975. This information was augmented by information derived from other published studies as well as information obtained from the Rent Stabilization Association and Conciliation and Appeals Board (CAB). Information relating to operating income and expenses for a sample of fifteen buildings which had applied for hardship increases during the 1974-1975 fiscal year was also obtained from CAB. Since the inception of the Rent Stabilization Law in 1969, 169 hardship applications were submitted to CAB. Of this total, 144 were submitted subsequent to October 1, 1974. This increase in applications was considered significant to the evaluation, especially in regard to the 1974 rent guidelines which were viewed as inadequate and largely responsible for the substantial increase in applications.

The sample of applications which were all still pending represents the total number of applications for which actual income and expense data was available for the "test" year (1974) as well as the preceding five years, required under then existent regulations. The backlog of cases as well as the small number of applications with complete information available was the result of changes in procedures and in the interpretation by CAB of the hardship provision of the Rent Stabilization Law.[2] Maintenance of the same "ratio" in net operating income as incorporated in the law was interpreted by CAB in May 1975 to mean maintaining net operating income ratios in dollar terms rather than the actual ratio. This interpretation reduced the number of hardship cases in the sample by one-third of the potentially eligible hardship cases. Applicants notified of this change in May 1975 were required to submit additional information including "actual" costs as opposed to annual estimates or projections which had previously been accepted.

The sample of fifteen applications provided "actual" 1974 income and expense data, either as a result of amended applications submitted since May 1975 or as supporting material originally submitted from which actual data could be verified.

### *Calculation of the Index of Gross Rental Income*

The index of gross potential rent income is based on assumptions regarding lease lengths and tenant turnover described below. The distribution of leases by term of lease was used to calculate the weighted average rent increase permitted for renewed leases. For new leases, the weighted average increase permitted under the guidelines and incremental rent allowances for new leases was calculated.

These calculations produced two estimates of permitted rent growth—one for lease renewals, the other for new leases. These estimates were then combined into an overall average rent increase for renegotiated leases, on the assumption that two-thirds of issued leases were renewals and one-third were new leases. From this average, an estimated average percent rent increase for each year was derived.

It was assumed that leases were issued on only one-half of stabilized apartments in any given year. Thus, the allowable rent increases for issued leases was divided by a factor of two. This estimated average increase in rent levels was then further adjusted to take into account the stabilizer adjustment which is applicable to rents charged on all apartments.

During the period in which rent increases on new leases were uncontrolled, it was assumed that rents on new leases would amount to the guideline rent increases permitted on renewal leases plus 10 percent. The resulting estimates of rent increases are in accord with the findings of the Stein Commission's report on rent increases on new leases issued in the stabilized sector of the city's housing stock during the same period.[3]

It is difficult to assess the adequacy of this rent index. Increases in the aggregate gross potential incomes of the fifteen buildings which have appealed for hardship rent increases suggest that our index does not understate potential rent increases (see Exhibit AIII-2). In four of the five years for which comparisons can be made, our index of potential rent increases exceeds the actual increase in the rent roll of these structures.

### *Lease Length in Stabilized Housing in New York City*

The Stein Commission assumed that one-, two- and three-year leases comprised 9, 50, and 41 percent of all leases, respectively.[4] A quick survey of eight major housing management companies in New York City determined that of fifty-seven leases expiring June 30, 1975, 18 percent were for terms of one year, 63 percent were for two years, and 19 percent were for three years. We assumed for our work that one-, two-, and three-year leases comprise 15, 50 and 35 percent of all leases, respectively.

### *Tenant Turnover in the Stabilized Sector*

George Sternlieb computed tenant turnover rates for rent-controlled apartments between 1963 and 1967. He found annual turnover rates to range from about 7 percent (in larger post-1929 apartment structures) to 15 percent (in larger old-law tenements).[5] It is very likely that turnover rates are somewhat higher in the stabilized sector. Based on a sample of apartments in elevator apartments in New York City, the Institute of Real Estate Management reported tenant turnover rates of 17.3 percent in 1973.[6] Data from the 1970 Census of Housing implies average residence terms for New York City tenants of 5.7 years and turnover rates of 17.6 percent.[7] We assumed tenant turnover in the stabilized housing stock to amount to 17 percent annually.

*EXHIBIT AIII-2*
*ANNUAL PERCENT CHANGE IN GROSS POTENTIAL RENTAL INCOME: ACTUAL CHANGE IN 15 SELECTED STRUCTURES VERSUS THE RENT INDEX*

| *Year* | *15 Selected[a] Buildings* | *Rent Index* |
|---|---|---|
| 1970 | 5.2 | 6.4 |
| 1971 | 6.2 | 7.3 |
| 1972 | 5.0 | 6.1 |
| 1973 | 4.7 | 6.4 |
| 1974 | 6.4 | 5.7 |

a. These buildings are those that have applied for hardship rent increases with the Conciliation and Appeals Board.

## *NOTES*

1. This report, "A Review of Rent Guidelines and The Economics of the Stabilized Sector of New York City's Housing Market" was prepared for the Rent Stabilization Association by the author in conjunction with Franklin James. The full report was subsequently submitted to the Rent Guidelines Board as input into the 1975-1976 annual rent guidelines determination.
2. It should be noted that in June 1975 the New York State Legislature amended the hardship provisions of the law, but the amended regulations did not apply to the applications then pending.
3. Temporary State Commission on Living Costs and the Economy of the State of New York, "Report on Housing and Rent of the Temporary State Commission on Living Costs and the Economy of the State of New York to the Governor and the Legislature," January 1974, p. 150. This commission reports an average increase in the decontrolled sector of 18.9 percent.
4. Ibid.
5. George Sternlieb, *The Urban Housing Dilemma: The Dynamics of New York City's Rent Controlled Housing* (New York: The City of New York Housing and Development Administration, 1972), Exhibit 5-6.
6. Institute of Real Estate Management, *Income/Expense Analysis: Apartments, Condominiums and Cooperatives, 1974* (Chicago: I.R.E.M., 1974), p. 50.
7. U.S., Bureau of the Census, 1970 Census of Housing, *Metropolitan Housing Characteristics: New York, N.Y.* (HC [2]-149), Table E-2.

# Appendix IV Selected Administrative Forms

The range of forms and schedules which have been used and are currently used in administering rent control are included as representative examples. The intricacies of individual municipality rent administration are evidenced by the forms which follow:

*Federal*



*Massachusetts*

Boston

Brookline



Cambridge



*Fort Lee, New Jersey*



*New York City*

## Specimen Fair Net Operating Income Form Under 1949 Federal Rent Control Legislation

**FAIR NET OPERATING INCOME FORM D-106**

| **Landlord's Petition For Increase In Rent To Secure A Fair Net Operating Income** | (Stamp of Issuing Office)<br>Maximum Rent Date | Docket No. |
|---|---|---|
| Address of Building for Which Increase is Wanted<br>Number and Street | City and State | Number of Dwelling Units in Building |

| I. Name and Mailing address of Landlord: | II. Name and Address of Tenant (If more than one tenant will be affected by your petition, do not fill in this item, but fill in Schedule D): |
|---|---|
| Name .................. Tel. No. ........ | Name ................................ |
| Number and | Number and ........................... |
| Street ................................ | Street ................................ |
| City, Zone No. and State ........................ | City, Zone No. and State ........................ |

For each building for which rent increases are requested, file two (2) copies of this petition with the Area Rent Office. You may be required to support the figures in this petition by submitting your books, records, receipts, or Federal Income Tax Return.

A. "TEST YEAR":

In order to determine the amount of certain expense and income items to be shown on this petition, you must select a "test year." The "test year" you select must be the most recent full calendar or fiscal year, or any twelve consecutive months ending not more than 90 days before the date of filing the petition.

**The "Test Year" I Have Selected Ended** .................... (Month) ........ (Day) ...... (Year)

| B. EXPENSES (except Repairs and Replacements): | Annual Expense |
|---|---|
| 1. HEATING FUEL USED IN TEST YEAR—Enter only if heat is supplied to the tenants by the landlord, without sharing the bills. | $ |
| 2. UTILITIES USED IN TEST YEAR.—Enter only if utilities are supplied to the tenants by the landlord, without sharing the bills. | $ |
| 3. PAY ROLL DURING THE TEST YEAR.—Do not include any salary for the owner or for corporate officers, nor any labor cost for repairs and replacements. | $ |
| 4. JANITORIAL MATERIALS USED IN TEST YEAR.—Do not include materials for repairs and replacements. | $ |
| 5. REAL ESTATE TAXES.—This is the amount of all real estate taxes (exclusive of penalties and overdue taxes for other years) shown on your latest tax bill. If taxes have increased since you received your latest bill you may attach a signed statement from your tax official showing the assessment and tax rate now in effect for the building, and enter your taxes on this new basis. | $ |
| 6. INSURANCE.—Divide the cost of each policy that is in effect on the date the petition is filed by the number of years that it covers, to obtain the annual expense. | $ |
| 7. INTERIOR PAINTING AND DECORATING.—Add the expenses for interior painting and decorating in the test year and the two preceding years, and divide the total by three (3) to obtain the annual expense. | $ |
| 8. DEPRECIATION.—Enter the depreciation figure shown on your last Federal Income Tax Return.<br>Note.—The amount of depreciation which will be allowed is the lesser of the following: (a) the amount shown on your tax return, or (b) 21% of the present annual income for buildings containing one to four units, or 16% of the annual income for buildings containing five or more units. | $ |
| 9. MISCELLANEOUS EXPENSES IN TEST YEAR.—This may include management fees actually paid. Show specifically the nature and amount of each miscellaneous expense. | |
| (a) ................................................ | $ |
| (b) ................................................ | $ |

NOTE: If you want to show an increase in pay roll or utilities which was not in effect during the entire test year, file Form D-100 in addition to this form.

**EXPENSES FOR REPAIRS AND REPLACEMENTS** may be shown on pages 2 and 3 of this petition. If you have no records of such expenses, or if the tenant is required to make all repairs, you may tear off pages 2 and 3 and file only page 1 and 4 with the Area Rent Office. **In any case, however, you must fill out page 4 of this petition.**

**Page 2**

**C. REPAIRS AND REPLACEMENTS:**

Expenses for repairs and replacements should generally not be charged entirely to the year in which they were paid. Instead, they should be "allocated" (that is, spread) over the period of years they normally last. For example, if a roof which normally lasts 15 years was replaced in the test year at a cost of $300, only one fifteenth or $10 is chargeable to the test year and $280 is chargeable to the other 14 years.

Similarly, if a roof was replaced any time within the last 15 years, one-fifteenth of the cost may be properly charged to the test year. Thus, it is proper for you to show not only a portion of the expenses incurred in the test year, but also the portion of the expenses incurred in previous years which is allowable to the test year. However, no portion of a prior year expense may be shown if the period between the date it was incurred and the end of the test year exceeds the proper "allocating period." The proper "allocation period" is the number of years shown in the Allocation Schedule below, unless it is established that an expense has been incurred more or less frequently.

In the table below, list on a separate line any repair or replacement item that is properly chargeable to the test year. In column 1 show the nature of the item. In column 2 show the year the item was purchased or completed. In column 3 show the cost. In column 4 enter the proper "allocation period," as shown in the Allocation Schedule, unless your records show conclusively that you have incurred the particular type of expense more or less frequently. Divide the cost of each item, as shown in column 3, by the number of years, as shown in column 4, and enter the result in column 5.

IMPORTANT NOTE.—The cost of capital improvements may not be included under repairs and replacements, since they are taken into account in the allowance for depreciation in table B on page 1.

ALLOCATION SCHEDULE

| Item | Allocation Period | | Item | Allocation Period | |
|---|---|---|---|---|---|
| | Repairs | Complete replacement | | Repairs | Complete replacement |
| Exterior painting | ..... | 4 yrs. | Sewers, sidewalks, masonry | 10 yrs. | 20 yrs. |
| Carpentry — doors, frames, sash, floors, siding, supports, weather stripping, storm windows, porches, insulation | 10 yrs. | 20 yrs. | Air conditioning | 5 yrs. | 15 yrs. |
| Plastering | 10 yrs. | 20 yrs. | Elevators | 5 yrs. | 20 yrs. |
| Electric wiring and plumbing | 5 yrs. | 20 yrs. | Refrigerators and electrical appliances | 3 yrs. | 8 yrs. |
| Heating equipment —boilers, radiators, pipe | 10 yrs. | 20 yrs. | Furniture, springs, mattresses | 5 yrs. | 10 yrs. |
| Hot water equipment—tanks, burners, fittings | 3 yrs. | 8 yrs. | Carpets, rugs, linolium, drapes, shades | ..... | 6 yrs. |
| Roofs | 5 yrs. | 15 yrs. | Blankets & spreads | ..... | 6 yrs. |
| Downspouts, eaves | 5 yrs. | 10 yrs. | Linens | ..... | 2 yrs. |
| | | | Venetian blinds, awnings, screening | ..... | 8 yrs. |
| | | | Kitchen and laundry equipment — sinks, tubs, cabinets, etc. | 5 yrs. | 15 yrs. |

| 1 | 2 | 3 | 4 | 5 |
|---|---|---|---|---|
| Description of Item | Year Purchased or Completed | Cost | Allocation Period | Charge (Col. 2+Col. 4) Test Year |
| | | | | |

[Ed. Note: Page 3 of this form was a continuation of the Allocation Schedule set forth above.]

Page 4

**D. RENTAL INCOME:**

Give the information required in the table below for every residential and commercial unit in the building.

Fill in column 4 for each unit according to the following instructions:

Units With Maximum Rents.. — Enter present maximum rent—even if vacant or occupied by the landlord, his employees, relatives, or other persons paying no rent or only a nominal rent.

Units With Voluntary Leases In Effect. — Enter the present rent payable under the terms of the lease.

Uncontrolled Residential and Commercial Units. — Enter the rent charged on the date the petition is filed. If no rent or only a nominal rent is charged, enter the full rental value. (Commercial units include garages rented to persons other than tenants of the dwelling units in the property. A single monthly or weekly total rent should be entered for all such garages, and the number of these garages specified in column 2.)

Units With Seasonal, Alternate, or Other Varying Rents. — —Enter the average monthly rent during the year ending on the date the petition is filed.

| 1 | 2 | 3 | | | 4 | 5 | | 6 \| 7 |
|---|---|---|---|---|---|---|---|---|
| Unit Number or Location (list every residential or commercial unit in the property on a separate line) | Name of Present Occupant (If occupied by landlord, enter "Landlord", if vacant, enter "Vacant") | Check (√) One | | | Present Rent | Check (√) One Rent Per | | Do Not Write In These Columns |
| | | With maximum rent | Voluntary lease in effect | Uncontrolled residential or commercial | | Month | Week | |
| | | | | | $ | $ | | |
| | | | | | | | | |
| | | | | | | | | |
| | | | | | | | | |

**E. TOTAL INCOME OTHER THAN RENTS FOR THE ENTIRE TEST YEAR:**

(Includes receipts for phone service, laundry equipment, utilities, alterations etc.) .......................................... $ ......................

CERTIFICATION

IT IS NOT NECESSARY THAT THIS PETITION BE SWORN TO, BUT ANY FALSE STATEMENT WILL RESULT IN THE DENIAL OF YOUR ENTIRE PETITION AND MAY SUBJECT YOU TO THE PENALTIES PROVIDED BY LAW.

I Hereby Certify That: (1) the information supplied by me in this petition is true and correct, and (2) I am maintaining all services required by the Rent Regulations, and will continue to maintain such services so long as any adjustment granted under this petition continues in effect.

........ (Date) ........ .......... (Signature of Landlord) ..........

Source:

Robert J. Galvin, Rent Control In Massachusetts, Reprint from the 1972 Massachusetts Lawyers Diary and Manual.

ALLOWABLE ADJUSTMENT COMPUTATION

1971 figures used [] [] allowed expense pg. 1a used
1970 figures used [] [] non-residential pg.1b used

1. Operating Expenses for 1973 $______
2. Operating Expenses for 1971 (1970 if applicable) $______
3. Increase in Operating Expense (line 1 minus line 2) $______

---

4. Property Tax for 1973 $______
5. Property Tax for 1971 (1970 if applicable) $______
6. Increase in Taxes (line 4 minus line 5) $______
7. Property Tax for 1972 (if lower than 1973 tax, use pg.2a Sec. A for adjustment) $______

---

8. Capital Improvements Since December 1971 (Dec. 1970, if applicable)

| | | | | |
|---|---|---|---|---|
| 8a) Apt. benefited/date | ______ | ______ | ______ | ______ |
| 8b) Amount | $______ | $______ | $______ | $______ |
| 8c) Useful Life | ______ | ______ | ______ | ______ |
| 8d) Monthly Amortization Rate (8 1/2%) | $______ | $______ | $______ | $______ |
| 8e) Line 8d x 12 | $______ | $______ | $______ | $______ |

8f) Increase in Capital Improvements (Total of line 8e) [Treat Capital Improvement to individual apartment(s) separately]. $______

---

9. Adjustment for gross inequity and extreme hardship (See pg. 2a Sec. B) $______

---

10. Potential Gross Income Dec. 1971 (Dec. 1970 if applicable) []Adjusted $______

---

11. Gross Allowable Income

| | |
|---|---|
| Line 3 | $______ |
| Line 6 | $______ |
| Line 8f | $______ |
| Line 9 | $______ |
| Line 10 | $______ |
| TOTAL | $______ |

12. Gross Allowable Monthly Rent (line 11 divided by 12) $______
13. Current Gross Monthly Maximum Rent $______
14. Allowable Increase in Gross Monthly Rent (line 12 minus line 13) $______
15. Landlord's Proposed Monthly Gross Rent $______
16. Current Gross Monthly Maximum Rent (line 13) $______
17. Proposed Increase in Gross Monthly Rent (line 15 minus line 16) $______
18. Percentage of Proposed Increase Allowable (line 14 x 100 ÷ line 17) ______%

---

Use 1970 figures where cost increases substantially exceeded rent increases during 1971.

II. GROSS INCOME, VACANCIES, COLLECTED GROSS INCOME

| | YEAR ENDING DECEMBER 31, or Fiscal year ending: | | | for office use only |
|---|---|---|---|---|
| | 1971 | 1972 | 1973 | |
| 1. Rents for residential units at 100% occupancy (from rent rolls in effect for each year or part of a year). | $ . | $ . | $ . | |
| 2. Non-residential units at 100% occupancy | . | . | . | |
| 3. Other income. Specify ______________ (include all income not included in rent above, including tax clauses, parking, vending machines, insurance proceeds, etc. Do <u>not</u> include abatements received). | . | . | . | |
| 4. Total Potential Gross Income | . | . | . | |
| 5. Rent loss due to residential vacancies | . | . | . | |
| 6. Total rent loss due to vacancies (include non-residential vacancies) | ( . ) | ( . ) | ( . ) | |
| 7. Uncollected residential rent | . | . | . | |
| 8. Total rent loss due to non-collection (include non-residential rent loss) | ( . ) | ( . ) | ( . ) | |
| 9. Total vacancies and uncollected rents (add lines 6 & 8) | ( . ) | ( . ) | ( . ) | |
| 10. Total Collected Gross Income (Subtract line 9 from line 4) | ( . ) | ( . ) | ( . ) | |

III. OPERATING EXPENSES
(Maintenance, repairs and miscellaneous expenses must be itemized on page 3).

| | 1971 | 1972 | 1973 | |
|---|---|---|---|---|
| Management select (a) or (b)<br>11. (a) Actual cash payment (a) | . | . | . | |
| 12. (b) 6% of gross income for self-management (6% of line 4) (b) | . | . | . | |
| 13. Heating Fuel (specify type________) | . | . | . | |
| 14. Electricity (other than electric heat) | . | . | . | |
| 15. Gas (other than heating fuel) | . | . | . | |
| 16. Water and Sewer | . | . | . | |
| 17. Insurance (fire and liability) | . | . | . | |
| 18. Total Maintenance (itemize on page 3) | . | . | . | |
| 19. Total Repairs (itemize on page 3) | . | . | . | |
| 20. Miscellaneous (itemize on page 3) | . | . | . | |
| 21. SUBTOTAL (ADD LINES 11-20) | . | . | . | |
| 22. Real Estate Taxes (after abatement) | . | . | . | |
| 23. Capital Improvements (amortization from page 4) | . | . | . | |
| 24 TOTAL (ADD LINES 21, 22 & 23) | . | . | . | |

V. REAL ESTATE TAX INFORMATION:

1. Assessed value as per 1973 tax bill:

   Building $_______.__   Land $_______.__   TOTAL $_______.__

2. Year assessment last changed 19__   Previous Assessment $_______.__
3. Property tax paid for 1971 $_______.__   1972 $_______.__   1973 $_______.__
4. Abatements Received:
5. Abatement for 1971 $_______.__   received in 19__
6. Abatement for 1972 $_______.__   received in 19__
7. Abatement for 1973 $_______.__   received in 19__

Pending Abatements:

List any abatement proceedings presently pending indicating the amounts and years for which claimed ______________________________

______________________________

______________________________

VI. Capital Improvements and Replacements (including replacement of appliances and equipment)

| Description (Indicate capital improvements made since Dec. 1970 Where improvement benefits less than all apartments, indicate apartments benefited). | | Apt. Benefited<br>--- | Date Work Started<br>mo/yr | Date Work Completed<br>mo/yr | Cost<br>$_______.__ | Estimated Life (yrs)<br>-- | Yearly amortization (divide cost by life)<br>$____.__ |
|---|---|---|---|---|---|---|---|
| New Plumbing | ....... | | | | . | | . |
| New Heating System | ....... | | | | . | | . |
| New Electrical Wiring | ....... | | | | . | | . |
| New Roof | ....... | | | | . | | . |
| New Appliances | ....... | | | | . | | . |
| Other (describe) | ....... | | | | . | | . |
| __________ | ....... | | | | . | | . |
| __________ | ....... | | | | . | | . |
| TOTAL | | | | | . | | . |

This financial statement including all accompanying schedules and attachments signed under the pains and penalties of perjury.

______________________________   ______________

Signature of landlord or authorized agent   Date

ST. 1970 C. 842 SEC. 12(c)

(c) Whoever willfully violates any provision of this act or any rule or regulation hereunder promulgated, or whoever knowingly makes any false statement in any testimony before the rent board or administrator or whoever knowingly supplies the rent board or administrator with any false information shall be punished by a fine of not more than five hundred dollars or by imprisonment for not more than ninety days or both; provided, however, that in the case of a second or subsequent offense, such person shall be punished by a fine of not more than three thousand dollars or by imprisonment for not more than one year, or both.

I have modified the following expenses claimed on the Property Financial Statement:

| OPERATING EXPENSES | CLAIMED AMOUNT | YEAR | ACCEPTED AMOUNT | REASON |
|---|---|---|---|---|
| ________ | $________ | 197__ | $________ | ________ |
| ________ | $________ | 197__ | $________ | ________ |
| ________ | $________ | 197__ | $________ | ________ |
| **PROPERTY TAXES** | | | | |
| ________ | $________ | 197__ | $________ | ________ |
| ________ | $________ | 197__ | $________ | ________ |

I have accepted all other expenses as stated on the Property Financial Statement (Form 3). I have determined the total Operating Expenses to be $________for 1971
$________for 1972
$________for 1973.

I have determined the total Property Taxes to be $________for 1971
$________for 1972
$________for 1973.

I have modified the following Capital Improvements claimed on the Property Financial Statement:

CAPITAL IMPROVEMENTS

| | YEAR | AMOUNT CLAIMED | CLAIMED USEFUL LIFE | ACCEPTED AMOUNT | ACCEPTED USEFUL LIFE | REASON |
|---|---|---|---|---|---|---|
| ________ | 197_ | $______ | ______ | $______ | ____ | ________ |
| ________ | 197_ | $______ | ______ | $______ | ____ | ________ |
| ________ | 197_ | $______ | ______ | $______ | ____ | ________ |

I have accepted all other Capital Improvements as stated on the Property Financial Statement (Form 3). I have determined the total Capital Improvements to be $________for 1971
$________for 1972
$________for 1973.

**Boston**

To be used when computing an increase for a building with non-residential units.

1. Average Potential Gross Income of Total Units plus other income:
   a. Total Potential Gross Income for 1971 (1970 if applicable) = $________
   b. Total Potential Gross Income for 1972 = $________
   c. Total Potential Gross Income for 1973 = $________
   TOTAL = $________ ÷ 3 = $________

2. Average Potential Gross Income less non-residential units:
   a. Total Potential Gross Income less non-residential for 1971 (1970 if applicable) (transfer to pg.3 line 10) = $________
   b. Total Potential Gross Income less non-residential for 1972 = $________
   c. Total Potential Gross Income less non-residential for 1973 (divide by 12 then transfer to pg. 3 line 13) = $________
   TOTAL = $________ ÷ 3 = $________

3. Average Percentage of residential rents in building for 1971, 1972 and 1973
   $________ (Total, line 2) x 100 ÷ $________ (Total, line 1) = ________% (Average Percentage)

4. Adjusted Operating Expense for 1973
   $________ (Operating Expense 1973) x ____% (line 3) = $________ (transfer to pg.3 line 1)

5. Adjusted Operating Expense for 1971 (1970 if applicable)
   $________ (Operating Expense 1971) x ____% (line 3) = $________ (transfer to pg.3 line 2)

6. Adjusted Property Tax for 1973
   $________ (Property Tax 1973) x ____% (line 3) = $________ (transfer to pg.3 line 4)

7. Adjusted Property Tax for 1971 (1970 if applicable)
   $________ (Property Tax 1971) x ____% (line 3) = $________ (transfer to pg.3 line 5)

8. Capital Improvements (see note)
   8a. Amount of Capital Improvements $______ $______ $______ $______
   8b. Adjusted Capital Improvements
   $________ (Capital Improvement) x ____% (line 3) = $______ $______ $______ $______ (transfer each cost to pg.3 line 8b)

**NOTE:** Use 100% of Capital Improvements if attributable solely to residential units.
Use 0% of Capital Improvements if attributable solely to non-residential units.

**APPLICABILITY:** Use 1970 figures where cost increases substantially exceed rent increases during 1971.

COMPUTATION FOR DETERMINATION OF FAIR NET OPERATING INCOME 1971.

Form 1a used []
Form 1b used []

[] 1-6 units: 20%-35%
[] 7 units & above: 25%-40%
[] buildings completed after 1960: 35%-50%

A. CASH FLOW/NET INCOME STATEMENT 1971

1. $________ 100 % $________ 100 %
Potential Gross Income — Potential Gross Income
(i.e. annualized Dec. 1971 rents as per Registration, plus other income from Form 3, Pg.2 line 3.)

2. $________ ___%
Operating Expenses

3. $________ ___%
Property Taxes

4. $________ ___%
Capital Improvements (amortized)

5. $________ ___% $________ ___%
Sub Total (add lines 2, 3, & 4) — Sub Total

6. $________ ___% $________ ___%
Net Profit Before Financing (line 1 minus line 5) — Net Profit Before Financing (See part B, Below)

7. $________ ___%
Annual Principal & Interest

8. $________ ___% $________ ___%
Cash Flow (line 6 minus line 7) — Cash Flow

9. $________ ___%
Interest Only

10. $________ ___% $________ ___%
Net Income (line 6 minus line 9) — Net Income

---

B. If net profit before financing at the base year falls outside the guidelines as set in BRCA, Reg. 6, Sec. 5b, 1(a)(b)(c), do the following to get adjusted gross income.

$________ ÷ [] .80 or .65 / [] .75 or .60 / [] .65 or .50 = $________ (transfer to line 1, Sec. C below and to line 10 pg. 3)
Sub Total (line 5) — Adjusted Potential Gross Income

---

C. ADJUSTED CASH FLOW/NET INCOME STATEMENT 1971 (if needed) [] Upward []Downward

1. $________ 100 %
Adjusted Potential Gross Income (Sec B)

2. $________ ___%
Sub Total (line 5, Sec. A)

3. $________ ___%
Adjusted Net Profit Before Financing

4. $________ ___%
Adjusted Cash Flow

5. $________ ___%
Adjusted Net Income

IV. ITEMIZED EXPENSES FOR MAINTENANCE, REPAIRS AND MISCELLANEOUS EXPENSES.
INSTRUCTIONS: Where work is done by the owner or an employee of the owner, state the total cost for supplies and labor and indicate by an "*" next to the amount. Where work is done by a contractor, state the contract amount.

| | YEAR ENDING DECEMBER 31, or Fiscal year ending | | | for office use only |
|---|---|---|---|---|
| MAINTENANCE | 1971 | 1972 | 1973 | |
| 1. Janitorial Payroll (include all maintenance performed by janitor) ...... | $ . | $ . | $ . | |
| 2. Cleaning ...... | . | . | . | |
| 3. Extermination ...... | . | . | . | |
| 4. Rubbish Removal ...... | . | . | . | |
| 5. Snow Removal ...... | . | . | . | |
| 6. Interior painting & decorating ...... | . | . | . | |
| Other Maintenance (describe) | | | | |
| 7. ______ ...... | . | . | . | |
| 8. ______ ...... | . | . | . | |
| 9. ______ ...... | . | . | . | |
| 10. Total Maintenance ...... | . | . | . | |
| REPAIRS | | | | |
| 11. Plumbing ...... | . | . | . | |
| 12. Electrical ...... | . | . | . | |
| 13. Heating Plant ...... | . | . | . | |
| 14. Roof ...... | . | . | . | |
| 15. Carpentry ...... | . | . | . | |
| Other Repairs (describe) | | | | |
| 16. ______ ...... | . | . | . | |
| 17. ______ ...... | . | . | . | |
| 18. ______ ...... | . | . | . | |
| 19. Total Repairs ...... | . | . | . | |
| MISCELLANEOUS | | | | |
| 20. Advertising ...... | . | . | . | |
| 21. Brokerage ...... | . | . | . | |
| 22. Legal ...... | . | . | . | |
| 23. Audit ...... | . | . | . | |
| Other Expenses (describe) | | | | |
| 24. ______ ...... | . | . | . | |
| 25. ______ ...... | . | . | . | |
| 26. ______ ...... | . | . | . | |
| 27. Total Miscellaneous ...... | . | . | . | |

A. CASH FLOW/NET INCOME STATEMENT 1973

1. $________ 100 % $________ 100 %
Potential Gross Income — Potential Gross Income
(Annualized current maximum rent plus other income from Form 3, Pg. 2 line 3).

2. $________ ___%
Operating Expenses

3. $________ ___%
Property Taxes

4. $________ ___%
Capital Improvements (amortized)

5. $________ ___% $________ ___%
Sub Total (add lines 2, 3, & 4) — Sub Total

6. $________ ___% $________ ___%
Net Profit Before Financing (line 1 minus line 5) — Net Profit Before Financing

7. $________ ___%
Annual Principal & Interest

8. $________ ___% $________ ___%
Cash Flow (line 6 minus line 7) — Cash Flow

9. $________ ___%
Interest Only

10. $________ ___% $________ ___%
Net Income (line 6 minus line 9) — Net Income

---

B. CASH FLOW/NET INCOME STATEMENT WITH ALLOWED ADJUSTMENT

1. $________ 100 % $________ 100 %
Potential Gross Income (Gross allowable Income, pg. 3 Line 11) — Potential Gross Income

2. $________ ___%
Operating Expenses

3. $________ ___%
Property Taxes

4. $________ ___%
Capital Improvements (amortized)

5. $________ ___% $________ ___%
Sub Total (add lines 2, 3, & 4) — Sub Total

6. $________ ___% $________ ___%
Net Profit Before Financing (line 1 minus line 5) — Net Profit Before Financing

7. $________ ___%
Annual Principal & Interest

8. $________ ___% $________ ___%
Cash Flow (line 6 minus line 7) — Cash Flow

9. $________ ___%
Interest Only

10. $________ ___% $________ ___%
Net Income (line 6 minus line 9) — Net Income

RETURN ON ACCUMULATED EQUITY ANALYSIS 197__

1. $__________________ Potential Gross Income *

2. $__________________ Vacancies (lesser of actual or 5% of gross income)

3. $__________________ Operating Expenses

4. $__________________ Property Taxes

5. $__________________ Capital Improvements (amortized)

6. $__________________ Interest Only

7. $__________________ Total Expenses — $__________________ Total Expenses (Add lines 2,3,4, 5 & 6)

8. $__________________ Net Income (line 7 minus line 1)

---

9. Accumulated Principal (Mortgage $__________@____% for ____yrs) $__________________

10. Equity $__________________

11. Accumulated Equity (line 9 plus line 10) $__________________

---

12. $__________________ Net Income (line 8) ÷ $__________________ Accumulated Equity (line 11) = ______% Return on Equity

13. $__________________ Accumulated Equity x .06 = $__________________ Net Income needed for 6% return

---

If line 12 (Return on Equity) is les than 6%, do calculation below:

$__________________ Net Income needed for 6% Return (Line 13) - $__________________ Net Income (Line 8) ** = $__________________ Yrly. Increase needed for 6% return ÷ 12 = $__________________ Mthly. Increase needed for 6% return

* If an increase is warranted under Reg.#6, use New Allowed Potential Gross

** If Net Income (Line 8) is a negative figure, add instead of subtracting it from Net Income needed for 6% return (Line 13).

Form 27 (6/5/73)

BROOKLINE

DEPRECIATION SCHEDULE

The proper "depreciation period" is the number of years shown in the Depreciation Schedule below, unless it is established that an expense has been incurred more or less frequently.

Repairs and/or replacement of any of the items below which total $150 or less will not be depreciated.

In cases where the total improvement costs exceed the sum of $2,500, and it has been necessary to obtain a property improvement loan to cover the cost of such improvement, reasonable financing costs will be included in the depreciated cost of the item in question.

| Item | Depreciation Period (years) | |
|---|---|---|
| | Repairs | Complete replacement |
| Exterior renovation and construction | | |
| Exterior painting | ..... | 4 |
| Glass, glazing | ..... | 7 |
| Screens, awnings | ..... | 4 |
| Storm windows | 4 | 8 |
| Weather stripping, insulation | 5 | 10 |
| Masonry, including concrete & stucco, sidewalks | 5 | 10 |
| Pointing (grouting) | 5 | 15 |
| Metalwork: doors, fire escapes, flashing, gutters, siding (aluminum) | 5 | 10 |
| Woodwork: doors, porches, siding, trim, windows, frames, sash, supports | 5 | 10 |
| Roofing | 5 | 10 |
| Downspouts, eaves | 3 | 6 |
| Sewers | 5 | 10 |
| Structural additions and alterations | 5 | 15 |
| Landscaping | | |
| Fences, lawn furniture | ..... | 4 |
| Gardens, lawns, shrubs, trees | ..... | 2 |
| Masonry, hard surfacing | 5 | 10 |
| Interior renovation and construction | | |
| Painting, wallpaper | ..... | 3 |
| Cabinets, cabinetwork, interior doors | 5 | 8 |
| Ceilings, floors, walls | 5 | 10 |
| Plastering | 5 | 10 |
| Fixtures: electrical and plumbing | 3 | 10 |
| Linoleum, floor varnishing, soft tiles | ..... | 5 |

(continued on other side)

-2-

| | Depreciation Period (years) | |
|---|---|---|
| | Repairs | Complete replacement |
| Interior renovation and construction (cont.) | | |
| Locks, miscellaneous hardware | ..... | 5 |
| Tiles, terrazzo | ..... | 8 |
| Utility and service systems | | |
| Heating equipment: boilers, radiators, pipes | 3 | 15 |
| Hot water equipment: tanks, burners, fittings | 3 | 5 |
| Electrical wiring, plumbing system | 5 | 10 |
| Flues | 3 | 5 |
| Incinerators, smoke alarms | 3 | 5 |
| Compactors, dumpsters | 3 | 5 |
| Elevators | 5 | 15 |
| Cooling systems | 5 | 10 |
| Doorbells, mailboxes, security systems | 4 | 8 |
| Appliances | | |
| Air conditioners | 3 | 6 |
| Refrigerators | 3 | 5 |
| Dishwashers | 3 | 5 |
| Washers, dryers | 3 | 6 |
| Compactors | 3 | 5 |
| Disposals | 2 | 5 |
| Fans | 2 | 5 |
| Stoves and ovens (gas or electric) | 4 | 8 |
| Space heaters | 2 | 5 |
| Hot water heaters | 3 | 5 |
| Other electrical appliances | 3 | 6 |
| Furnishings | | |
| Beds, springs, mattresses | ..... | 5 |
| Bureaus, chairs, desks, sofas, tables | ..... | 5 |
| Carpets, rugs | ..... | 5 |
| Drapes | ..... | 3 |
| Window shades | ..... | 3 |
| Venetian blinds | ..... | 4 |
| Other furniture | ..... | 5 |

TOWN OF BROOKLINE

BEFORE THE RENT CONTROL BOARD

FORM 7(12/21/70)

TOWN HALL
BROOKLINE, MASS.

In the Matter of:
[Addresses of property]

____________________

____________________

____________________

____________________

BLOCK & LOT________________

DOCKET #__________

LANDLORD PETITION FOR ADJUSTMENT

I hereby petition for adjustment of my rents at the above named property.

This petition including the accompanying schedules and attachments signed under the pains and penalties of perjury.

______________________________ __________

Signature of landlord or authorized agent Date

______________________________________

Address (residence of individual / if not individual, then residence of officer, trustee, or authorized agent)

G.L. c. 842 §12(c)

(c) Whoever willfully violates any provision of this act or any rule or regulation hereunder promulgated, or whoever knowingly makes any false statement in any testimony before the rent board or administrator or whoever knowingly supplies the rent board or administrator with any false information shall be punished by a fine of not more than five hundred dollars or by imprisonment for not more than ninety days or both; provided, however, that in the case of a second or subsequent offense, such person shall be punished by a fine of not more than three thousand dollars or by imprisonment for not more than one year or both.

Article XXX, §12(c),
By-law of the Town of Brookline

(c) Whoever willfully violates any provision of this article or any rule or regulation hereunder promulgated or whoever knowingly supplies the rent board with any false information shall be punished by a fine of not more than one thousand dollars.

FORM 7 (Rev.2/6/74) Block & Lot ____________

SCHEDULE A --- EXPENSES

Please indicate your actual expenses for the years listed below.

| ITEM | EXPENSE ITEM | (A) 197 EXPENSES | (B) 197 EXPENSES | (C) 197 EXPENSES |
|---|---|---|---|---|
| 1. | Total payroll expenses (except management and painting) | | | |
| 2. | Supplies (janitorial, light bulbs, uniforms, etc.) | | | |
| 3. | Electricity | | | |
| 4. | Water | | | |
| 5. | Gas (excluding heating fuel) | | | |
| 6. | Heating fuel | | | |
| 7. | Painting and decorating (interior only; include wages) | | | |
| 8. | Maintenance and repairs (interior and exterior) | | | |
| 9. | Services (window washing, exterminating etc. not maintenance) | | | |
| 10. | Insurance (exclusive of FHA mortgage and employee Group Insurance) | | | |
| 11. | Real Estate Taxes | | | |
| 12. | Other taxes, fee and permits, personal property, franchise, etc. | | | |
| 13. | Miscellaneous operating expenses (specify) ____________ | | | |
| 14. | Management [Select either a or b]<br>a. Actual cash disbursement [ ]<br>b. 6% for self-management [ ] | | | |
| 15. | Depreciation on capital improvements (from line 6, Schedule C) | | | |
| 16. | TOTAL | | | |
| | | (A) | (B) | (C) |

FORM 7 (Rev.2/6/74) Block & Lot______________

SCHEDULE B --- CONTROLLED RENTAL UNITS

Instructions: In Column A put the present maximum monthly rent for each controlled rental unit (even if you do not propose an increase for that unit). In Column B enter the proposed maximum monthly rent for those units for which you are requesting a rental increase. This schedule provides space for income information on 20 units. Please use additional pages of this schedule for more units if necessary.

| STREET ADDRESS | FLR. | UNIT # | NAME OF TENANT | NO. OF ROOMS | (A) PRESENT MAX. RENT | (B) PROPOSED MAX. RENT | DATE LEASE EXPIRES |
|---|---|---|---|---|---|---|---|
| | | | | | | | |
| | | | | | | | |
| | | | | | | | |
| | | | | | | | |
| | | | | | | | |
| | | | | | | | |
| | | | | | | | |
| | | | | | | | |
| | | | | | | | |
| | | | | | | | |
| | | | | | | | |
| | | | | | | | |
| | | | | | | | |
| | | | | | | | |
| | | | | | | | |
| | | | | | | | |
| | | | | | | | |
| | | | | | | | |
| | | | | | | | |
| | | | | | | | |
| MONTHLY TOTAL__________ | | | SUBTOTAL__________ | | | | |
| | | | | | (A) | (B) | |

FORM 7(11/16/70)

Block & Lot________

SCHEDULE C--THE CONDITION OF THE PROPERTY

1. What is the assessed value of the property? $______________

2. Are abatement proceedings pending? yes___ no___

3. In your opinion is the assessed value the fair market value? yes___ no___

4. If your answer is no, what is in your opinion the fair market value?

$___________

[IF YOU CLAIM THAT THE ASSESSED VALUE IS NOT THE FAIR MARKET VALUE ATTACH A SEPARATE SHEET HEADED "FAIR MARKET VALUE" OUTLINING WHAT KIND OF TESTIMONY AND/OR DOCUMENTATION WILL BE PRODUCED TO PROVE A DIFFERENT VALUATION IF A HEARING IS HELD. IF YOU DO NOT SUBMIT THIS SEPARATE SHEET, THE RENT CONTROL BOARD WILL USE THE ASSESSED VALUE AS THE FAIR MARKET VALUE.]

5. CAPITAL IMPROVEMENTS TABLE

| DESCRIPTION [Indicate capital improvements made since March, 1970] | DATE MADE | COST | ESTIMATED LIFE | YEARLY DEPRECIATIO [divide cos by life] |
|---|---|---|---|---|
| | /70 | $ | yrs | $ |
| | | | | |
| | | | | |
| | | | | |
| | | | | |
| | | | | |
| | | | | |
| | | | | |
| | | | | |
| | | | | |
| | | | 6. TOTAL | |

7. Have there been increases or decreases in living space, services, furniture, furnishings or equipment since March, 1970 not reflected in the above CAPITAL IMPROVEMENTS TABLE? yes___ no___ [If yes, describe. Attach an additional sheet if necessary]

8. Has there been substantial deterioration of the housing units other than as a result of ordinary wear and tear since March, 1970? yes___ no___ [if yes, describe. Attach an additional sheet if necessary]

9. Has there been failure to perform ordinary repair, replacement and maintenance since March, 1970? yes___ no___ [If yes, describe. Attach an additional sheet if necessary]

10. Do the affected rental units comply with the state sanitary code, the Brookline Building Code and Zoning By-Law? yes___ no___ [If no, please explain on a separate sheet headed "SCHEDULE C, ITEM 10" how such lack of compliance is not due to the failure of the landlord to provide normal and adequate repair and maintenance.]

CAMBRIDGE DEPRECIATION
SCHEDULE

TABLE OF YEARLY COSTS ALLOWED FOR EACH $1.00 OF CAPITAL EXPENSE ITEM BASED ON THE USEFUL LIFE OF THE ITEM.

| USEFUL LIFE OF THE ITEM | FACTOR FOR THE YEARLY COST TO BE MULTIPLIED BY THE TOTAL COST | USEFUL LIFE OF THE ITEM | FACTOR FOR THE YEARLY COST TO BE MULTIPLIED BY THE TOTAL COST |
|---|---|---|---|
| 1 | 1.0523 | 9 | .1657 |
| 2 | .5510 | 10 | .1553 |
| 3 | .3845 | 11 | .1469 |
| 4 | .3016 | 12 | .1400 |
| 5 | .2521 | 13 | .1343 |
| 6 | .2194 | 14 | .1295 |
| 7 | .1962 | 15 | .1254 |
| 8 | .1790 | 20 | .1120 |

To use this table multiply the total cost of the capital item times the factor determined by the useful life of the item.

NOTE: THIS IS A REVISED SCHEDULE AND MAY BE USED TO DETERMINE THE EXACT AMOUNT OF THE EXPENSE. PLEASE DESTROY YOUR OLD SCHEDULES THAT WERE USED FOR ESTIMATES.

LANDLORD APPLICATION FOR CAPITAL IMPROVEMENT SURCHARGE
SHALL BE ACCOMPANIED BY THE FOLLOWING INFORMATION:

---

A. THE BUILDING GENERALLY

1. Number of units.

2. Name and apartment numbers of all tenants to be effected by proposed rental increase (use separate sheets).

3. Monthly rent roll. (If income is received for garage parking, swimming pool or club membership fees, commercial rentals, etc., provide separate operating statement for each such activity.)

4. Vacancy experience past 12 months in percentage _____.

5. Year purchased _____; purchase price $__________.

6. Financing:

   1st mortgage at ____% for ___ years in face amount of $____.
   2nd mortgage at ____% for ___ years in face amount of $____.
   Initial equity investment (Down Payment) $____.
   Assessed valuation: Land $____ Bldg. $____ Total $____.
   Initial basis of depreciation $____.
   Method of depreciation ______________________.
   Useful life expectancy ____________.

7. Operating statement: % of Gross $ Dollars

   Gross income 100% $__________

| Annual operating expenses: | % | $ |
|---|---|---|
| Payroll | ______ | ________ |
| Electricity | ______ | ________ |
| Water and sewerage | ______ | ________ |
| Heating fuel | ______ | ________ |
| Maintenance | ______ | ________ |
| Decorating | ______ | ________ |
| Administration and Management | ______ | ________ |
| Other (Explain) | ______ | ________ |
| ____________________ | ______ | ________ |
| Property taxes (Indicate whether tenants pay in accordance with tax clause apart from rentals. Omit if paid 100% by tenants). | ______ | ________ |
| Total non-financing expenses | ______ | ________ |
| Net operating income | ______ | ________ |

   Annual rate of return on purchase Price: $\frac{\text{net operating income}}{\text{purchase price}} =$

```
8.  Net operating income          % of gross              $ Dollars
      Financing expenses
        1st mortgage
          interest    _____                   $_______
          principal   _____                   $_______
            Total     ______                      $______

        2nd mortgage
          interest    _____                   $_______
          principal   _____                   $_______
            Total     ______                      $______

        Total financing expenses  ______%                $________
        Cash flow                 ______%                &________
    Annual cash rate of return on initial equity: $cash flow =  %
                                                  down payment

9.  Total profits
      Cash flow                                          $_______
      Equity build up:
        1st mortgage  __________
        2nd mortgage  __________
        Total equity build up
      Total                                               ________
      Total annual rate of return on initial equity:
                                               $total profits ≐  %
                                                down payment

10. Income tax
      Gross income                                       $_______
      Deductions:

        operating expenses          _________
        property tax                _________
        interest

          1st mortgage  ________
          wnd mortgage  ________

        total depreciation          _________
        Total tax deductions        _________
```

B. THE CAPITAL IMPROVEMENT

1. Does the improvement effect habitability? If so, designate which classification same falls within: (check one)

/__/ a) structural shell of building and all integral parts thereof;
/__/ b) equipment that services normal heating;
/__/ c) " " " plumbing;
/__/ d) " " " air conditioning;

☐ e) equipment that services illumination;

☐ f) " " " fire prevention;

☐ g) " " " power requirements;

☐ h) " " " movement of passengers and freight within the building:

☐ i) other, explain ______________________________

2. Will the tenant have free access to the improvement or will a service charge for use of same be charged to the tenant in addition to rental?

3. What is the cost of the capital improvement?

4. How is the improvement being paid for?

☐ cash

☐ mortgage loan

☐ improvement loan

☐ other (give details)

5. What is the basis of depreciation?

What is the method of depreciation?

What is the useful life expectancy?

6. Date improvement was contracted for?

7. Date improvement was completed or is scheduled for completion?

8. Attach copies of all relevant documents relating to the above.

I hereby certify that the above information is true to the best of my knowledge and belief. I am aware that if any of the information supplied above is willfully false, I am punishable under the penal provisions of the Rent Leveling ordinance

______________________________
Signature

LANDLORD APPLICATION FOR HARDSHIP INCREASE
SHALL BE ACCOMPANIED BY THE FOLLOWING INFORMATION:

---

1. Number of units.
2. Name and apartment numbers of all tenants to be effected by proposed rental increase (use separate sheets).
3. Monthly rent roll. (If income is received for garage parking, swimming pool or club membership fees, commercial rentals, etc., provide separate operating statement for each such activity.)
4. Vacancy experience past 12 months in percentage ________.
5. Year purchased _____; purchase price $________.
6. Financing:

   1st mortgage at ____% for ___years in face amount of $________.
   2nd mortgage at ____% for ___years in face amount of $________.
   Initial equity investment (Down Payment) $________.
   Assessed valuation: Land $_____ Bldg. $______ Total $________.
   Initial basis of depreciation $________.
   Method of depreciation ____________________________.
   Useful life expectancy __________________.

7. Operating statement:

| | % of Gross | $Dollars |
|---|---|---|
| Gross income | 100% | $_______ |

| Annual operating expenses | % | $ |
|---|---|---|
| Payroll | ______% | $_______ |
| Electricity | ______% | $_______ |
| Water and sewerage | ______% | $_______ |
| Heating fuel | ______% | $_______ |
| Maintenance | ______% | $_______ |
| Decorating | ______% | $_______ |
| Administration and Management | ______% | $_______ |
| Other (Explain) | | |
| ____________________ | ______% | $_______ |
| Property taxes (Indicate whether tenants pay in accordance with tax clause apart from rentals. Omit if paid 100% by tenants). | ______% | $_______ |
| Total non-financing expenses | ______% | $_______ |
| Net operating income | ______% | $_______ |

Annual rate of return on purchase price: $\frac{\text{Net operating income}}{\text{purchase price}}$ = %

8. Net operating income % of gross $Dollars
   Financing expenses
   1st mortgage
   interest ______ $______
   principal ______ $______
   Total ______ $______

   2nd mortgage
   interest ______ $______
   principal ______ $______
   Total ______ $______

   Total financing expenses ______% $______
   Cash flow ______% $______
   Annual cash rate of return on initial equity: $cash flow / down payment = %

9. Total profits
   Cash flow $______
   Equity build up:
   1st mortgage ______
   2nd mortgage ______
   Total equity build up
   Total ______
   Total annual rate of return on initial equity: $total profits / down payment = %

10. Income tax
    Gross income $______
    Deductions:

    operating expenses ______
    property tax ______
    interest

    1st mortgage ______
    2nd mortgage ______

    total depreciation ______
    Total tax deductions ______

I hereby certify that the above information is true to the best of my knowledge and belief. I am aware that if any of the information supplied above is wilfully false, I am punishable under the penal provisions of the Rent Leveling ordinance.

______________________

Signature

TENANT'S FORM RLB-1(74)

Tenant's Name ______________________ Claim No. __________

Street Address & Apt. No. ____________________

Home Phone No. _______________ Business Phone No. __________

Landlord's Name _________________

Address _______________________ Phone No. _____________

Name of apartment complex _________________________

Check one: High Rise ☐ Garden Apt. ☐ Mobile Home ☐ Other ☐

How notice received: Regular Mail ☐ Certified Mail ☐ Hand-Delivery ☐

Date notice received: __________

FOR LEASED TENANT

Expiring lease was: 1 year ☐ 2 year ☐ 3 year ☐ ___Year ☐

Date Began _____________ Date ended ________________

Rent $_______ Was there an increase in rental during the term of your lease? Yes ☐ No ☐. If yes, how much and when:

_______________________________________________

New Lease Date Begins __________ Date ends __________

Proposed increase in dollars: $_______

Proposed new rent: $__________

FOR PERIODIC TENANT

1. Terms of tenancy: Month-to-month ☐ week-to-week ☐ other ☐
2. Date entered tenancy __________
3. Date tonancy terminated ________
4. Old rent $_______________
5. Proposed new rent $__________

SIGNED ________________
DATE ____________

FOR ALL TENANTS WHEN FILING THIS COMPLAINT
PLEASE enclose the following:
Photocopy of old lease (or agreement);
" new lease and notice of increase;
" any pertinent communications between you and your landlord;
Check or money order (payable to the Borough of Fort Lee) for the $2.00 filing fee.

FOR MISCELLANEOUS COMMENTS, PLEASE USE REVERSE SIDE

THE CITY OF NEW YORK — HDA
DEPARTMENT OF RENT and HOUSING MAINTENANCE
OFFICE OF RENT CONTROL

Docket No. 2AO ..........

## LANDLORD'S APPLICATION FOR INCREASE OF MAXIMUM RENT (FAIR RETURN)

**(See Section 33.5 of the Regulations)**

**NOTE: This application must be typed, or printed clearly in ink. Instructions for the preparation and filing are contained in Instruction Sheet No. 2.**

1. MAILING ADDRESS OF LANDLORD (See Instruction 1):

NAME.......................................... TEL. NO..........................

NUMBER AND STREET..........................................

CITY, STATE AND ZIP CODE..........................................

2. MAILING ADDRESS OF TENANT (See Instruction 2):

NAME.......................................... APT. NO..........................

NUMBER AND STREET..........................................

CITY, STATE AND ZIP CODE..........................................

(Number and Street) (Borough and Zip Code)

3. **Address of subject building(s)** (See Instruction 3):..........................................

4. **Building Data:** (See Instruction 4): No. of dwelling units..................No. of professional or business units including stores............

No. of garages.........................Total Units...........................Total No. of rooms (excluding bathrooms)..................................

### THE NOTICE

*(NOT TO BE COMPLETED BY LANDLORD)*

**TO: Tenant named in item 2 above:**

The following is an application filed by your landlord for increase of the maximum rent for the housing accommodation occupied by you on the ground that his property is not earning the net annual return provided for in Section 33.5 of the City Rent and Eviction Regulations.

Under the provisions of this Regulation, if your landlord proves that the net rental income from the property is not yielding a net annual return of 6% of the valuation of the property as defined in the Regulations, the Administrator may increase the maximum rents for the controlled housing accommodations in the property.

The landlord has certified that he is maintaining all essential services provided or required to be provided with the housing accommodations. *Complaints concerning essential services may only be considered in this proceeding if filed within the period during which the tenant may file an answer to the landlord's application herein.*

You are hereby afforded an opportunity to oppose this application by filing an answer thereto in duplicate upon the answer forms enclosed herewith. The original of your answer must be signed and must be returned to this office together with one copy within **fifteen** days from the date appearing at the bottom of this notice.

**The original of your landlord's application and all required supporting schedules may be inspected at the District Rent Office.**

..................................................
(Date of Mailing) District Rent Director

### THE APPLICATION

5. **Acquisition and Construction Data** (See Instruction 5):

a. Date property acquired...................... Cost $......................... Purchase ☐ Otherwise ☐ Construction Year (approx.)............

b. Number of stories................Elevator(s)? "No" ☐; "Yes" ☐. If "Yes", No. of "Automatic"................. "Manual"................

c. Type of fuel used.................................... Capacity of fuel tanks or bins ..........................................

6. **Assessment Data** (See Instruction 6):

a. Assessed Valuation in effect at time of filing this application:

Land $............................ Building $............................ Total $..............................................

b. Tax Year for which valuation was assessed: from July 1, 19........ to June 30, 19........

c. Block........................ Lot No.........................

d. Are proceedings now pending to reduce the Assessed Valuation for the Tax Year indicated in b. above or for the prior Tax Year? "Yes" ☐; "No" ☐. If your answer is "Yes", indicate which of such Tax Years are so affected.

.................................................. ..................................................

e. Was the Assessed Valuation for the Tax Year indicated in b. above or for the Tax Year prior thereto reduced by settlement or court order? "No" ☐; "Yes" ☐. If "Yes", supply the following data:

Tax Year.......................... Original A. V.......................... Final A. V..........................

Tax Year.......................... Original A. V.......................... Final A. V..........................

6A. Have rent increases pursuant to Section 33.5 of the City Rent and Eviction Regulations been granted in a prior application? "Yes" ☐; "No" ☐. If your answer is "Yes", indicate the Docket No. 2AO.......................................... of the last application, the date it was filed .................................. 19........ and be sure NOT to file this present application unless TWO years have elapsed since such date.

APPLICATION FORM **A-33.5** *(Rev. 1-69)* (see other side) Filing of Application (See Instruction 23)

**The items, schedules, and amounts listed below are to be supported by such evidence as bills, cancelled checks, and books of account. These are to be submitted in accordance with detailed instructions in Instruction Sheet No. 2.**

**OPERATING STATEMENT**

7. INCOME AND EXPENSES FOR TEST YEAR ENDED Month................ Day................ Year................ (See Instruction 7)

State the period covered by your latest Federal Income Tax Return: from............................19........ to............................19........

| INCOME | ANNUAL INCOME |
|---|---|
| 8. Annual Rental (From Schedule A—Form A-33.5A) } See Instruction 8 | $ |
| 8a. Vacancy Allowance—Compute at 1% of Item 8 } See Instruction 8 | |
| 8b. Net Annual Rental—Item 8 minus Item 8a } See Instruction 8 | $ |
| 9. Miscellaneous Income (Other Than Rents) (From Schedule B. See Instruction 9) | |
| 10. TOTAL INCOME (Lines 8b and 9) (See Instruction 10) | $ |

| EXPENSES | ANNUAL EXPENSE |
|---|---|
| 11. Fuel (From Schedule C. See Instruction 11) | $ |
| 12. Utilities (From Schedule D. See Instruction 12) | |
| 13. Payroll and related costs; or Owner's Janitorial Allowance (From Schedule E. See Instruction 13) | |
| 14. Real Estate Taxes (From Schedule F. See Instruction 14) | |
| 15. Insurance (From Schedule G. See Instruction 15) | |
| 16. Management Allowance (From Schedule H. See Instruction 16) | |
| 17. Repairs and Maintenance (From Schedule I. See Instruction 17) | |
| 18. Replacements and Improvements (From Schedule J. See Instruction 18) | |
| 19. Miscellaneous—not otherwise classified (From Schedule K. See Instruction 19) | |
| 20. Depreciation (From Schedule L. See Instruction 20) | |
| 21. TOTAL EXPENSES (lines 11 through 20) | $ |
| 22. NET RETURN EARNED IN "TEST YEAR" (Line 10 minus line 21) | $ |

COMPUTATION OF NET ANNUAL RETURN AND RENT ADJUSTMENT INDICATED

| VALUATION-BASIS (Fill in Items 23 and 24 below) | | |
|---|---|---|
| 23. Assessed Valuation (Total Assessed Valuation per Item 6a on reverse side) | $ | |
| 24. Purchase Price of Property (if acquired since February 1, 1961). (See Instruction 21, Part B) | $ | |
| 25. Net Annual Return claimed (6% of Item 23 or 24 above) | | $ |
| 26. Rent Adjustment indicated (Item 25 minus Item 22) | | $ |

**NOTE: If Item 22 equals or exceeds Item 25, there is no basis for an adjustment under Section 33.5 of the Regulations.**

The landlord states that (s)he is (one of) (the.......................................... of................................................................ Corp.—Inc.—Corporation), the owner(s) of the building(s) mentioned and described in this application; that (s)he is fully familiar with the physical condition of said building(s); that the landlord is maintaining and will continue to maintain all essential services provided or required to be provided with the housing accommodations involved to the date of issuance of any order herein adjusting the maximum rent(s) and will thereafter continue to maintain such services so long as the increase in such maximum rent(s) continues in effect.

**I have read the foregoing application, including the accompanying documents, and I hereby affirm under the penalties provided by law that the contents thereof are true of my own knowledge.**

*It is not necessary that the foregoing be sworn to but false statements may subject you to the penalties provided by law.*

..............................................................................
(Signature of Landlord)

Dated................................................................ 19........

**CONCILIATION AND APPEALS BOARD**
**N.Y.C. RENT STABILIZATION LAW OF 1969**
**666 FIFTH AVENUE, NEW YORK, N.Y. 10019**

You will be advised in **writing** about the disposition of this application by the Conciliation and Appeals Board

**O-M**

**Docket No.**

**OWNER'S APPLICATION AND NOTICE—(MULTIPLE TENANT)**
**(FILE IN DUPLICATE)**

1. **MAILING ADDRESS OF TENANT:**

NAME ........ TEL. No. ........

NUMBER AND STREET ........

CITY, STATE AND ZIP CODE ........

2. **OWNER INFORMATION**

a. Owner's Name ........
b. Owner's Mailing Address ........
c. Multiple Dwelling Registration Number # ........
d. Managing Agent (Natural Person Only) ........
e. ........ Business Address ........ Telephone No.
f. Owner's Membership Number in Rent Stabilization Association # ........
g. Number of apartments in property ........

**FILING INSTRUCTIONS:** Complete an original and one copy of this form and accompanying schedules and file with the Conciliation and Appeals Board at the address indicated above.

3. **NOTICE TO TENANT:**

The owner has filed an application for a rent adjustment on the ground indicated in item 10. If the Conciliation and Appeals Board approves the owner's application, the stabilized rents for the dwelling units in the property will be increased. **THE OWNER'S APPLICATION CLAIMS AN INCREASE OF % IN YOUR MONTHLY APARTMENT RENT.** A copy of the owner's application is available for your inspection in either the Superintendent's or Resident Manager's office. If you wish to interpose an answer to the owner's application you may do so, on the "Tenant Answer Form" enclosed herewith, within 10 days from the date of mailing of this notice.

If the Conciliation and Appeals Board issues an order increasing the stabilized rent, such order will be effective as of the thirtieth day from the date of the completion of the filing of this application, or the date of the Conciliation and Appeals Board's Order, if issued prior to such thirtieth day. However, if your current lease does not contain a clause authorizing such increase during its term pursuant to Section 42(b) of the Rent Stabilization Code, such increase will be effective upon the renewal of your lease.

If the order is issued because of owner hardship (item 10a) the tenant may, within thirty days of his receipt of a copy of the order of the CAB, cancel his lease on sixty days written notice to the owner. During said period the cancelling tenant may continue in occupancy at no increase in rent.

**This application is subject to the Presidential Stabilization Order of August 15, 1971 and any subsequent limitations imposed by the Federal Government.**

4. Property name—if any ........
5. Property address/location (List All Addresses) ........
6. Description of Property: Number of: Buildings ........, Stories ........, Apartments ........, Rooms ........, Garages or Spaces ........, Stores ........

☐ Garden Apartments; ☐ Elevator Number ☐; Automatic ☐ Operator; Walk up; ........

Fuel: ☐ Oil—Type ........; ☐ Steam; ☐ Other ........ . Air Conditioning: ☐ Central; ☐ Individual Units; ☐ None

7. Date property acquired by present owner ........
8. Date of certificate of occupancy (Permanent) ........
9. Tenant services included in rent or other charges to tenant. (Check those applicable)

☐ GAS ☐ ELECTRICITY ☐ AIR CONDITIONING UNITS ☐ T.V. ANTENNA ☐ DISH WASHER ☐ OTHER (Describe)

10. Application is filed under: (Check applicable box)
a. ☐ Comparative hardship—Section 43a (Use Form 3-M-43a.1 and Form 3-M-43a.2 with this application and see instructions 43a)
b. ☐ Major capital improvement—Section 41 (Use Form 3-M-41 with this application and see instructions 41)— briefly describe the improvement here.

11. **LANDLORD'S AFFIRMATION:**
I have read the foregoing application and the other required statements and schedules and documents, and I hereby affirm that the contents thereof are true of my own knowledge.

**It is not necessary that the foregoing is sworn to but false statements may subject you to the penalties provided by law.**

........ Owner
By ........
Date ........

Form CAB – 3M Rev. 10/71

**O-M**

Docket No. ____________

**CONCILIATION AND APPEALS BOARD**

**STATEMENT IN SUPPORT OF COMPARATIVE HARDSHIP**

**UNDER SEC. 43a OF THE RENT STABILIZATION CODE OF THE CITY OF NEW YORK**

**RATIO OF OPERATING EXPENSES TO GROSS RENTS FOR THE CURRENT ANNUAL PERIOD**

Name of Applicant (Owner) ....................

Location of Property ....................

Current Annual Period (See Instruction Booklet) From .................... To ....................

**GROSS RENTAL INCOME** (Omit Pennies)

1. Gross apartments and garage rental income—CAB-3-M—Schedule 1 $____________
2. Gross commercial rental income—CAB-3-M—Schedule 2 $____________
3. Other rental income .................... $
   (a) Washing Machines and Dryers .................... ____________
   (b) Vending Machines .................... ____________
   (c) Pool Club .................... ____________
   (d) Other .................... ____________

3(a) to (d) Total other Rental Income .................... ____________

4. **Total gross rental income items 1, 2 and 3** .................... ____________

**OPERATING EXPENSES** $

5. Fuel .................... ____________
6. Electric ☐; Gas ☐ (Check applicable boxes) .................... ____________
7. Operating Payroll .................... ____________
8. Operating payroll costs .................... ____________
9. Insurance .................... ____________
10. Service contracts .................... ____________
11. Painting, repairs, maintenance and supplies .................... ____________
12. Replacements and improvements .................... ____________
13. Real Estate Tax .................... ____________
14. Water and sewer charges .................... ____________
15. Other operating expenses .................... ____________
16. **Total operating expenses (Items 5 to 15)** .................... ____________
17. Ratio of operating expenses to gross rental income (Item 16 ÷ Item 4) .................... ____________%
18. Average ratio for the five (5) year period (item 23 Form CAB-3-M-43a.2) .................... ____________%
    If the percentage at Item 18 is equal to or greater than the percentage at Item 17, there is no comparative hardship and the owner is not entitled to a rent adjustment. If Item 18 is less than Item 17, complete Items 19 to 22 to compute rent adjustment.
19. Adjusted gross rental income (Item 16 ÷ Item 18) .................... $____________
20. Amount of annual gross rent adjustment (Item 19 less Item 4) .................... $____________
21. Amount of monthly gross rent adjustment (Item 20 ÷ 12 months) .................... $____________
22. Monthly gross rent adjustment as a percentage of monthly apartment rents (Item 21 ÷ Column 5 of Schedule 1) .................... ____________%

Form CAB-3-M-43a.1

**O-M**

Docket No. ____________

**CONCILIATION AND APPEALS BOARD**

**STATEMENT IN SUPPORT OF COMPARATIVE HARDSHIP**

**UNDER SEC. 43a OF THE RENT STABILIZATION CODE OF THE CITY OF NEW YORK**

**RATIO OF OPERATING EXPENSES TO GROSS RENTS**

**FOR THE PRECEDING FIVE (5) YEAR PERIOD**

Name of Applicant ..............................

Location of Property ..............................

| | PRECEDING FIVE YEAR PERIOD | | | | |
|---|---|---|---|---|---|
| | Year (a) | Year (b) | Year (c) | Year (d) | Year (e) |
| **GROSS RENTAL INCOME** | $ | $ | $ | $ | $ |
| 1. Apartments, garages and other charges to apartment tenants | | | | | |
| 2. Commercial rental income | | | | | |
| 3. Other rental income | | | | | |
| 4. Vacancies and concessions claimed | | | | | |
| 5. **Total gross rental income (Items 1 to 4)** | | | | | |
| **OPERATING EXPENSES** | | | | | |
| 6. Fuel | | | | | |
| 7. Electric and Gas | | | | | |
| 8. Operating payroll | | | | | |
| 9. Operating payroll costs | | | | | |
| 10. Insurance | | | | | |
| 11. Service contracts | | | | | |
| 12. Repairs and maintenance | | | | | |
| 13. Painting | | | | | |
| 14. Janitorial supplies | | | | | |
| 15. Replacements and improvements | | | | | |
| 16. Real Estate Tax | | | | | |
| 17. Water and sewer charges | | | | | |
| 18. Other operating expenses | | | | | |
| 19. **Total operating expenses (Items 6 to 18)** | $ | $ | $ | $ | $ |
| 20. Ratio of operating expenses to gross rental income (Item 19 ÷ by Item 5) | % | % | % | % | % |

21. Total operating expenses for the five (5) year period (Total of Item 19 Columns (a) to (e) ) .............. $____________

22. Total gross rental income for the five (5) year period (Total of Item 5 Columns (a) to (e) ) .............. $____________

23. Average ratio for the five (5) year period (Item 21 ÷ Item 22)—(Enter at Item 18 of Form CAB-3-M-43a.1) .............. ____________%

Form CAB-3-M-43a.2

**O-M**

Docket No. ____________

**CONCILIATION AND APPEALS BOARD**

**APARTMENT AND GARAGE RENTAL INCOME—SCHEDULE 1**

**(USE SEPARATE SCHEDULE 2 FOR COMMERCIAL OCCUPANCY AND GARAGE RENT WHERE GARAGE IS LEASED TO A GARAGE OPERATOR)**

Name of Owner ..........................................................................

Address of Property ..........................................................................

| 1 | 2 | 3 | 4 | 5 | 6 | 7 | 8 | 9 |
|---|---|---|---|---|---|---|---|---|
| | | | | Present Monthly Rent | | | Apt. Adjustment | |
| | | | | As of (Date) ________ | | | | |
| Apt. No. | No. of Rooms | Tenant Names or "Vacancy" (List All Units In Accordance With Instructions Attached Hereto.) | Lease Expiration Date | Apt. | Garage | Other | Amount of Increase % of Col. 5 | New Rent Col. 5 Plus Col. 8 (See Instructions) |
| | | | | | | | | |
| | | | | | | | | |
| | | | | | | | | |
| | | | | | | | | |
| | | | | | | | | |
| | | | | | | | | |
| | | | | | | | | |
| | | | | | | | | |
| | | | | | | | | |
| | | | | | | | | |
| | | | | | | | | |
| | | | | | | | | |
| | | | | | | | | |
| | | | | | | | | |
| | | | | | | | | |
| | | | | | | | | |
| | | | | | | | | |
| | | | | | | | | |
| | | | | | | | | |
| | | | | | | | | |
| TOTALS—ON A MONTHLY BASIS | | | | $ | $ | $ | $ | $ |
| TOTALS—ON AN ANNUAL BASIS | | | | $ | $ | $ | $ | $ |
| Totals of Columns 5, 6 and 7 On An Annual Basis $ | | | | | | | | |

**Use Additional Sheets If Necessary—Carry Forward Totals.**
**Only Annualize Final Totals And Enter On Operating Statement For Either Comparative Hardship (Form CAB—3-M-43 a ) Or Operating Loss (Form CAB—3-M-43 b ) Or Major Capital Improvement (Form CAB-3-M-41)**

Form CAB—3-M—Schedule 1 (12-69)

11

**CONCILIATION AND APPEALS BOARD**

**COMMERCIAL RENTAL INCOME—SCHEDULE 2**

**O-M**

Docket No. ________

Name of Owner ..........................................................

Address of Property ..........................................................

| 1<br>Designation of Commercial Tenant<br>(List By Office and/or Store All Units In Accordance With Instructions Attached Hereto) | 2<br>Lease Expiration Date | 3<br>Present Monthly Rent As Of<br>Date________ | 4<br>Additional Rent — Annual Amount |
|---|---|---|---|
| | | | |
| | | | |
| | | | |
| | | | |
| | | | |
| | | | |
| | | | |
| | | | |
| | | | |
| | | | |
| | | | |
| | | | |
| | | | |
| | | | |
| | | | |
| | | | |
| | | | |
| | | | |
| | | | |
| | | | |
| | | | |
| | | | |
| Total On A Monthly Basis | | $ | |
| Totals On An Annual Basis | | $ | $ |

Total of Columns 3 and 4 On An Annual Basis $

Use Additional Sheets If Necessary—Carry Forward Totals. Only Annualize Final Monthly Total of Column 3.
Enter Final Total Of Columns 3 and 4, On An Annual Basis, On Operating Statement
For Either Comparative Hardship (Form CAB—3-M-43 a) or
Operating Loss (Form CAB—3-M-43 b)
Or Major Capital Improvement (Form CAB—3-M-41)

Form CAB—3-M—Schedule 2 (12-69)

FUNDERBURG LIBRARY

MANCHESTER COLLEGE

352.75
L569r